# Food Cop

*Yolanda, Tell Us
What to Eat!*

# Food Cop

## *Yolanda, Tell Us What to Eat!*

## Yolanda Bergman

with Daryn Eller

**BANTAM BOOKS**
NEW YORK • TORONTO • LONDON • SYDNEY • AUCKLAND

FOOD COP

*A Bantam Book / August 1991*

Library of Congress Cataloging-in-Publication Data

Bergman, Yolanda.
    Food cop : Yolanda, tell us what to eat! / by Yolanda Bergman with Daryn
Eller.
        p.   cm.
    ISBN 0-553-07337-0
    1. Nutrition. I. Eller, Daryn. II. Title.
RA784.B393   1991
613.2—dc20                                                    90-25848
                                                                   CIP

ISBN 0-553-07337-0

*Published simultaneously in the United States and Canada*

*Bantam Books are published by Bantam Books, a division of Bantam Doubleday*
*Dell Publishing Group, Inc. Its trademark, consisting of the words ''Bantam Books''*
*and the portrayal of a rooster, is Registered in U.S. Patent and Trademark Office*
*and in other countries. Marca Registrada. Bantam Books, 666 Fifth Avenue, New*
*York, New York 10103.*

PRINTED IN THE UNITED STATES OF AMERICA

RRH    0  9  8  7  6  5  4  3  2

I dedicate this book with all my love and gratitude to my daughter, husband, parents, and very close friends. All who have always believed in me, supported me in my efforts, and who, to this day— look good.

With great thanks for unending support:

Barbara Alpert
Michelle and Arlen Andelson
Gail Barton
Casey Carsten
Paul Cooper
Susan Geliebter
Carla Glasser
The Entire Gonda Residence
Mel Harris
Wendy Harris
Robert Kahan
Susan Kay
Amanda Kempley
Dr. Arnold Klein
Anne LeGassick
Hope Boonshaft Lewis
Charles Matthau
Shelley Naphtal
Positive Ray
Kimmy Robertson
Michael Romanelli
Marcia Russell
Janet Sheen
Cotter Smith
Paul Stanley
Dan Strone
Madeleine Stowe
Ian Weiss
Brian Wilson
Francis Yonan

Also, thanks to Gary Bernstein, Jeff Jones, Robin Riker, and Anastasia Wellington.

—Y.B.

With much appreciation to my family, friends and colleagues for their encouragement and support. Special thanks to Carla Glasser, Barbara Alpert, and Janis Jibrin.

—D.E.

# Contents

# Introduction:
# All About Yolanda

*People* magazine called me a "food cop," *Vogue* referred to me as a "food coach," *Self* coined the phrase "food guru," and *Mirabella* went on to make me the "junk food buster." Whatever the name attached to me, the fact is, I know food! And I should—I've been on every diet in the book. As a former ballerina, I really learned the true meaning of starving yourself thin—it's not fun, it's not healthy, and it's no way to live. But you'll never catch me on a starvation diet or acting neurotic about food again. Now I eat as much as I like (and believe me, I eat a lot), give in to my cravings for sweets, drink wine, dine lavishly in restaurants, and even binge when I'm feeling stressed out. Yet here's the kicker: I'm very thin and have been able to stay that way now for a long time. That's because I combine my indulgences with healthy, nonfattening foods—some I make myself, others I have found by researching what's new and nutritious in the food marketplace—and I stay away from oils and other fats. It's a mix that has not only kept my body at its best, but has inspired many people to hire me to help them learn to eat the same way. So now, much of what I do is to work with people one-on-one, educating them on how to bring food back into their lives so that it's a pleasure, not a problem. That's what food has become for me—in fact, I like to call myself the fat person who won.

Don't get me wrong. Just like anyone else who maintains a slim and healthy physique, I work at it. I have to exercise and watch what I eat in order to stay this way. And while I've found a healthy way to do so now, I didn't start out that way. The first time in my life I ever had a weight problem was the year I turned fifteen. Ironically, it was a time when I especially wanted to be thin because, after years of dance lessons, I had decided to pursue a career in ballet. And ballerinas, as you know, don't have room for one extra ounce of fat.

So I started putting a lot of effort into paring down. Growing up in a show-biz household (my father was a TV writer and producer on, among other programs, *The Merv Griffin Show*), I was hip to every Hollywood diet that existed—and I tried them all. My mother was an excellent gourmet cook, and she, too, was always going on and off the diet of the day. After years of everything from the "Potato Diet" to "Dr. Atkins" to grapefruit diets to a diet based on Ayds diet caramels (I ate the whole box), I found the answer. Starvation. By the time I received a scholarship to dance with the Harkness Ballet in New York City a few years later, I was about as lithe and lean as you can get. I was also consumed with trying to avoid consuming any food. Like a true bulimic, if I broke down and overate, a quick trip to the bathroom was all I needed to repair the damage. Yes, I was thin all right, but not exactly healthy or happy about how I had to live to stay that way.

In 1979 I moved to Los Angeles and continued dancing with various companies including the Los Angeles Ballet, Americana Dance Theater, and a spin-off of the Joffrey Ballet. Keeping my weight down remained a high priority; however, my life began to change in ways that would eventually cause the way I ate to change, too. First, I began living with Richard, my future husband. That in turn inspired me to start cooking (I had learned from my mother), something that would come in particularly handy down the line. I started to eat a little more with Richard, but it was after we got married and I became pregnant that I knew my days of starving and purging were over for good. By allowing myself to eat exactly what I wanted to eat when I was pregnant, I realized all that I had been missing. I really loved food! And it felt so good to eat—really eat—again.

But I wasn't prepared to carry a lot of extra weight around purely for the pleasure of eating. The birth of my daughter, Nolina, left me with about twenty extra pounds, and a goal: To find a way to incorporate food into my life *and* get back to my old slim self—I had no intention of blaming pregnancy and childbirth for a fat behind the rest of my life. So I started experimenting with the gourmet cooking techniques my mother had taught me. But instead of using the classic, fattening ingredients she had always used, I replaced them with some nontraditional, nonfattening ingredients of my own. I also scoured the supermarket shelves to find other low- or no-fat foods I could serve with meals or just keep around for snacking. As it turned out, there were tons more than I'd ever expected to find.

Things started coming together. I had found an appealing, satisfying style of cuisine that would let me eat all I wanted to and also get back into dancer-thin shape. It was exciting to realize I had discovered the secret to eating and enjoying food without having to wear it, although it wasn't until a few years later that I would start getting paid for revealing my strategy.

During the time I was experimenting in the kitchen and experiencing the first joys of motherhood, I decided not to go back to ballet classes. Still trying to lose those pregnancy pounds, I found it hard to face my svelte dancing peers. So despite having had a C-section just three weeks earlier I began taking the advanced exercise class at Jane Fonda's Work-out Studio in Beverly Hills. The instructor asked me to hold off on some of the exercises when she learned of my condition but, insisting that I knew what my body could and couldn't do, I pressed on and did well. Five months later I was teaching the class, and Jane herself was one of my students. People flocked to my classes, drawn to the dancers' techniques I incorporated into the exercise routine. Yet many students were still frustrated by the minimal amount of personal attention given in large studio classes. A lot of them started asking me to work with them privately. I left Fonda's and became a personal trainer.

While working with people individually, I discovered that even though they were exercising enough, they weren't losing the weight they wanted to. One look inside their refrigerators and cupboards revealed why. "You say you want my legs," I'd admonish them. "Well, if I ate the kinds of foods you eat, they would blow up overnight!" I was adamant that my clients relearn their eating habits and even stopped working with a few who continued to sabotage both of our best efforts. They weren't going to get results, and because many of them blamed the exercise routine, I felt my integrity was at stake.

Eventually, with each client I fell into the natural habit of giving them tips on how to eat more healthfully. At one point, I went as far as to cook meals for one couple myself after we'd finished their workouts. Most of the time, though, what I'd do was clean out my clients' kitchens, tossing all the foods that were making them fat into a big garbage bag. Then I'd restock their refrigerators and cupboards with more nutritious, nonfattening groceries. I'd even teach them (or their personal chefs) how to cook without fat, just as I had been doing for myself at home. I never put anyone on a restrictive diet but rather introduced them to foods that would allow them to eat well and satisfy their cravings without ending up with clogged arteries and excess pounds. Because people in LA, as in so many cities, tend to eat out much of the time, I also started giving them tips on how to order nonfattening meals no matter where they were dining—Spago, Tommy's burger joint, any-eatery-USA. Sometimes

I'd even call ahead to make sure the restaurant would serve them the right kind of food.

My reputation as a good trainer began to spread around LA, and before long I got a call from a well-known dermatologist who wanted to hire me—but not as a personal trainer. He already had one of those. He wanted me solely to help him lose weight. "But I'm not a nutritionist," I told him. He insisted that I had made my clients look great and that they raved about my food counseling. Still, my first instinct was to put on the brakes: Again, I thought, I'm not a nutritionist . . . but I had found a very safe, nongimmicky way to help people lose weight and lower their cholesterol. I had several doctors' approval, and my eating philosophy, after all, is simply common sense. But many people cannot determine what is sensible on their own, and even fewer people know how to adjust their eating habits to a high-stress lifestyle. That's where I could be particularly helpful: my strong point is putting balance back into out-of-balance lives. So, forward I went.

One of my first clients as a "food coach" was Paul Stanley, lead singer/guitarist of the rock group KISS. It was also Paul who gave me the incentive to take my business, which now included both food counseling and fitness training, a step further. Known as one of rock's bad boys, he was just as naughty when it came to eating. This was a man who could go a whole day on nothing but cookies, cake, and candy; if a bowl of whipped cream was the only thing in the fridge for breakfast, no problem, he'd polish it off. But he came to me because he wanted to change his ways—and he did, successfully decreasing his cholesterol level and increasing his energy level at the same time.

For someone who's on the road a lot, part of doing that was just learning how to eat right in restaurants. Easy enough, but because Paul doesn't cook, finding a solution for when he was home was more difficult. "Why don't you cook for me?" he asked.

Once again I protested, "I'm not a cook!"

He said, "Just make some of the things you talk about, like turkey breast, grilled veggies, and turkey meat loaf, then stock my fridge."

The next thing I knew I was delivering Tupperware containers full of food to his door; then, once his friends heard about it, all over town.

I began my catering business more than four years ago, an operation whose customers included Bill Murray, Brian Wilson, Carrie Fisher, Robin Williams, Kate Jackson, Martin and Janet Sheen, Lisa Hartman, Ozzy Osborne, Emilio Estevez, Rick Springfield, Linda Ronstadt, the rock group The Scorpions, Mel Harris, Madeleine Stowe, Brian Benben (*Dream On*), and many others. As the business expanded, so did the menu, which eventually came to include everything from Cajun quesadillas with tomatillo salsa and nonfattening lasagna to roast turkey breast with mustard herbes de Provence sauce and home-style turkey meat loaf, plus a whole line of nonfat sauces and salad dressings. Paul Stanley still placed his orders regularly, and when he moved back to New York, my staff would send them packed in dry ice and delivered via Federal Express.

Presently, I still offer diet counseling and nutritional guidance locally in LA, as well as by phone and mail. I have appeared often on local and national television and various radio shows, and have been consulted for numerous magazine and newspaper articles. I often lecture on healthier eating tactics these days, too. My catering business has evolved into a select-client service, so now I provide food for just a few, like Mel Harris, Madeleine Stowe, Emilio Estevez, and Robin Williams.

The one thing that hasn't changed is my goal: to teach you to eat healthily and well without giving up the pleasure you find in food. I hope this book will give you a fresh outlook on eating and help you learn to enjoy it again—without all the usual worries—as much as I do.

# 1

# *Shut Up and Eat!*

I COME FROM THE dance world, where I'm used to hearing the expression "Shut up and dance!" In other words, don't talk about all the difficulties of dancing or how many pirouettes you're going to do or how much thinner you will be by perform-ance time—*just dance*. Do the steps, do the work. Granted, the world of ballet is disciplined, demanding, and basically nonverbal. But what I learned is that there are people who *talk* and people who *do*. That's the difference I'm trying to point out by calling this chapter "Shut Up and Eat!" Shut up and eat should be to food what Nike's "Just do it" campaign is to exercise.

Obviously, I don't tell my clients just to shut up and eat. I put a lot of hard work into helping them overcome their individual problems so they can begin to eat without being afraid of food (or at least begin to under-stand those fears). But, admittedly, after years of hearing excuses, more excuses, and endless babble about the newest gimmicks, pills, and sur-gical solutions, I got a little tired of it. Really, aren't we all a little sick of hearing each other discuss the intricacies of every meal and whether what we ate was "bad" or "good?" Aren't we all tired of having problems with food? I believe it's time to stop worrying about every morsel we put into our mouths, time to enjoy eating again. That's what I'm talking about when I say shut up and eat. And what it amounts to is freedom: The freedom to sit down and eat without having to agonize over how it's going to affect your body. The freedom to flip through a magazine and skip the latest fad diet because you don't need it—you already know how to stay consistently thin and healthy. The freedom to satisfy all your needs and cravings without feeling guilty and acting crazy. The freedom, for once, to shut up about food and just eat and *enjoy* it.

Life is stressful enough without having to feel stressed out about eating. Eating should be soothing and pleasurable. Food is one of the most wonderful, life-sustaining things we have on this planet, yet somehow we've managed to turn it into an enemy. Here we are in the nineties, headed for the 21st century with a quantity of technical advances that exceeds what we ever could have hoped for. But at the same time, the quality of our lives has regressed; we've lost touch with home base in many ways. Several of the more sensual, relaxing activities we used to enjoy are missing—and eating is one of them. Instead, chronic dieting, nutrition-related illnesses, and eating disorders sweep this country. Food, glorious food has become a problem and eating, a dilemma.

The people who come to me for a consultation are, excuse the pun, fed up with their food problems. They want to eat again. To enjoy a life *with* food, but *without* being fat and/or unhealthy. Many times what they're looking for is a day-by-day, meal-by-meal prescription of foods that will make their troubles disappear. But if that's the case, they've come to the wrong person. Although I do introduce my clients to foods that are healthy and nonfattening, I never give them a *diet* (see the "Glossary of Terms" at the end of this chapter, which explains how I define *diet* and several other terms you'll see throughout this book). Instead, I put them in "school," and with each "class" I try to teach them something—from understanding their emotional ties to food, to knowing how to order in restaurants—that will help them eat more healthfully. The way I've designed this book is similar to the way I work with my clients. Think of each chapter as a lesson, the sum total of which I hope will make you an expert in both your own needs and wants as well as the world of food around you. Upon graduation, you'll be able to achieve both your health and weight goals.

## Tapping Into the Source of the Problem

The first lesson, and perhaps the most important lesson of all, is one aimed at helping you get to the bottom of what's making you struggle

with your eating habits and, usually by extension, your weight or cholesterol. Nine times out of ten, the clients I see have already tried a billion
different ways to make peace with food, but without success. How could
so many fail so often? Once I begin talking to clients about all the different things they've tried, it becomes clear that each "remedy" was usually
nothing more than a Band-Aid fix—that is, a superficial solution for what
really is a deep-seated problem. The diet book(s) or professional(s) they
consulted didn't help them tap into the source of their eating problems;
they just treated the symptoms.

So when I begin consultations, I start by investigating both my client's
emotional relationship with food and the practical details of their lives.
The first questions I ask include "When was the last time you were
satisfied with your body?" and "When was the last time you felt healthy
and energetic?" My goal is to find out what was going on in their lives at
that time that let them enjoy food without worrying or feeling guilty about
what they ate. I also ask "What meal are you most satisfied with?"
"What particular foods do you like the best?" "What foods do you turn
to when you're stressed out?" "When do you find yourself binging?"
"What kind of food did you have in your house growing up?" and "Food-
wise, how would you define your lifestyle—do you eat out a lot, do you
cook for yourself, does someone else cook for you?" If you ask yourself
these questions, I think you will find that, like most of my clients, the
trouble is not that you went on the wrong diet in the past or that you just
simply have no willpower. Take a look at these classic traps—five that I
find people are most likely to have fallen into—and see if you don't recognize one or more patterns that describe your approach to food.

**Trap #1.** *You can't help it.* Your cravings for certain foods are just too
strong to ignore, so you satisfy them . . . and now that you've eaten one
"bad" thing—meaning you went off your "diet"—you might as well eat
everything you desire because pretty soon you'll just have to starve yourself again. This is the all-or-nothing syndrome, a cycle of gluttony and
deprivation that (here's that pun again) literally feeds off itself.

**Trap #2.** *To eat healthfully requires too much time and energy and means
you'll be reduced to eating boring, tasteless food.* Besides, you don't want
to act like some kind of food weirdo in front of your family and friends.
This is a classic trap for men, who still think it isn't really macho to diet
or be particular about food. A classic example of this is the scene in *When
Harry Met Sally* when Meg Ryan rattles out an entire speech just to order
one lunch and Billy Crystal, giving her a deadpan stare, simply orders

the number 9. Believe me, we would all like to be naturally thin and healthy and never have to worry about what goes into our mouths, but the truth is most of us aren't. If you don't accept it, you're likely to find yourself deep in Trap #3 . . .

**Trap #3.** *The point-the-finger trap.* "I'm fat and unhealthy because of my mother, brother, father, sister, boyfriend, ex-boyfriend, husband, bratty child, too many children, my job, lack of job, and, of course, STRESS, STRESS, STRESS!" You're just a poor victim of circumstance. Yeah, sure.

**Trap #4.** *You want to eat healthfully but you love the taste of junky foods and just can't stay away from them.* This is like saying, I didn't want to litter but I couldn't find a garbage can. I've heard every excuse in the book. One of the best was my client who poured fatty powdered creamer into his coffee, and looked me straight in the eye and said, "I use Coffee-mate because it doesn't cool my coffee down."

"Well," I countered, "neither does nonfat powdered milk."

This pushed him to admit that it was the taste he was after. It also revealed a host of other junky foods he was addicted to. Taste buds are creatures of habit—and habits can be changed. I'm not talking about turning your love of potato chips into a passion for carrot sticks. There are other, better alternatives.

**Trap #5.** *The food confusion trap.* This is one of the most pervasive traps. Every day you hear something new, and one thing contradicts the next. All the hype has got you running around the supermarket like a lost soul, and too often you fall for those alluring labels that shout "no cholesterol" and "low fat." Suddenly, you're finding oat bran in your laundry detergent, calcium in your toothpaste, and biodegradable cereals in your cupboards! Once you learn what foods you really do and don't need, though, you can clean up 90 percent of your food intake and not get swept up into every new commercial craze.

## Finding What Works for YOU

People who fall into the trap of believing that they must eat like a saint—or eat like the devil—or who have decided that eating healthfully will infringe on their lifestyle too much are usually people who have had tons of diet experience. The diet industry is one of the biggest businesses in America and not surprisingly: many people have reached a point where they'll buy into anything that seems like a half-decent plan for eating—even if what it asks of them is next to impossible. Then, when it doesn't work, they'll try the next new diet that comes along. But underlying each of these diets is the premise that "Sure, I'm going *on* this diet for a while, but one of these days I'm going to go *off*." On, off, on off, on on on, off off off. . . . Enough already!

When I ask clients about their past history, they usually say something like, "I was on the Dr. Atkins diet—and it really worked!" Well, of course it worked. Most diets do if you follow the prescribed rules and stay *on* them. But losing weight by following a prescribed eating plan doesn't make you a success. Success is when the weight *stays* off or you *continue* to eat healthfully (which obviously my new clients haven't if they're hiring me). One man told me that a certain diet worked for him until his mother's death sent him on an emotional roller coaster; seven months later he was still eating poorly. Again, that's not success. Success is when you change your attitude toward what you put into your mouth for good. Success is when you create an eating style for yourself that pulls you through a crisis, a vacation, stress, and the many ups and downs in life. You may gain three to five pounds here and there and you may even fit cookies, candy, and ice cream into your life, but the bottom line is that the bulk of what you eat is lean and healthy. The goodies have their place, but they don't dominate.

One of the saddest things I have to report is that there are very few people who have managed to lose weight and keep it off to their satisfaction. To be successful, whether it's permanent weight loss you're after or whether you are trying to lower your cholesterol or just want to stop putting poisonous foods into your system, it's necessary to make healthy eating your "eating style." That means that instead of following a short-lived plan that you abandon once you feel fit, you simply eat the right foods all (or at least 90 percent) of the time. That becomes your style, just as you have spiritual or religious beliefs, standards of education, literary and musical tastes, fashion rules, and a certain home style. It becomes part of who you are, not what has happened to you. It's a choice.

After years of following diets, many people are at a loss about how to proceed without a prescription telling them precisely what they can and cannot do. Because, it's true, we all need some kind of rules to live by. That's why the next chapter in this book is all about rules—about making rules for yourself that take into account such simple things as what foods you like, what foods satisfy your mind and body, where you eat, and when you eat. Rules that take into account, for better or for worse, your lifestyle and the eating habits you already have. And the great thing about the rules you make for yourself is that they're much easier to follow, let alone remember. You're not going to have to check a list of regulations every time you get hungry to make sure you do the right thing.

Chapter 2 is also designed to help you take a look at rules you've conceded to following in the past—and why, in the end, you probably broke them all. The reason we so often go on and off diets in the first place is because the rules are so hard to abide by; any given diet plan may suit your best friend's style, but not necessarily suit yours. I saw evidence of this again and again when I was teaching at Jane Fonda's Workout Studio years ago. The classes were packed wall to wall with women who were working hard to get into shape, but it wasn't long before they realized that all that sweating, grunting, and jumping wasn't going to change their bodies that much unless they also got a handle on what they were eating. So inevitably, they'd turn to some trained professional (often not in much better shape than themselves) or they'd hop on the latest fad-diet bandwagon. And they'd almost always fail, although not for lack of trying. The trouble was they'd usually choose a weight-loss program that a friend or someone on TV (like Oprah Winfrey) had told them was the ultimate answer. And maybe it was the ultimate answer—for those women singing the diets' praises (although they probably eventually gained back the weight themselves). But that didn't mean those diets would be the ultimate answer for everyone, and judging by the failure rate of the women I saw, they weren't.

As I said in the introduction to this book, I consider myself the fat person who won. I won the battle. But that doesn't mean that I get to eat anything I want. I have learned that my physical needs for food are different from my emotional needs, so I have made rules for myself that will allow me to satisfy both. Likewise, you must find what works for you. For example, you're trying to lose weight, but you absolutely have to have the bread at your Thursday girls-night-out dinner, you know you can't resist it. Great! Then don't have bread at lunch and dinner that day and don't have the bread with a heavy pasta dish. Have a grilled fish or chicken, veggies, and a salad (bring your own oil-free dressing), dunk the great bread in the dressing and have fresh fruit for dessert. That's your rule, you have the bread and you make alterations to compensate for the added calories. Say you absolutely have to have the Caesar salad. Fine, just keep the rest of your meals that day light and lean, and perhaps exercise a little harder the next day to burn the calories. It's the same idea.

*Balance* may quite possibly be the most boring word in the English language. However, a balanced approach to eating is exactly what your rules should give you. This means accepting yourself when you're out of balance as well. I want to go back for a minute to the idea of all or nothing. Just as seeing food in black-and-white terms trips people up, so do the words *good* and *bad*. What's labeled good and bad changes on a daily basis, plus what's good for one person might be bad for another. They are words that bring instant affirmation or instant guilt; they stand for weakness and strength. But in reality, they are just labels that allow us to become all the more obsessed with the foods we eat. The good/bad syndrome makes eating a stressful affair: instead of helping us cope with stress, eating becomes stressful in itself. Worst of all, labeling foods good or bad keeps us from getting to the root of why we eat them, or don't eat them, in the first place. Instead of thinking of a food as good or bad, you need to look at it in terms of your total diet and how your particular body will use, or burn, that food.

Americans feel guilt about many things: drinking; smoking; suntanning; sex; and eating sugar, salt, and fat. We even experience guilt about relaxing. But we are human. Sometimes we break under pressure, and sometimes we do things that aren't in our best interests. Sometimes. Not all the time. The problem is that most people feel they can only live one way or the other—all or nothing, perfect or out of control. Out of control, obviously, is out of the question. But so is perfection. Everyone knows that perfection is boring. As a wise person once said "Do everything in moderation—even moderation." We want, need, and crave the physical pleasures of life, and food is one of those pleasures. There's no reason to feel guilt or have anxiety about it.

## Placing the Blame Where Blame Is Due

It's all well and good to have rules that are specific to your desires and lifestyle, but while they may be easier to follow than standards imposed on you by someone else, those self-made rules are no good if you just throw them away every time a sticky situation comes up. Later in this book I'll talk about why it's so easy to blame food problems on anything or anyone—your mother, spouse, children, dog—other than yourself. But the truth is, *you* and *only you* are responsible for what goes into your mouth.

I once had a client who had gone completely overboard with junk food. He was not only fat because of it but felt miserable about it too. He is one of the top entertainment business managers in the world and boasts some of Hollywood's hottest stars as his clients. I had already heard about the famous parties at his LA mansion as well as those at his Malibu estate long before he called me into his Hollywood office. When I went to see him he spent a lot of time ranting and raving about how poorly he ate. Two of his underlings were sitting in on the meeting and I could tell from their expressions that this was not the first time he had cried out for help with his diet.

Finally, when he was through, I looked him square in the eyes and said, "You must be very intelligent to have come this far in business." He agreed. "Obviously you have money, status, position. You only associate with the cream of the crop." He agreed again. "Then why do you eat cheap garbage junk food? Why do you eat worse than a family on welfare?" His colleagues turned pale. He hired me.

As it turned out, this client was an excellent "blame artist." One of his problems was that whenever they had staff meetings in the office, they'd order pizza and he just couldn't avoid eating it. "You're the boss," I told him. "You can have them order whatever you want for staff meetings. Take control of your eating life just as you've taken control of your business life." There was no reason that this man had to eat junky food. His office is located near some of the best restaurants in town. In LA anything and everything is available for takeout (salads, grilled chicken, turkey sandwiches, and more). Yes, he should satisfy his cravings and indulge on occasion, but what he had been doing—eating junk food night and day—had just become a habit. He wasn't thinking about other options, and there are many.

You don't have to be wealthy to eat healthy foods. Fast foods and convenient junk foods may be cheap, but healthy foods don't cost much more. I used to say to the celebrities I worked with, "I ate better than you do now when I was first married and living on a dancer's salary. I had no money, but I wasn't willing to live on junk food." Now that food is available in such amazing variety, it's a breeze to eat nutritiously and without gaining weight. There's no excuse.

A lot of women these days think it's clever when they say, "Cook! I can't even boil water." While I understand that they're proud of not being confined to the kitchen like the generations of women before them, I also think they use their inability to cook as an excuse not to take responsibility for the food in their lives. Once they're out of their mothers' houses where good food may (or may not) have been provided for them, they head straight for Mama McDonald's or Mama Convenience Store. What they don't think about—because they're too busy blaming all their troubles on their lack of time and knowledge—is that it's just as easy to stop at the market and pick up some grapes, pre-cut veggies, and low-fat cheese or even some roasted chicken (everything doesn't have to be a three-course meal) as it is to stop at a fast-food joint. No cooking involved, no artery-clogging, fat-producing food down the hatch either.

These are the kinds of issues you need to deal with if you're going to make the necessary changes in your eating habits. Dealing with how stress—the scapegoat of the eighties and now the nineties—affects your eating habits is essential too. You will never succeed in losing your food neuroses if you don't learn to accept that *everybody* has an emotional relationship with food. Just like a relationship with a spouse, boyfriend, mother, sister, or brother, it takes some work to keep it healthy.

Let me give you an example of how my client Harold dealt with his dependence on food during times of tension. When events in his life began to build to a nervous crescendo, Harold would decide to have Harold Day, a day when he would do nothing but be Harold, which included indulging himself with two boxes of Kraft Macaroni and Cheese. Obviously, this was a meal that his mother made (fifties-type food), and it was comforting to him. He was surprised when I told him he could—and should—bring Harold Day back into his life. However, whereas in the old Harold Days he'd make himself two boxes of Kraft Macaroni and Cheese—not only filled with fat, but chemicals as well—on the new Harold Day he switched to Hain's healthy version of macaroni and cheese, which has no preservatives, uses defatted cheese powder, and is made with skim milk. It's just as easy to prepare and tastes incredible. He could enjoy being Harold without hating himself the next day for destroying his health. As you read on, those are the kinds of options you'll find in this book. Because it just doesn't make sense to deny the fact that we turn to food for comfort. It does make sense, though, to give in to your most destructive cravings once in a while. Then, that's it—you don't go hog-wild, but just get back on track. It also makes sense to find smart alternatives that will let you indulge when you need to, but won't make you feel even worse the next day.

## Your Body, Your Self

Learning more about yourself is one of the most important ways to get a handle on your diet. It doesn't, however, stop there: you have to know what that knowledge means in practical terms. For one thing, you need to understand how foods are processed by the body in general—

just like information in a computer—as well as how foods are processed by *your* body in particular. When I meet with clients I also ask a lot of questions about how their bodies respond to food. Not everyone, for example, gains weight when they eat olive oil; not everyone has to watch his cholesterol like a hawk. Some people's bodies are satisfied with just two cookies and others crave the whole bag. All these personal idiosyncrasies are essential to take into consideration, because not only is it true that "You are what you eat, but it is also true that who you are defines what you *can* eat.

With so much media coverage of nutrition and weight loss these days, the average person is an expert on the subjects—or at least thinks she or he is. What I find, though, is that while the new awareness of food and its effect on our health has brought about a lot of beneficial changes it has also caused a lot of confusion. Most people are mixed up about food today and understandably so. The reports and so-called facts and figures on what's healthy and what isn't change everyday. Unless you make a career or regular pastime of it, you'd be hard pressed to keep up. It's also difficult to know what to do with this newfound knowledge. The information about food coming out now makes you feel like you should have a completely clean diet—no chemicals, no fat, sugar, salt, and so on—but the fact is, that's virtually impossible: There's no way to have a perfect diet unless you raise everything yourself (if you can even find perfectly clean soil) and never, never indulge. Some of your food is going to have chemicals in it. Sometimes you're going to eat fat, sugar, and salt. The difference is that you don't have to be eating them all the time. What you need is to get a handle on how, when, and where to let these things into your life so that your diet is 90—or at least 85—percent healthy. Strive for perfection and you'll most likely fail; admit you're human and that we live in a polluted world and be realistic about indulging when it's appropriate—and you'll succeed.

Chapter 4 is designed to help you get the facts straight about what foods your body does and doesn't need. And I hope that the information throughout this book will give you insight into the truth about which foods are nonfattening, which foods are healthy—and which foods are neither. One way I uncover what misconceptions my clients have about certain foods is to have them keep a diary of everything they eat for four days to one week (in Chapter 6 I'll show you an example of a daily food journal, plus some menus that make a lot more sense). Some things are obvious—a client knows that having a chocolate cookie *and* a piece of shortcake all in one day isn't going to do her hips any good. But when we go over the diaries, I also find not-so-obvious mistakes a client is making.

Kate Jackson thought her cereal choice was fine because it said "natural" on the package. Well, the word *natural* is one of the most abused in the food industry. The cereal was loaded with sugar, salt, nuts, and several other euphemisms for sugar such as dextrose, sucrose, corn syrup, and so on. I threw out the cereal.

One client I had was making a drastic mistake understanding the difference between "healthy" and "non-fattening" when she first consulted me. She was taking five advanced aerobics classes a week at Jane Fonda's studio, but hired me because she wasn't losing weight. She told me that she was a vegetarian and that she usually ate either fruit or a muffin in the morning, salads with no dressing for lunch, and steamed vegetables for dinner. Still, she was carrying an extra eight pounds and they weren't coming off. Something was obviously wrong—she should have been quite thin if that was all she was eating. My diet detective's mind started working. Everything else seemed okay, so what were her breakfast muffins like? Did they have nuts and raisins in them? No nuts, she said, but raisins and raisins are okay—they're *healthy*. I snack on them all day at the office, I eat a box a day. One of those mini boxes, I asked? No, no, no—the big kind. Well, my jaw dropped and so did hers when I told her that the box of raisins she ate daily totaled close to 900 calories! That's a lot when you're trying to lose eight pounds . . . and a lot more than she was burning in her one-hour aerobics classes. Sure, you can burn off some sugar, but not as much sugar as all those raisins contained.

Another thing that confuses a lot of people is exercise. This book is not about exercise, but as long as healthier eating is being discussed let's deal with exercise too.

It's a common misconception that if you work out you can eat whatever you please. I've found that many exercise trainers these days have terrible eating habits. But it's an even worse misconception to think that if you watch what you eat, you don't have to exercise too. Fitness might have seemed like just a fad when jogging first became the rage ten to fifteen years ago. But, in fact, fitness has turned out not to be a fad at all—rather, it's an important way of life for all people. We now understand that even if your diet is beyond reproach you have to move your body in some form or another to maintain good health and extend your life. And, of course, if you want to lose weight you have to engage in some kind of physical activity too. Even if you don't think you have the time or energy, at least make time to walk. Walk anywhere—walk with your friends, children, lover, spouse, or dog. This is exercise that everyone can do. It is also why many people in foreign countries are physically fit—their lives require them to walk everywhere. If you're not doing anything—and if you want to get the most out of this book about healthy eating—start walking or exercising now!

Of course, if you are already on a regular exercise program at a gym or are willing to start one, great. Remember, your workout program is the way you force your body to burn more fuel, increase circulation, strengthen your heart and lungs, and relieve stress. But also keep in mind that your body will adjust itself to the level of energy you expend during your program. If you want to budge a few more pounds, then lengthen the duration or raise the intensity level of the cardiovascular section of your workout. But don't turn an exercise program into a barter system for junk food. Being in shape and working out regularly doesn't justify eating lousy foods. You will eventually pay for it. It's one thing to use a workout to burn the extra calories after overindulging; it's another to continue to give your working body lousy fuel.

When she came to me with a heavy sugar addiction, my client, actress Madeleine Stowe, said, "It's as if all the work I do in my exercise program is completely undone with I eat too much candy. My muscles don't feel the work and it never shows on my body!" Madeleine was 100 percent right, and later I'll tell you how she overcame her addiction, and why she looks so great in such films as *Revenge, The Two Jakes, China Moon,* and *Closet Land.* When you overindulge in sugar, your body is spending its energy just to burn the sugar (simple carbohydrates, as opposed to complex) and barely has time to get to the important work of burning fat. It's like going into your workout with an extra burden to burn. Remember, you exercise with more energy when you've been eating correctly.

## Putting Theory into Practice

When the Los Angeles edition of *City Sports* magazine did a cover story on me, the headline read, "Yolanda, tell us what to eat!" Not surprisingly, "What should I eat?" is still the question I'm most often asked today. But before I introduce my clients to the healthy, nonfattening foods I think will suit their needs, we do a little cleaning out first. I examine every product in their kitchen cabinets, refrigerators, office desks, car glove compartments, closets, vacation homes, and the menus of the restaurants they frequent, and take a good clear look at exactly what is going into their bodies.

In the chapters ahead, that's what we'll do for you, too. We'll look at foods that you most likely have in your lives and learn alternatives. You'll learn how to eat less fat so that you'll not only be eating fewer calories, you'll be eating fewer of the most fattening calories. But don't expect me to tell you, "Oh, have an apple here, four ounces of this or that at a certain hour, or just eat oat bran and tofu—they're nutritious and they won't make you fat." This is meaningless. We are all aware of what we *can* eat to be healthy, but you really want to enjoy eating and not deprive yourself. When my clients ask me what they should eat, I take into consideration the foods they like and crave as well as their lifestyle. Then, instead of recommending carrots and fruit, I explain what a wonderful dinner they can prepare for themselves tonight or how to handle the movie munchies or, if they're going out, how to order a great meal, including bread and wine, and still lose a few pounds. In other words, how to make the food in their world work for them.

This book is about eating, *really* eating, not deprivation. It's not necessary to live an ascetic life to be thin and healthy, and I speak from personal experience. Because I wanted to enjoy food, I went out and found new foods that would suit both me and my family. I brought food back into my life and began to eat real meals again, as a great and *healthy* family affair.

What follows will educate you about the growing number of revolutionary low-fat and fat-free foods becoming available in stores and restaurants today, as well as the many new cooking techniques that will allow you to make meals without added fat. There are also lots of satisfying foods that are not new, but I'm willing to bet you never thought of eating them as an alternative to the junk you usually consume. I'm going to give you suggestions about what to eat when you're home, when you're alone or with your family, when you're at work, when you dine out, even when you go to a baseball game. Everywhere and anywhere. The upcoming chapters will fill your head with new ideas on how to—literally—eat to your heart's content. Consider the recipes and food suggestions here as tools for putting into practice what you learn about your eating needs.

For a lot of people, the concept that you can actually eat well and be happy with your body is too good to be true. Back in the days before I changed my "eating life," I also had no idea that it was possible to be both satisfied by food and satisfied with the way I looked. In fact, when I was pregnant, I was so thrilled to be eating real food again that I gained forty pounds! It was then that I realized I had to find a way to keep food in my life (but lose the weight). I embarked on a mission, and, much to my surprise, I began to discover exciting new products almost on a daily basis. It seemed that the food industry was responding to my very wants and needs and, in the process, reinforcing the direction I was going in.

This added to my joy of cooking and sparked my creativity. I found that old classics like meat loaf could even be made healthy now that ground turkey was available. I found that I could even get by in restaurants just by asking that my meal be prepared without oils.

Everything started to come together, partly because I decided not to be forced to eat foods I didn't want, partly because a revolution in the food industry had begun. More and more people now want to know what's in their food—and they're not going to eat it if it's not satisfactory. The food industry *has* to respond to people's health concerns if it wants to stay in business. Restaurants, too. The big trend on the West Coast now is open kitchens that allow patrons to actually see how chefs are preparing their meals.

## To Think About Before You Begin

Most of the time, I find that what my clients are eating isn't even making them happy on an emotional or a physical level. This is nonsense. It's time to stop and find workable solutions. I'm happy to say they definitely exist. After nearly a century of overrefined, chemical-infused foods full of sugar and fat, the food industry is changing. Eating healthfully now doesn't have to mean eating wheat grass, plain tofu, and tasteless brown concoctions from a health food store. And losing weight doesn't have to mean following one of the zillions of diets whose rules are so strict they make you feel like you've been inducted into the army.

I'm not going to tell you how to lose 20 pounds by Friday or even 2 pounds in two weeks. This is not a "miracle diet" book. This is not the latest gimmick or fad. This is about common sense. Granted, in our instant gratification society this is the harder road. Truly educating yourself is obviously going to be more difficult than following a map. So take a deep breath and forget everything else you have learned about diet and weight loss. This is a book about reeducating yourself about food and how it affects your body. Your individual body. Your particular set of circumstances. If you have a serious eating disorder or are extremely obese, this book is probably not going to give you all the answers you require. Most likely, you need to work one-on-one with someone who can help you deal with the complex health (and emotional) concerns of those problems. But in addition to getting personalized help, I hope you will use this book to help you bring food back into focus.

I also hope that in using this book you will become comfortable enough with food to avoid becoming obsessed with your body. When I was a dancer I learned a lesson that later served me well when I was working with clients. Because I had to keep myself rail thin, which is a job in itself, every time my weight varied a pound or two, I would wail and complain about how fat I was getting. A dear friend pointed out the truth to me: one day he jokingly asked, "Who's looking at you?" What he meant was, don't take yourself so seriously. Not everyone is noticing or even cares about your every pound. He also meant, "Get over yourself!" Sure, when you're dancing, you're always being observed, but the observers are only going to notice a major weight gain, not one or two pounds. I also realized then that I was focusing on my "fatness" to avoid the real problems in my life. Carrying a few extra pounds didn't make me fat, but by controlling those pounds I felt I could control other things—such as the fact that I was lonely and terrified by the competition in the dance world.

Taking weight control to extremes is so common these days. If you're going to be using the tips in this book to lose weight it's really a wise idea to take a good look at yourself—at your body and at your motives for wanting to be thinner. And it's important to know when to stop. One client first came to me at age 30, married, and 15 pounds overweight. She was taking five exercise classes a week as well as working out privately with me three times a week. In the beginning I admired her perseverance. She was working hard at getting the weight off and then, I expected, she would settle in with a good balance of eating well and exercising that would help her keep it off. But instead weight loss began to rule her life. She left a decent job so that she could exercise more, and she began to arrange her life around eating and working out. Eventually, so much of her conversation was about weight that it became difficult to be around her.

By this time she was seeing a therapist, trying to work out some family problems. I often wondered why her therapist didn't pick up on the fact that she was obsessed with food and weight, but she said she didn't discuss it with him. It occurred to me that perhaps this woman who was now 89 pounds was not talking to him about *any* of her real problems. It was obvious that her body dominated her attention because she was avoiding other more serious problems.

This, of course, is a worst-case scenario. What started as an attempt to get healthy turned into an unhealthy way of expressing her more deep-seated troubles. But let me tell you about Michelle, a client who has a very balanced attitude about food and her weight. When I began working with her she was 36, happily married with two daughters ages 3 and 5. She was also about 25 pounds overweight. As we began to work together, I would talk to her about her diet, the foods she kept in the house, and the changes she should make. Week by week she would report back to me about how well she was faring with her new eating habits; she'd tell me about the times she slipped up too.

What was so unusual—and so refreshingly healthy—about Michelle is that she never felt remorse or guilt about slipping up. She'd go out to dinner and just eat what she pleased one night, or she'd drink beer at a family picnic or have a piece of bacon at brunch and never make a big deal out of it. Instead she'd just cut back on her fat and calories for the next few days, eating nothing but "clean" foods.

Michelle eventually lost 26 pounds, *but not overnight*. She'd go down five, up one, down three, up two, down five more—you get the picture. She took her time and was intelligent about losing the weight. When a few pounds would come back, she dealt with it instead of getting crazy. She allowed food into her life. The result? A woman who is now 39 and looks better than she did at 26!

It may sound complicated, but it's really so easy. The truth of the matter is that once you start to make a few alterations in the way you eat, you'll never want to go back to eating the way you did before. You'll be so happy with the delicious foods you're able to eat and have so much more energy that you'll stop craving lousy oily, heavy, junky foods. Eating those foods, you'll find, are really only force of habit. I'm not saying you're suddenly going to want to buy a year's supply of wheat germ, but that your body will adjust—and eventually even crave—a better way of eating. You'll find yourself loving food for all the right reasons.

## A Glossary of Terms: What They Do and Don't Mean in This Book

One of the things that makes food so confusing these days is that the media, product manufacturers, nutritionists, and doctors—just about everybody—are tossing around terms without ever really defining what they mean. When you come across keywords in this book, unless otherwise stated, the following is what I will, and won't, be referring to.

### DIET

What it *doesn't* refer to:
• Adhering to a specific set of rules or a daily menu plan to lose weight.
• Counting ounces or calories.

- Starving or depriving yourself.
- Altering your lifestyle.

What it *does* refer to:
- The foods you consume.
- Your daily fare.
- What goes into your mouth.

## HEALTHY (NOT HEALTH) FOOD

What it *doesn't* refer to:
- Wheat grass, granola, sprouts, and foods that taste like sand.
- That eating it means leading a life where any pleasurable or junk foods (see below) are completely verboten; you can still have chocolate cake in your life and put Equal in your coffee and be a healthy person.

What it *does* refer to:
- Foods in their purest state, unadulterated by chemicals and overprocessing.
- Foods that do not present a health problem for you specifically, e.g., eggs aren't healthy for a man with high cholesterol but, in moderation, aren't fattening and are fine for a woman who can use the added protein.
- Foods that are not overloaded with salt, sugar, or fat.

## NATURAL

What it *doesn't* refer to:
- Foods called natural just for marketing purposes. A manufacturer of white bread, for example, could label his product all-natural because it contains flour, eggs, and water—all those ingredients are fundamentally naturally occurring. However, the flour could be refined and that takes a lot of its natural fiber, vitamins, and minerals away—so labeling that product natural is misleading. Plus, don't confuse natural with healthy—that product could contain twenty high-cholesterol egg yolks.

What it *does* refer to:
- Unprocessed (or minimally processed) foods made without any preservatives, artificial flavors, or chemical additives.

## FATTENING

What it *doesn't* refer to:
- Foods with healthy complex carbohydrate calories that the body can readily utilize as fuel.

What it *does* refer to:
- Foods that contain dietary fat, which the body can readily store as body fat.

## JUNK FOOD

What it *doesn't* refer to:
- Solely foods like the obvious: McDonald's hamburgers, Twinkies, Hershey bars.

What it *does* refer to:
- All the "fifties foods"—that is, overprocessed, chemically adulterated, artifically flavored foods (like TV dinners, cake mixes, spaghetti in a can, sugared cereals, and so on), that came of age in the fifties and have been popular ever since.
- Fast and poor-quality restaurant food.
- Any food overloaded with sugar, salt, fats, or chemicals.

## CALORIES

What it *doesn't* refer to:
- Numbers you should obsess over.

What it *does* refer to:
- Numbers you should be concerned about when they apply to fat—fat calories are the least healthy and most fattening kinds of calories because they're not readily burnable.

## SHUT UP AND EAT!

What it *doesn't* refer to:
- Rude disregard for the willpower and energy it takes to change your eating habits for the better.
- Stop talking and stuff your face.

What it *does* refer to:

- Stop talking, thinking, and obsessing about food.
- Learn the facts, learn about yourself, learn what healthy foods are out there in the marketplace—and then eat in peace!
- Do the work, go through the steps, and stop fooling yourself and everyone else.

# 2

# *Eat for Your Needs: The Best Rules to Live by Are Those You Make Yourself*

**S**HOULD YOU LET someone else tell you when you're hungry, what you crave, how much of it to eat, and what to eat with it? The answer, flat out, is no. Should you try time and time again to change your personality to fit someone else's ideas/rules for eating? Again, the answer is no.

We all spent our childhoods with someone telling us what and how much to eat. Part of growing up and leaving the roost is learning to make your own food choices. Yet it continually amazes me how many adults are not capable of taking responsibility for what they eat. Instead, they spend endless amounts of money on books and diet programs, on diet consultants, doctors, and nutritionists—anyone or anything that will act as a "food mom" and make healthful choices for them. Obviously, I am a food mom, too, but my aim is to get my "kids" to stop depending on me as soon as possible. Even from the very start, I explain to my clients, "I cannot hold your hand, I cannot be there every second. You have to learn to make food decisions on your own."

I could easily give those clients an arbitrary set of rules to follow when they're away from me, but that would never work. I'm not saying that you shouldn't abide by any rules at all. Otherwise we might all end up eating whatever we pleased, overweight and unhealthy and generally leading a slothful life. What I'm saying is that it's essential to establish rules that are right for *you*—rules based on facts about food and nutrition interwoven with facts about your own personal needs, preferences, and lifestyle. Rules that will come so naturally to you, that making the right food choices will be relatively easy. Not rules someone else says will "cure" you of all your dietary woes. And not rules from some regimented diet plan that works on paper, but disrupts your life—the old "oh, it was great while it lasted" syndrome. Because, say you go on a diet that tells you to drink water all day to quench your appetite. Well, if you don't like to drink water all day—or simply can't remember to drink water all day— the diet is not going to work. Drinking water all day is not you. It's not one of your habits. You're going to eventually drop any kind of diet that imposes rules too uncomfortable for you to abide by.

Does this mean you can't be thin and healthy? No! The people I know who have succeeded in changing their eating habits for the better have usually tried tons of different diets then, using bits and pieces of each one, have created rules of their own. Through all the ups and downs of those diets, they finally got enough education to figure out what works for them. For instance, after years of ping-ponging from one diet to another, losing, then gaining again each time, my client Dr. Fletcher finally went to Jenny Craig Weight Loss Center. Their diet didn't completely work for him, but the food helped because, although it's low cal, it appeals to his taste for junk food. "I eat the Jenny Craig food when I'm home and use what I learned from you about restaurants when I go out," he told me. "I sort of combine the two."

That's what works for Dr. Fletcher. Similarly, you have to find out what works for you. **You.** You are number one. You are an individual, your body is a unique "computer," and you live each day with your own stresses and emotional needs. Everyone has his or her own particular food cravings, whether it be a sweet tooth or a weakness for bread and pasta. It's also important to recognize that some desires—like those for salt and sugar—are innate and natural and that cravings are often a signal of what your body really needs. Trying to ignore them is not going to help you lose weight or eat healthfully. It's just going to turn what are natural desires into guilty binges. Instead, you've got to satisfy them in healthy, nonfattening (i.e., nondestructive) ways.

The minute you begin to listen to yourself and not the fad diet of the moment, eating well will become a natural part of your lifestyle—not something you do one day, don't do the next. Listen not only to the needs of your body, but your emotional needs and even your own personal complicated food hang-ups—everything! That's the biggest difference between the rules you make for yourself versus the rules someone else provides for you: your rules allow some leeway. They allow you to accept and accommodate your relationships with food that are other than saintly. I talk a lot about food being a joy, but not only is it a joy it is soothing, comforting, filling, and sensual. Most people have a complex relationship with food, which is why so many of them are obsessed with what they eat, even to the point of being "eating-disordered." I can only think of a handful of people—my husband is one of them—who don't ever think about what they eat. And even Richard, although he does not have a weight or health problem, has a relationship with food. He has to have his pizza and beer after his Saturday baseball game, he loves his mother's pot roast, and he would never have married a woman who couldn't cook.

It is my belief that all people need foods in their lives that are not particularly healthy. We all have times when we must say, "I don't care anymore, I'm going to have all of the ___(you fill in the blank)___ I want!" For one of my clients, it's a chopped chef's salad at her favorite restaurant, for another it's macaroni and cheese. For me it's cookies. The more you try to tell yourself that you do not need to have these so-called sinful urges to indulge, the more urges you will have and the more out of control you'll feel. You might as well tell yourself you can never have sex again either. Let your desires out of the closet, get to know them, acknowledge them, hell . . . embrace them! And then take them into account when making rules for yourself.

Let me use my client Madeleine Stowe as an example. Madeleine is a very centered, even-tempered, lovely, and talented young actress. Any of you who have seen her in films (mentioned earlier) know that she's naturally gorgeous too. But when she came to see me she was slightly plump and not surprisingly: as a way of handling stress or relieving boredom she was going through close to a half pound of See's chocolate candies a day. On top of that, heavy Italian food was the base of her diet. It was not only affecting her looks (it was a wonder she wasn't obese!), it was affecting her energy and health too. Just talking about what that candy was doing to her body helped inspire Madeleine to give it up. I explained that the sugar was sitting in her body and not allowing her to get the benefits of her exercise program. Plus, chocolate candy is not just sugar, it's filled with fat, fat, fat. Madeleine is by nature very slender, but she had been overloading her body with fats and sugars for so long that it was starting to show in her body shape and her skin. I helped her increase the cardiovascular section of her workout and introduced her to a diet of lean/fat-free foods. She was allowed her beloved Italian food once or twice a week—no more. Madeleine lost the weight quickly and really enjoyed the way her body looked and responded to her exercise program and filled her with increased energy. But when she started a new and particularly difficult movie, she would tend to hit the candy again. This time she made it a "rule" that the See's chocolates were part of her keep-my-sanity-while-working program—and she was able to limit it to just a few pieces. She wasn't being "bad," so she didn't have to binge. She also knows that one or two nights of fatty Italian food aren't going to make her blow up, as long as the following day is full of lean, clean foods. Now she has a lifestyle that allows her indulgences, without letting them ruin her. Madeline is proof that your body will benefit most from a good mind-set about food.

Another part of making your own rules is learning to accept your personal taste preferences, not the ones a diet book or program tells you you must acquire. In most cases, you're not going to be able to make your food cravings go away; it's better to pay attention to them and let them work for instead of against you. The same goes for acknowledging and learning to eat according to your lifestyle, then finding foods that jibe with the way you live, not the way a typical diet assumes that you do. Most diets are created in an effort to give you some control over your food intake. But what they really do is put you under someone else's control and eventually you're going to try to break free. And who could blame you? All the rules go contrary to the way you live your life. Later on in this book, you'll find some sample menus, and that's just what they are—samples, not "musts" that will dictate your life. They should serve as guidelines to educate you, get you going in the right direction, and give you some tangible ideas on how to eat better according to your own rules.

Before we start to explore how to find your own rules, consider some of the common—but unreasonable—diet rules you're used to hearing . . . and why they probably made you head straight for the cookie section of your supermarket instead of helping you eat more wisely.

**Unreasonable Rule #1:** *Measure your portions.* You have to have a lot of free time if you're going to measure and weigh each meal. And what about those days when you're absolutely starving and feel the need to eat more than the prescribed three ounces of chicken? By the time you've eaten your fourth ounce you'll feel like you've broken your diet so why not eat everything else you've been dying to have, too? What have these prescribed amounts got to do with the many ups and downs we go through? If the way we eat was as uncomplicated as ABC, we would all be thin and healthy.

Although the body is a creature of habit that strives for balance and, for the most part, runs like clockwork, it also has mood, or what I like to call need, swings, which affect what and how much your body tells you to eat. Women, with their frequent hormonal ups and downs, are particularly prone to these swings. And everbody, even children, is subject to the kind of stress that contributes to them.

When we turn to food because we're feeling tense or anxious, we turn to it because it's calming. Think of a baby nursing itself to sleep, the relaxed feeling after a good meal—it's a natural phenomenon. Why are athletes told to never eat a full hot meal before a competition? Mainly because it's too relaxing. The body's energy shifts to the stomach to digest the food, and the heavier the meal, the more energy required. On the other hand, certain kinds of stress and nervousness can also deaden the appetite. The opiate of romance can cancel out any desire for food; so can being nervous because of a new job. Even certain kinds of sadness or depression will make food completely unappealing. No doubt about it, just like the body, the mind has a lot to do with how hungry we are and what we want to eat.

What I'm trying to say is that there's no telling how much you're going to feel like eating at a given time. Measuring food to keep portions strictly under control usually only lasts until the dieter craves more than a half cup of rice—in other words, not very long. Measuring does not teach you to listen to your body's own needs, either physical or emotional. Many diets even want to restrict the amount of nonfattening foods you have. Going ahead and having a whole six ounces of chicken isn't going to make you fat if it's *prepared correctly,* but it will keep you satisfied. And it's being happy and satisfied with the food in your life that will help you lose the weight you want. I, for one, could never give up eating the amount of lean and healthy protein foods (fish, turkey, and chicken) I crave, although I gave up eating them prepared with oil or butter. For that reason, I don't have to measure my portions. I eat to my heart's content—and my body isn't fat!

**Unreasonable Rule #2:** *Never eat after six P.M.* GET REAL! In this day and age, no one even gets off work until six or seven o'clock. What are you supposed to do after a long day at the office, brush your teeth and go to bed? Or have a little salad and some Perrier? Gee, that's a great reward for working hard. It would be one thing if we lived in a European society that allows time for a major meal (and nap) in the middle of the day. But, no, America keeps running, looking forward to a satisfying meal at night instead. Granted, having a larger lunch than dinner is not a bad idea, because you'll have all afternoon to burn off the calories. However, skipping or severely limiting dinner will sabotage your good weight loss intentions: With your willpower weakened by hunger and your body simply worn down from a hectic day, you're only going to be digging into a bag of cookies or bag of oil-soaked popcorn before the evening is through. About 90 percent of my clients are weakest in the evening, and even those who aren't beaten down by the day want to eat at night—the reality is most people just love to eat at night.

The problem is not eating after six P.M., it's *what* you eat after six P.M. A dinner that's satiating but low in fat is ideal and, for most people, it will be enough to squelch the need for night binges. But others are irrepressibly prone to night snacking. One of my clients, a high-powered agent—who told me that she would give me a million dollars if I could help her lose weight—had especially strange eating habits, which she attributed to stress. She had been to every doctor, including a couple of shrinks, she'd tried every diet program in town and had had a few minor forms of plastic surgery. Still, she couldn't manage to change her eating habits, which went something like this: She wouldn't eat a thing all day, then she'd have dinner out at a restaurant virtually every night with business associates. But her real downfall was that, even though she'd eaten a substantial dinner, she'd get up at two A.M. without fail, walk down to the kitchen, and stuff herself with Wheat Thins, staring out the kitchen window as she munched. "I know, I know," she said. "You're going to tell me not to do that. I know you should never eat at two in the morning."

"No, I'm not going to tell you not to do that," I told her, "although you might want to talk to your shrink about why you're awake at two in the first place. But if you're going to continue to be up at two, you're going to eat at two in the morning no matter what I tell you. It's who you are, it's the way you deal with stress. So what you can do is eat something that will satisfy your desire for crunchy, salty food, but won't make you gain weight." I then gave her 7-calorie, oil-free onion-garlic crackers that are much less addictive—and much, much less fattening—than the

Wheat Thins. That, combined with learning how to order more wisely in restaurants, really worked; she lost the weight. (Funny thing, though, I never got the million dollars.)

**Unreasonable Rule #3:** *Never mix certain foods, always mix others.* Basically, this rule comes with the *Fit for Life* diet. Fit for exactly whose life is what I always ask. This diet has so many rules: never mix this with that, but mix these with those, and so on. Can you imagine not being able to have fish and rice together? Or a combination of chicken and noodles? Being restricted to having cereal without milk?

One of the rules *Fit for Life* is adamant about is that you must not eat fruit with or closely after eating any other types of food. What, no watermelon or fresh berries after dinner on warm summer nights? According to the authors, fruit will rot and ferment the other foods in your stomach, but even they admit there's no medical evidence to back this theory up. And as if it weren't enough to have to worry about when you can eat fruit again after consuming other foods, there are different time limits for different foods, e.g., wait two hours after eating raw vegetables; four hours after eating a meal that included fish, chicken, or meat; and so on. Most people have more important things to do than to spend time planning their digestive system's schedule. With stipulations like these, you're finally just going to say, the heck with it, give me everything at once. Man is meant to have a bounty of wonderful foods on his plate at the same time. One of the great joys of eating is to choose flavorful bits of this and bits of that and eat them all on the same forkful. It's human nature!

As far as I'm concerned, the strict *Fit for Life* diet is devoid of pleasure and has little, if any, scientific merit. Only a food fanatic could adhere to this eating plan.

Singer Stephen Bishop is one of my favorite examples of someone caught up in the *Fit for Life* frenzy. Stephen called me and said he needed to lose about twenty pounds. When I arrived at his house, my grocery bags in tow, he sat me down in a kitchen loaded with junk and proceeded to go on and on about how great the *Fit for Life* diet was. As he talked about the wonders of food combining, I was scanning the kitchen to see what he possibly could have found in that disaster area worth combining. "Oh, I haven't been on *Fit for Life* for months, but," he emphasized, "it's the only way to go."

At that point, I looked him square in the eye and asked, "Stephen, if *Fit for Life* is so fabulous for your *life*, why aren't you *fit*?"

"Well," he said, "I couldn't stay on it."

Exactly. The bottom line was that it did not *"fit"* his real *"life."* I then attempted to work with him to find what indeed was fit for keeping him, not anyone else, fit. Because for Stephen, as for most people, it isn't when or where you eat or how you combine your food that will help you get and stay thin and healthy. It's understanding your needs and your motivation for eating as well as understanding the truth about how your body processes food.

**Unreasonable Rule #4:** *Forget real food—try a liquid fast.* If you have fifty pounds or more to lose, fine—if you do it under medical supervision. Because, obviously, drastic measures are necessary. But even so, you will eventually have to go back to eating. Food will have to become a part of your life again. Going on a liquid fast may work for some obese people for a while because it helps them make a clean break with old bad eating habits that are threatening their lives, much like smokers and drug addicts have to go cold turkey. And if the supervision is good, liquid dieters can learn how to bring food back into their lives. But this does not happen overnight and involves a lot of psychological training. Then there's the question of whether or not they'll even be able to stick to the diet/fast. Fasting is a difficult and seriously involved procedure and it must include a long period of reentry into regular eating, otherwise it will have all been for nothing. Unfortunately, Oprah Winfrey is a classic—and highly visible—example.

This kind of diet never works for the average person trying to drop a few pounds: Nine out of ten people gain back the weight they lost. This is mainly because they use it as a quick fix, then just return to eating the same old fat-filled foods as they did before the diet. The average person doesn't need the type of severe counseling most obese people do, but they do need to make changes. Remember, when you tell yourself you're going *on* a diet, subconsciously you are setting yourself up for going *off* it, and that won't help you make the changes necessary to eat healthfully for life.

**Unreasonable Rule #5:** *No sugar or salt.* First (I will talk more about this in Chapter 4), sugar and salt are not the bad guys they're made out to be, unless you have a specific medical problem. Our cravings for salt and sugar are natural; our taste buds are primed to desire products made with them. And if they're eaten in moderation, they're not unhealthy or fattening. It's only when they are abused or eaten in foods that are cooked with fattening ingredients that they present a problem. Keep in mind that 90 percent of our processed food in this century contains about

50 percent sugar and is likewise oversalted. No wonder salt and sugar have become demons, and no wonder we're so used to overeating both.

Consequently, with our natural cravings and our habits of eating salt and sugar too often, any diet that tells you to eliminate them is setting you up for failure. And because you've been told they are bad, when you decide to be "bad" yourself and give into your cravings for salty or sugary foods, you'll go for the most forbidden ones you can get your hands on. Instead of acknowledging your salt craving and satisfying it with something like onion-garlic rice snaps or teriyaki rice cakes you'll probably have potato chips or Chee-tos. Instead of quenching your sweet desires with low-sugar candies or sorbet you'll probably have a Hershey bar or ice cream. A lot of the decisions we make about food are tied into guilt and defiance.

**Unreasonable Rule #6:** *Fats are fattening—never have any of them.* YES! Fat eaten is fat on the body . . . BUT—and I repeat BUT—if you crave something with oil or a delightful cheese now and then, have it in moderation. Most of the time it is not the actual fat you are craving. Otherwise you would munch on a stick of butter or drink a bottle of olive oil or chew on the ring of lard around a steak. (Keep in mind that chicken, fish, and turkey contain all the natural fat you need.) What you really want is a food with fat mixed in. Try to figure out what it is that you're craving: Is it really something fatty? Or is it something sweet or salty? Perhaps it's really something crunchy that you want.

You should always limit the amount of fat you eat if you want to maintain your weight and stay healthy. If you're trying to lose, cut it out all together except for those times when you desperately need a fat fix. Then find that low-fat substitute or have the real thing, eat it with gusto, and clean up the next day.

**Unreasonable Rule #7:** *Stay away from alcohol when you're trying to lose weight.* While it goes without saying that alcohol abuse is detrimental to your body, mind, and spirit, life is too short to eliminate all pleasures completely. Enjoy your glass of light beer or wine—the calories are not that high, and because they're carbohydrates, they're very burnable. One of my clients, a successful business manager for some of the world's top performers, is about fifty years old and belongs to a generation of men who work hard, golf hard, think dieting is for women, and have a few drinks every night. He worked hard to get where he is, and he doesn't want to hear from any nutritionist or diet counselor that he should cut out all drinking to drop pounds. He wouldn't do it.

He typically has a few drinks per night, nothing more; he works hard, and he enjoys those drinks. It was not my job to get him off alcohol, but to get weight off him. So what I did was just suggest that he keep his drinks to a minimum and change what he was drinking slightly. Thinking it was healthy, he had been mixing vodka with cranberry juice. Yet the cranberry juice he was drinking was loaded with sugar and corn syrup and was very high in calories. I got him to switch to unsweetened grape-fruit juice, a less caloric choice. By shaving off a few calories here, plus a few calories from his meals, he is slim to this day. What was important here was dealing with the realities of his life and his personality, not making a moral judgment about what he should and shouldn't do.

While that particular client wouldn't have listened to anyone telling him how much to drink, another client of mine did, much to her disadvantage. This client was always either on a diet prescribed by one of the many nutritionists she had been to or, on the other end of the spectrum, eating absolutely anything she pleased. One of this woman's pleasures was to have a glass or two of wine with her husband at the end of the day. It was a nice—and not fattening—break for her, but the various diet coun-selors she'd gone to had made it seem like a negative and told her to cut it out.

Except for the last nutritionist she went to before seeing me: that one said she could have one glass three times per week or two glasses twice a week or three glasses in one sitting—in other words, a prescribed number of ounces. (Confused? So was she.) At the end of the first week of her new diet, her son walked in and announced that he had totaled her husband's new Porsche. After realizing that her son had no injuries—and controlling the desire to injure him herself—she decided to wait and tell her husband when he got home. In the meantime, she examined the damages to the car, talked to the other party involved, discussed the insurance, and went over all of the other problems related to accidents. By the time she was done—and completely stressed out—she had poured herself a few glasses of wine. Before she knew it, she realized that she had gone beyond her prescribed wine limit for the week (at that point, who cared about counting ounces), so figuring she'd already bro-ken her diet, she overate at dinner, then again after dinner, and never looked at that diet again.

In reality, the wine wouldn't have done too much damage to her waist-line. A slight headache the next day maybe, but that comes with having children. Believe me—I'm a wine lover myself—it's not that fattening. But because most people have been forewarned about alcohol, probably because of the heavy sugary drinks that were once so popular, drinking anything at all makes them think "I've blown my diet. I might as well go the distance and pig out." What I taught my client was that she, in fact, hadn't screwed up and that drinking a bit too much wine wasn't any reason to let it all go. She felt stressed out about the car and needed an outlet. She was entitled to those glasses of wine and, really, any extra calories they added she could have made up for by just exercising more or cutting back a little on her food intake the next day. Wine does not have fat calories, just extra carbohydrate calories, which are easier to burn than fat. Her downfall was that she didn't make up a rule—a rule that allowed her to have her wine and eat too. Just because you want some wine, light beer, or a few drinks doesn't mean that you might as well eat what you please. Keep your drinking light and your food light and you'll be fine.

**Unreasonable Rule #8:** *Have five to eight mini meals a day.* If you're like me, you probably don't have five to eight mini seconds most days. When are you supposed to have all this time to prepare eight mini meals? And if you're not preparing them, then you're probably grabbing eight mini junk meals a day. If you can have lots of healthy mini meals prepared without added fats, great, it's a very good way to eat. It is the way most children eat in the first few years, but keep in mind that someone (like mom) is preparing those meals. Also, you can't just eat a little of any old thing all day long and expect that the fat and calories won't add up just because you didn't eat them all at once.

The truth is, this rule doesn't work out for most people. It's just too demanding to have to stop and eat several times a day. At one time it was very hip—remember "grazing?"—but the problem, once again, is that it rarely fits into our fast-paced lives.

**Unreasonable Rule #9:** *Have breakfast like a king, lunch like a prince, and dinner like a pauper.* What if I feel like a pauper at breakfast (not to mention a grump), a princess at lunch, and a queen at dinner? Maybe the next day I'll feel like none of the above at breakfast and lunch, all three at dinner. With PMS I have been known to vary my meals in much stranger ways. This prescription is as old as the idea of royalty. In theory, it might be a smart way to eat—since everyone is generally less active after dinner, more active throughout the day, it makes sense on a calorie-burning level—but, again, things just don't work out that way for everybody. For example, if I ate a huge breakfast, I would go back to bed. This book would never get written, let alone would my daughter get to school on time. And I wouldn't stick to it, because I personally hate eating that way. Plain and simple. Eat your biggest meal when you feel you need it. Just make it a big meal of healthy, low- or no-fat foods and you'll be eating just as wisely as the king, prince, and pauper—only on your terms.

**Unreasonable Rule #10:** *Don't turn to food when you're stressed out.* Let's face it, we don't eat solely for survival anymore. In this day and age, many of us also use food to relieve stress—although most people feel so guilty about eating poorly, they wind up even more stressed out than when they started. Why neglect the simple fact that when we're sad or mad or nervous eating is an excellent source of comfort? You cannot live in these high-pressure times and not have something to relax you. You don't want to abuse drugs, cigarettes, and alcohol, or take it out on your children or mate. So what's left? We are human and certain foods act somewhat like opiates; they soothe the nerves. It feels good to indulge in sugary foods when you're depressed. It feels good to munch on something crunchy when you're anxious. Stop trying to pretend that food is not a comfort. Eating for emotional reasons is not a sin! You just need to know what foods will help you cope with stress (certain flavors, textures, and temperatures are more comforting than others) but not make you fat. Food should satisfy your emotional needs, but not damage you. You should be able to use it as a comfort and not feel terrible the next day, which will only lead to more stress.

I was giving a lecture once and a young woman raised her hand and told a story of how when she had a fight with her boyfriend, she walked out, went directly to the store, and bought a pint of Häagen Dazs. She ate it, then went back to the store for more. I could see she was miserable about drowning her sorrows in ice cream and she was more than a little surprised when I said, "And you'll do it again. If it's not the problem with this boyfriend, then it will be one of life's other disappointments and you will nurse it with ice cream. And that's okay!" I could see she was totally confused. "First of all, pat yourself on the back because you are not drowning your sorrows with drugs or alcohol, then admit that ice cream comforts you. Keep some healthier, lower-fat types around the house for those occasions. Set yourself up for the blows of life. I always have diet candies squirreled away somewhere in the house. If Ice Bean [a non-dairy frozen dessert] or frozen yogurt doesn't cut it, have the Häagen Dazs and clean up your diet the next day. Exercise a little more and carry on!"

**Unreasonable Rule #11:** *Never eat too much protein (or carbohydrate).* I absolutely have to have a lot of protein for dinner. If I listened to that rule, I would leave the dinner table feeling unsatisfied and end up in the cookie jar or eating bread or crackers to fill the gap. I also stick to very lean proteins, which is a lot different than downing lots of pork products or fatty steaks. I have learned my computer, that is, my body, and I know that I can handle a lot of protein and stay healthy and thin. True, someone else may not. But what is good for the goose is not always good for the gander. Madeleine Stowe can consume olive oil on a very moderate basis and she doesn't blow up. I cannot consume one drop. If you are running marathons or exercising strenuously or simply just don't gain weight when you eat them, you can afford more carbohydrates than average. There's nothing unhealthy about them. Too much is relative to who you are, what your body needs, and how it functions.

## How to Decide What Rules Are Right for You

I could go on and on about unreasonable rules: there are thousands of them out there, and those of you who have tried diet after diet, nutritionist after nutritionist, book after book, gimmick after gimmick know all of them. The rules—or "shoulds" as they really ought to be called—that are reasonable are the ones that take into account the food and nutrition facts discussed in Chapter 4, but also apply specifically to your body, to your lifestyle, to your wants and needs, and, of course, to your goals. "Shoulds" that are reasonable are shoulds that you'll be able to adhere to in the long run.

Does this mean it will be easy? Not too long ago a television producer and writer by the name of Ken Hecht wrote a very right-on-the-mark essay in *Newsweek*. Hecht, who had once carried 315 pounds on his six-foot frame, but is now a slim 167 pounds, called his piece "Oh, Come On Fatties!" and wrote, "the obese [and, presumably, the overweight] will latch onto any excuse for failing to lose weight." One excuse might be that it's not easy enough. Well, face the truth right now: anyone who keeps their weight down consistently WORKS AT IT! I work at it, Madeleine Stowe works at it, Cher works at it, my girlfriends work at it. Just as we work on the relationships in our lives (they don't just happen), we work at eating right and exercising. So don't assume that anything is going to be a snap.

On the other hand, know that if you make your own rules, it will definitely be easier than following a formatted diet, but you have to be realistic: If you have high cholesterol, then there are certain foods you just cannot eat on a regular basis or you may eventually die of a heart attack. If you are fat, there also certain foods you cannot eat regularly or you will continue to be fat. Yet making individualized rules is also about making individualized compromises and that can make the whole process of changing your eating habits a lot less difficult. For instance, although I love peanut butter, I can live happily without it. But I can't live without candy, although if I ate as much as I wanted to, I'd be twice my size. So I limit my candy times to when I go to the movies or to times when I'm suffering the effects of PMS, and I stick to low-sugar candies. This is a "should" that works for me. Yours might be something else: switching from Ben & Jerry's Heath Bar Crunch to no-fat raspberry sorbet, eating pretzels (they contain no fat) instead of potato chips, or forgoing filet mignon for filet of sole. Maybe you can't live without olive oil on your salad. Fine, just don't have oil on any of the other foods you eat.

"Rules" imply rigidity, but they don't have to. One of your rules might even be that you're flexible: When you're at someone's house for dinner and they serve, say, crème brûlée for dessert, your rule might be to just go ahead and eat it—and then cut out all fats the next day to make up for the indulgence. I have one client, Gail, who can eat just two or three cookies, then put the bag away. I find this amazing and admirable. Even if I put the bag away, I'd have my hand back in it ten minutes later (and I hate to admit it, but if I threw the rest away, I'd have probably fish them out of the garbage). Gail, though, avoids fats elsewhere in her diet and so lets herself have a few cookies occasionally. Not on a regular basis, but occasionally. She knows the rules that work for her and they help her maintain a healthy, thin body.

These are the kinds of specific trade-offs and self-imposed rules you'll have to decide for yourself. We all feel a little out of control when it comes to food so we turn to the latest set of popular rules hoping they will help. But if you stop and think about it, you know best what you need from food. I can't tell you what exactly will work for you, but I can help you ask yourself the right questions and give you some basic guidelines to help you develop a personalized plan for eating. First off, take the time to do a little self-examination about . . .

■ YOUR FOOD WANTS AND NEEDS. When do you need to eat and what satisfies you? Heavy breakfast and light dinner or big lunch and no dinner? What kinds of food cravings do you get? And, no guilt attached, what do you need from food? Further along, in Chapter 6, I'll show you how to keep a food journal, which will help you see more clearly just what is going into your mouth and body.

■ YOUR LIFESTYLE. All of our lives are stressful in one way or another and stressed to different levels. When do you eat to deal with the stress? Does your job dictate that you eat at odd hours? Do you have frequent business meals? Do you sit down to big family meals or are you single and always on the run? If you examine it, you'll find that the way food and stress intertwine in your life always falls into a pattern.

■ YOUR BODY. Considering that one body may take a tablespoon of ice cream and apply it right to the hips, while another won't even register the fat from a full carton, it's crucial to consider your body when making rules. I'll deal more with this issue in Chapter 4, but for now, consider some of these questions: What problems does your body have now . . . or what potential problems do you want to work on avoiding? Are you overweight or do you have a tendency to put on pounds easily? Do you have high cholesterol? Do you feel lousy—listless, uncomfortable—most of the time? Is your goal to eat more healthfully so that, even though you look and feel fine now, poor eating habits don't catch up with you later? Think of your body as a computer: How does it compute food information?

## Making Rules Based on Your Wants and Needs

There's a fine line between what you want and what your body needs. What we *want* is mostly determined by habits we've formed—our minds, that is, not our bodies. Dennis wants a big brunch on Sunday because that was the only time his family ever got together, so he finds it both emotionally and physically fulfilling. Suzanne wants a McDonald's cheeseburger at 12:30, because she's been having one at 12:30 since she was six, not because her body needs a cheeseburger to function. Robert wants to have mayonnaise on his sandwich because that's the flavor he's used to tasting. It's just not a sandwich without it! Alice wants popcorn at the movies because that's what you're *supposed to have* at the movies.

We are conditioned to taste certain things in certain forms at certain times, and this is especially true when it comes to fat, sugar, and salt taste sensations. Dennis could still have brunch on Sundays and just choose something like a mushroom omelet made with one yolk and several whites instead of the eggs, pancakes, and bacon he's used to ordering. Suzanne might sit down and realize that the cheeseburger really isn't that important to her, just convenient. Alice could skip the popcorn (she doesn't even really like it) and have grapes or a roll of Lifesavers instead. Robert really isn't after a sandwich—those come in many forms—he's after the taste of mayo. Likewise, people who have been eating butter on bread all their lives can't imagine the bread without. Yet my daughter only knows—and loves—plain bread. Butter is truly out in our house.

I particularly have difficulty getting older clients to change their way of eating, because they are so used to eating the fatty and overprocessed foods endemic to this past century. The old meat, potatoes, and vegetables cooked until they're mush and covered with salt and butter dies hard by them. Habits. Remember, we have relationships with food. Once you're comfortable with those relationships it's damn hard to change unless you can see how destructive they are to your life.

Unfortunately, what most people want to eat is not what their bodies need. *Wants* are brain based, linked up with emotions and conditioning. *Needs* are simply what man as a human animal needs to survive, not emotionally, but in pure physical terms. What everyone needs are the basics: lean proteins, fresh fruits and vegetables, whole grain foods, and (wise but not essential on a daily basis) legumes and limited nonfat dairy products.

Often your body will crave what it needs, often times it will crave what it wants. Should you only satisfy your needs and not your wants? As I keep saying, it's important to satisfy both—but while the foods you need can basically be eaten in generous amounts, the foods you want usually cannot. Still, wants, whether they're due to habit or the desire for emotional sustenance, can feel as urgent as needs and they must be addressed. Here are some issues to consider. I believe they'll help you understand the differences between the body's healthy wants and the minds needs (which aren't always as healthy) and guide you in making your own rules accordingly.

**I. Don't sacrifice needs for wants.** In other words, don't give in to what you need emotionally until push comes to shove. For example, you never have time for lunch, which irritates you, so you just down a bag of m&m's because you're so frustrated by your overtaxing job. However, you're not getting revenge, you're just getting a big behind. Even though a bag of m&m's may have fewer calories than a sandwich and piece of fruit, if you have the candy instead of a traditional lunch you miss out on the vitamins and minerals the sandwich and fruit provide. That's why sugar foods are called empty calories—they might not kill you, but they won't add many life-sustaining nutrients to your system either. Also, we know now that a calorie is not a calorie. Chocolate contains a lot of fat. The calories you get from the m&m's might be fewer but can ultimately be more fattening than calories from a lean meat sandwich and piece of fruit. When you're in crisis, allow yourself to indulge, but don't make a regular habit out of subjugating your needs for your wants.

**2. Don't be so quick to sacrifice your wants for what you've been told your body needs.** Common sense will tell you that you shouldn't have a croissant every morning—the butter content will not only clog your arteries, it will most likely make you wind up with croissant-size slabs of fat on your thighs. But what about common diet wisdom that says you should have fruit for breakfast? I, for one, love fruit, but not for breakfast. I crave some kind of bread in the morning. So instead of a fat-filled croissant, I have a huge fat-free blueberry muffin for breakfast. Maybe it's habit, but it's a good habit. If your habits aren't hurting you, keep them. Say you don't like to eat lunch. Ideally, you should eat lunch (building up your hunger all day might make you overeat at night), but don't force yourself. As long as you're getting enough nutritious foods the rest of the day, you're not hurting yourself and you should be able to eat as you please. I hate lunch, but I have a few pieces of fruit, or some steamed veggies during the day as I need them. Also, eating when you please will help you to maintain a consistent diet—and that is the healthiest thing you can do. The person who achieves a balance of eating 85 to 90 percent healthy lean foods, with 15 to 10 percent treat foods will find success over years, not the horrible nightmare of yo-yo dieting, which, as news reports have made clear recently, is extremely unhealthy.

**3. Anticipate your wants and prepare for them with guilt-free foods.** One of my clients had a habit of having a handful of peanuts at four o'clock every day, but now that his cholesterol has shot up, he's had to make a switch. A carrot stick or piece of fruit at four o'clock would never satisfy him, so instead he now has a handful of soy-based nuts or stone-ground crackers—foods that provide him with a similar flavor sensation, but are low in saturated fat.

**4. Selectively give in to your wants and make trade-offs.** There will be times when nothing less than the real thing will do. Robert, the mayo lover, might go ahead and have his mayonnaise on a sandwich only on the weekends, or at his favorite deli, and not have any mayo any other time, as well as keep the oil out of his diet the rest of the time. One friend of mine has a thing for Ben & Jerry's ice cream. Her trade-off is that she doesn't have any desserts the whole week, then has a big bowl of Heath Bar Crunch on the weekend. Frozen yogurt just wouldn't do, so she saves up for a real indulgence. It's important to recognize your

need for fattening, sugary, salty, just plain old no-good foods AND AL-
LOW THEM INTO YOUR LIFE AS THE (LITTLE) PLEASURES
THEY ARE MEANT TO BE, NOT AS THE BASIS OF YOUR EN-
TIRE DIET. I have a client who, instead of going home and having a
drink at night like a lot of people do, is happy with a few *teaspoons* of
peanut butter. And she can afford to do it. She has cut oils out of the
rest of her diet.

**5. Keep a mental record not only of what you've already eaten
that day, but of what you're going to eat later.** Here's my own personal example. I wake up and have a muffin with my coffee, then I do my
workout. I skip lunch (my rule: I hate lunch so I don't have it), then pick
up my daughter from school at 2:30 and take her for frozen yogurt. I
stop and think: should I have a non-fat yogurt or just ask for a cup of
fresh fruit (the kind they have on hand for toppings)? If I am having dinner
at home, something like fish and vegetable, I go for the yogurt. If I'll be
eating out that night and know I'll want to eat the basket of bread, I skip
the yogurt and plan on having dessert at the restaurant. Keeping a mental slate of what's going into your body on a daily basis will help you plan
for excesses so that, all told, you maintain a very balanced diet.

. . . . . . . . . . .
## Making Rules Based on Your Lifestyle

Weren't there once such things as sit-down breakfasts, lunch time,
coffee breaks, tea time, family dinners? Didn't we once read about it or
see it on *Leave It to Beaver* or *The Donna Reed Show*? It's been so long I
can hardly remember.

Who has a normal eating lifestyle anymore? Everyone is always grabbing a bite when they can. (For a while it even had a name, grazing, which
really meant that, because there was no time for sit-down meals, people
were just eating finger foods all day long. See Unreasonable Rule #8.)
The leisurely meal has now been relegated to Sundays and holidays only.
And then only sometimes. Those who don't use the catch-as-catch-can
technique of eating are most likely eating out a lot, or eating at times
that don't jibe with the traditional three-meals-a-day framework, let alone
any diet prescription.

Musician Paul Stanley, for example, could never stay on a diet that told
him not to eat after six P.M. He gets up at eleven, goes to work at the
studio about one, writes and records until eight, then goes out to dinner

at about ten. That's Paul's lifestyle. He can't change it, nor did he want to when I was working with him. So I didn't try to make him. I just tried to help him eat well within that framework.

One of his pitfalls was that he always craved something sweet to eat when he got home at night. Unlike physically stressful work, which usually brings on cravings for substantial foods like pasta, mentally stressful work—like writing music—often inspires a desire for sugar. In Paul's case, he figured that his cravings were just plain "bad" so he would eat the worst thing he could think of, usually something rich and chocolate like Black Forest cake. It reminded him of his childhood in a home filled with wonderful baked goods. However, he felt so guilty about the cake and his sugar cravings that he simply decided his whole diet was rotten and went completely out of control.

When we worked on getting him to eat more healthfully, one of the things I told Paul was to go ahead and keep satisfying his sugar cravings, but to do it with diet chocolate mousse, low-calorie fudge bars, or low-sugar candies instead. Knowing he had those alternatives in the house— and that it was okay to go ahead and eat something sweet—ultimately kept him away from the Black Forest cake.

What, you're probably asking yourself, do I have in common with a rock star with eccentric hours and eating habits? Maybe not too much, but I like to use Paul as an example to show that it's possible to find answers no matter how unusual your lifestyle or how crazy the way you eat seems. In this day and age, very few people really eat three meals a day at regular hours and with nothing in between. We all have our own food craziness; sometimes it's just better to admit it and then try to work with it.

And it's not when or where you eat, it's what you eat that counts. I eat my biggest meal at night, which according to most nutritionists should doom me to being overweight. But I have maintained a lean, healthy body for sixteen years because what I eat at night is lean and healthy. And I'm happy eating that way. *Happy* is the operative word. I don't have to struggle to do the "right" thing, because the way I eat *works* for my lifestyle.

If my lifestyle dictated that I eat out every meal, it would be the same thing. I would have to find restaurant foods that were lean and healthy too. What's important is that you take a close look at what your life is really like instead of hoping it will change and you will be able to eat three square textbook-perfect meals. Just because you eat out all the time is no reason to order the fattening chef's special at every meal. If you eat out all the time, how special can it be? It's routine. Likewise, if you eat at odd hours. Two o'clock in the morning might traditionally be a time for sneaking a sugary, nutrient-empty snack from the refrigerator, but if you eat at two o'clock every morning, there's no reason not to be prepared with something more nutritious. Say that, like Paul Stanley, you have dinner at ten P.M. Just because the time seems wrong (in fact, it's right—right for you), don't think that it's okay to order poorly too.

A client of mine who works in real estate likes to have breakfast with her two young children in the morning. The rest of her day is spent zooming around in her car showing homes. Her two biggest mistakes were (1) eating the same things she prepared for her kids in the morning and (2) stopping at fast-food joints and ordering something like a chicken sandwich loaded with sauce or salad loaded with ham, cheese, and dressing for lunch. I explained that while it was great that she had breakfast with her children, there was no need for her to eat scrambled eggs and buttered toast like them (and, in fact, she'd be doing them a favor if she cut the fat and gave them a healthier cereal or fat-free muffins instead). Likewise, even though she's on the run during the day, it's just as easy to stop in a supermarket and pick up some fruit and crackers or a deli where she could find a lean turkey sandwich or less fat-packed salad to go. Don't change your lifestyle, I told her, just make some very convenient adjustments.

Much of what negatively affects our eating habits is the stress in our lives. Men and women are working hard, men and women are stressed. I needn't go into the pressure of the work force, coping with rapidly growing technology, raising children, and just keeping fit and healthy. As everything moves faster, we find ourselves moving faster just to keep up. When we need to eat, we want to eat what we want to eat. Unfortunately, that ultimately leads to more stress as what's put down the throat one day begins to show up in ever-thickening rolls around the stomach the next. "I'm fat!"—more fat, more stress!

Try to figure out the times that you usually eat because of stress. Do you run for sweets after a bad date? A bag of chips and a six-pack after a crazy day at the office? Do you get anxious, wake up in the middle of the night, and head for a midnight snack? Are you likely to pig out on ice cream on the weekends because you feel lonely? Or do you hit a pint of ice cream at 3:30 on weekdays because you've been driving the kids around all day and they've been driving you crazy? Do you go to your desk and get out the Pepperidge Farm Milanos after a presentation at work? I once had a surgeon-client who, before he went into surgery every Thursday morning, would dive into the doughnuts at the coffee cart. This was a time when nothing was on his mind but the upcoming operation (thank goodness!) and he just ate what was there. I arranged for there to be fat-free bran muffins right next to the Danish and other junk, and he felt much better.

Everybody has a breaking point, a time when sinning seems necessary and food in various forms becomes comforting, fulfilling, even sensual. But the comfort lasts only as long as the time you're eating it. So you lengthen the comfort time—until you find you're in the middle of the famous, full-scale binge. Being aware of what provokes these forays into food marathons can help you prepare for them. Have foods around that you can indulge in—like low-cal baked cheese puffs or animal crackers (sweet, but not too high in fat)—without being destructive. Allow yourself to eat when you're feeling stressed out, but choose foods that, while satisfying to your particular needs, won't make you more stressed out in the end. Naturally there will be times when you have to have the real thing. It has to be Häagen Dazs coffee ice cream, not blueberry sorbet. Don't feel guilty—that's only more destructive. Have it and keep your diet clean the next day.

I said this before, and I'll say it again: stress isn't going to go away and neither are the needs you associate with it. But you can help yourself by not compounding your stress level with junky foods and learning about all the new foods out there to help you.

# 3

# *You're Not Helpless: There Are No Victims*

**HERE IS A** very hip saying going around these days in response to anybody who complains about a bad relationship, a bad deal, a bad job, a bad day, a bad habit—a bad anything. It goes like this: "There are no victims." What happens to you happens because you create it, you allow it, you buy into it. Nobody does it to you, you do it to yourself. The very bottom line of hard-core reality. Sound harsh? Perhaps in some instances it does, depending on what it applies to. But not when it comes to the way we eat. In that instance, what's harsh are the diet-failure statistics in this nation. What's harsh is how desperate people are to get their eating habits balanced and under control in this day and age. I say, enough excuses, enough talk, enough gimmicks. Deal with it: get your body the way you want it.

One of the major reasons people fail to get and keep their bodies slim and healthy is because they so often feel compelled to consume the wrong foods simply because of circumstance. They feel it is out of their control and that they're victimized. Women in particular often feel like they have to eat the same foods—even if they are fattening and unhealthy—as their boyfriends or husbands, their children, mothers-in-law, even housekeepers, simply because to do otherwise would "upset the balance of the meal." When eating with friends or business associates, the tendency is to follow their lead as well. Men, especially, have a difficult time admitting they're watching what they eat when they're dining with colleagues. It still has a female stigma attached to it. And nobody, male or female, wants to be known as the chronic dieter who sits at the table with his or her mouth shut while everyone else enjoys himself.

Ken Hecht, who wrote the piece in *Newsweek* I mentioned in Chapter 2, said something else quite astute: "Fat people have no experience that even remotely suggests such success [permanent weight loss] is possible. They love to wallow in failure and believe that in the end, that they really have no control over their weight. The fact is we have more control over what we put into our mouths than over almost any other aspect of our lives. Face it, Chubbo, when was the last time you were force-fed?"

And I thought I was tough! Hecht has experienced every facet of being fat and unhealthy so he's not without sympathy for others' struggles. But he also faced the facts: there's no justification for letting your body go to pot.

Nonetheless, I know it's difficult to stand your ground. Even those who care for you most may try to undermine your efforts at every turn. Recently, to celebrate one of my best friends' birthday, we went to the club to work out and sauna, then I took her to lunch. As she knows, I'm not a lunch eater and I usually just opt for a decaffeinated cappuccino. "It's my birthday! You have to eat lunch," she said.

"Marcia," I replied, "I fully intend to join you for lunch, but I really just want a cappuccino. I don't even eat lunch on my own birthday, let alone anyone else's. This isn't about who's eating what, it's about spending time together to celebrate your birthday. You have what you want and I'll have my cappuccino and we'll both enjoy ourselves."

She laughed and that was that, but this is the kind of subtle pressure that can easily trip you up. Just because someone else wants to indulge doesn't mean you have to. It's the same idea as when you're a kid and all the other kids are smoking so you think you should too. Eating, of course, is not as harmful as smoking, but it can still be harmful if you can't afford the extra calories. If you really want to indulge, do it. But when you're not in the mood, you're not in the mood. Once my husband brought me a beautiful chocolate cake for my birthday and I honestly didn't want it. It occurred to me that I wanted to feel good about myself on my birthday and that if I ate the cake (no, I never just eat one piece) that I would feel lousy, fat, and depressed. Not to mention that this was one of those birthdays that made me feel anxious just by its number alone. Who needed a fat hangover? I wanted a tasty swordfish dinner with a good loaf of bread and nice bottle of wine. I gave the chocolate cake away, although if I'd truly wanted it I would have allowed myself to have it. I decided not to let a social situation rule what I ate and, by extension, my health and weight. (And my husband, bless him, understood!)

Here's another typical story of someone feeling victimized at a meal. My client Carol not only needed to lose weight herself but hired me because her children were overweight as well. She said she was helpless when it came to eating out. For example, she had had lunch the day before with her daughter, her girlfriend, and her girlfriend's daughter. The friends, she said, were naturally skinny and could eat to their hearts' delight and never gain a pound (I personally don't buy this). After a full and fattening lunch, the friend ordered dessert. Carol turned down dessert, but gave into her daugher's pleas. When the dessert came, her friend put a big bite of it on her fork, thrust it within an inch of Carol's face, and said, "You absolutely MUST have a bite!" "Well," Carol told me, "what could I do? I didn't want to hurt her feelings."

*Her* feelings! What about *your* thighs and *your* daughter's bulging tummy and *your* guilty feelings for eating poorly? First of all, your girlfriend is not you, and I don't care what she says she and her daughter can or can't eat. You are responsible for yourself and most of all for your child. This woman is not force-feeding you. You are buying into her victimization because you really want to eat the dessert. If that's true, then accept the consequences. Or learn to order fruit. But most of all, learn to please yourself and not others. Get a grip on it. If it is a special occasion, then have a light lunch and go for dessert, or skip the dessert and have a big, satisfying meal. Don't allow your friend to make rules for you. Make a rule for you and your daughter and stick to it.

## Family Feuds: Asserting Your Right to Eat Right

The fact that most of us consider ourselves victims of circumstance is no wonder: it's something we got used to during our youth when the person wholly responsible for our consumption of food was our mother. She did the shopping and cooking, she decided what kind of food was served. Essentially you were a victim of her choices. Because my mother was a gourmet cook, we were introduced to a large variety of wonderful foods at our house. She was always serving different ethnic dishes, and meals were a main event. We four children all sat down to breakfast and dinner at the same time. Sunday dinners, in particular, were a major family occasion. They were always held in the dining room at about three or four in the afternoon. Polished silver, the good plates, and a bottle of wine were on the table, and the meal was huge, topped off by luscious homemade desserts.

I was so conditioned by the fact that we indulged all day on Sundays that even years later when I became a dancer, I always pigged out on Sundays, although because I had become so hyper weight conscious due to dancing, it was no longer a pleasure; it was just plain uncomfortable. Still, it was a habit ingrained in my psyche—and the guilt I felt because of it made me binge all that much more. There was no middle ground. Just like all the others with eating disorders in this country, I thought you either ate or you dieted that there was no in between. While I wasn't really a victim of circumstances, I was, like Pavlov's dog, a victim of past training: just the suggestion of Sundays made me want to eat.

Because family tradition can have so much influence on your approach to food, it's important to establish your own traditions, ones that won't thwart your goals to be thin and healthy. At the same time, you don't necessarily want to impose your way of eating on the people you dine with. But there is a happy medium. I found it when I moved to Los Angeles and met Richard, my husband to be.

During the time we were dating, I started to employ a few of my mother's skills and make him a meal or two. I knew he didn't have a lot of money to take me out so I'd often suggest cooking dinner at my place. It wasn't long before I had to stop worrying "Is he going to call?" "When will I see him again?" I knew he'd show up around dinnertime. Although he was too reserved to actually ask me to cook for him, he was burned out on bachelor spaghetti dinners and peanut butter survival kits. So he would just casually drop by or call around the dinner hour. I definitely had a hook. So there I was, terrified of gaining weight, yet madly in love and using food as an aphrodisiac!

As luck would have it, Richard is naturally thin, doesn't have a cholesterol problem, and is always hungry. I certainly couldn't have eaten everything he did or, in two weeks, I would no longer have looked like the girl he first met—and I probably would have been out of a dancing job. I had been through bulimia before (I was never a full-fledged bulimic, I'd just act like one once or twice a month, max) and I wasn't about to start excusing myself from the table to go throw up. I had to confront the problem and figure out a way to bring food back into my life. But it wasn't just my weight I was concerned about. It was fun making dinner for him every night. It was fun to sit down to eat together and talk. So, determined not to fall into the "oh, I gained ten pounds because of my boyfriend" syndrome, I started to come up with a way to prepare foods that would suit both of our needs and allow us to still share our meals. (Later I'll show you how to prepare meals that suit the needs of everyone at the table.)

The pressure to be inventive so I wouldn't gain weight was mostly a factor of my job as a dancer. But many women (this can be true for men as well) receive pressure from the very same significant other who has thrown their diet into turmoil in the first place. The Catch-22 is that you want to look attractive for that person, but eating with him or her can put an extra ten pounds on your rear end!

One of my clients is married to a very famous and handsome movie star. They have been married for many years and have two children. She has about 15 pounds to lose and speaks freely about the fact that her husband often does love scenes with younger women who are in better shape than she is. She feels the competition and wants to get the weight off, but she also frequently goes on location with him and the food available there always proves to be her undoing. Plus, her husband becomes very uncomfortable when, as he puts it, she "makes a big deal" out of ordering her way in a restaurant. He disapproves of her special ordering, but he also disapproves of her weight.

Again, Catch-22. People love to see their loved ones eat, but don't want to see them wear it. Or hear them talk about it, for that matter. Instead of being a victim, I told the actor's wife, level with the guy. If he wants you to lose the weight—or even if it's only you who wants to lose the weight—he should be more tolerant of how you order in restaurants and prepare food for yourself at home. You have an unalienable right to eat what you like.

## When Work Interferes with the Way You Eat

Barbara is an ex-dancer who still had a dancer's body when she took an office job a few years ago. Yet it wasn't long before she went from a dancer's overly body-conscious mentality to having an office worker's overly food-obsessed mentality. The dancer rarely eats, while the office worker, usually because she just needs a break, lives for her next meal. At Barbara's office there were always doughnuts around in the morning and, because everyone else was eating them, she almost subconsciously felt that she should too. She wanted to be part of the pack and liked the idea of convening with her co-workers. The result was that, feeling she had pretty much blown it with the doughnuts in the morning, she went on to order the classic mayonnaisey tuna salad sandwich or hamburger when she went out to lunch with her co-workers, just as they did. And it got worse: by four o'clock, when someone was passing around the Mrs. Field's cookies, she sighed and said, "What the heck." Soon her dancer's body was in trouble.

By the time I met Barbara she was disgusted with her body and how much weight she'd gained. When we talked, we discovered the fact that she didn't really want that morning doughnut, nor did she care about the burger at lunch. She did, however, really crave that cookie at four o'clock. Try bringing a low-fat bran muffin or bialy to the doughnut klatch in the morning, I told her, and go ahead and order some sliced white meat chicken or turkey for lunch—even if your work friends give you the evil eye. Then have the cookie at four o'clock and a healthy lean dinner. I also pointed out to her that while she had been dancing all day before, she was now sitting and burning nothing but nervous energy. She needed to get back to a class or two a week, not only to get a sense of her body back, but to relieve some of the office stress.

What Barbara needed to figure out was how not to be a victim of one lifestyle or another, but to blend the two. The point is, your eating lifestyle should stay constant no matter what other lifestyle changes you make or what situations occur. Don't let the situation dictate to you.

Sandy, another client of mine, fell into a similar predicament. She was about thirty-one and married. After having major surgery, she took her time recovering and gained thirty pounds. She realized that she had probably overnurtured herself, and instead of going straight back into the working world, she decided to get back into shape first. However, the exercise classes she was taking weren't getting to the specific areas where she wanted to see change and much of the class seemed like a waste of time. Frustrated, she came to me for private training. We worked closely on everything: her diet, her attitudes toward food, and those problem areas of her body where exercise could help. Sandy not only lost the weight, but she got her healthy self-image back. When it was time to return to work, she got a job at a major corporation and bought a whole new wardrobe—sized to fit her back-in-shape body—to go with it. She looked great.

But once Sandy began her new job, the peer pressure began immediately. It started with the cookie/doughnut/pastry break in the earlier part of the day, then escalated at lunch. Sandy would order black coffee and a plain salad only to find herself being stared at in disbelief by four resentful women (with fat thighs) downing chicken salad sandwiches drowning in mayonnaise and a side of potato chips. Just like Barbara.

Sandy came running back to me with five of her thirty pounds already back on. What should she do? "You've spent so much money on private training and worked so hard to get back into shape," I said. "Why are you letting other people destroy your best efforts? You go to work to earn a living and fulfill your intellectual potential, not to be accepted by the crowd. It's great to have friends at work, but if they smoked and drank heavily, would you do that, too?" Take care of yourself, I told her. Be responsible for yourself and here's one way to do it: take a drawer in your desk and stock it with things that will save you when the Danish or anything else fattening starts getting passed around. Then, when your work friends start snacking, pull out your own low-fat, healthy choices. Here are the twenty options I gave her:

1. An oat bran muffin.
2. Apple-cinnamon rice cakes (or teriyaki or popcorn cakes, any flavor).
3. Animal or graham crackers.
4. Low-fat baked cheese puffs.
5. Diet salad dressings in foil packets.
6. Weight Watchers nonfat milk powder for coffee (Coffee-mate is loaded with fat; if you can't find Weight Watchers, just get instant nonfat dry milk).
7. Instant soup broths (Westbrae makes a good mushroom and seaweed one).
8. Instant oatmeal.
9. Instant diet hot chocolate.
10. Fruit, fruit, and more fruit.
11. Low-cal diet candies or Lifesavers.
12. Microwaveable packages of fresh vegetables.
13. Fat-free cookies or fat-free granola bars.
14. Whole wheat pretzels (with mustard).
15. Oriental (oil-free) rice crackers.
16. Low-cal bialys.
17. Mini pop-top cans of water-packed tuna.
18. Mini lunch-size cups of applesauce.
19. Mini pop-top cans of no-sugar canned fruit.
20. Individually wrapped fortune cookies.

All of these things are perfect examples of how to take care of yourself diet wise. **Set yourself up for success, not failure.** Sandy also had to realize that she was more sedentary now that she was working than when she was training; she found a gym close to her office. The other great lunch alternative—work out! Sandy is still thin to this day.

Here's my own experience with work and food. Years ago, when the ballet company I worked for folded due to lack of funds, I decided to try out my other skills and took a job as an assistant to a television writer. I was petrified at the thought of a sit-down job, precisely because it was just that—sit down. All I could visualize was my rear end slowly starting to spill over the sides of my desk chair. At the writers' meetings we attended, the table was always piled high with fattening foods. It was as if the staff couldn't have a meeting without munching peanuts, croissants, popcorn, and cookies. I could tell the others in the meeting resented me for not indulging, that I was a threat to them. "Oh, look at Miss Skinny not eating. She must be neurotic." No, I just wanted to stay thin—and pigging out at writers' meetings was just not my thing. When they started giving me a hard time, I became even more conscientious about what I ate. The bottom line was that they were all overweight and I didn't want to look like them.

The funny thing is, though, that while at first most people feel uncomfortable when you're eating differently (and more conscientiously) from them, they usually begin to pick up on your healthy eating habits after a while. And better that you should influence them, than they influence you. It didn't take too long for the croissants to change to bran muffins, and the peanuts and popcorn into grapes. Everybody (except perhaps Roseanne Barr?) wants to be thin and healthy. Sometimes it just takes one person to take the lead.

The point here is, you have to stop making excuses for what you're "forced" to eat and start taking action. If I told you that a certain food would make your face break out in hives in three seconds or if that food was against your religion, you'd have no problem saying no to it. One case of hives and you'd avoid that food like the plague. If you skipped a food because of your religion or an allergic reaction, people would understand. Well, you should think of fat in the same way: It is your "religion" to avoid junky fattening foods. If you have a body that gains weight, you're "allergic" to junky fattening foods. You're allergic to fat! It's very simple! If people think you're crazy, that's their problem. People used to think I was crazy when I would eat out and order my way. "But you're so thin!" they'd say, thinking I was a nut. How did they think I stayed thin?! It's better to be considered slim, healthy, and clear about food, than fat and compliant, but guilty inside.

# Taking Responsibility for Your Body

True, our families, friends, and even our co-workers don't always make it easy for us. There are things in life we are not responsible for, that just simply happen. For the most part, though, weight gain is not one of them and, while we can't help that we're predisposed to, say, large bones or heavy muscle mass, high cholesterol or high blood pressure, there's no excuse for exacerbating the problem. Unless someone is holding you hostage and forcing fat calories through an IV, you are ultimately responsible for your own actions. It's all too easy to name excuses such as . . .

1. I just quit smoking.
2. I just broke up with someone.
3. I just got together with someone.
4. My new boyfriend/girlfriend eats junk food.
5. A relative, dog, cat, bird, fish, or other significant other died.
6. I am stressed by my job, in-laws, children, parents, school, friends.
7. I don't have time to worry about what I eat.
8. I just had a baby (blameworthy for six months and no more).
9. Everyone at my new job eats constantly.
10. I just love to eat (we all do).
11. I am going to die someday anyway, so I might as well go down eating foods that I like. (Sure, but you'll go down a lot earlier and uglier.)
12. I am just out of control! This is a *choice* you make consciously, a definite cop-out.

I also love to eat and want to enjoy my life and indulge in the sensuous pleasures of food. But I hate to be overweight and I certainly don't want to be unhealthy. I don't buy all those excuses. In this day and age when there are so many wonderful things to eat, you don't have to be deprived to be thin and healthy. The more you blame something or someone else for your troubles, the more you avoid confronting and dealing with them.

This sounds unforgiving, I know, and there are times when you really do need the comfort of food. But if you let it get out of hand, allow food to become primarily a soothing thing—a drug—you are in for a destructive end. The eating might feel good, but when it's over you're only left with guilt and remorse. It's not worth it.

And blaming outside factors for bad eating habits is not the answer. You are responsible for educating yourself about food and for controlling what goes in your mouth. If you feel the problem is out of control, then there are groups that can help you. But many people, for instance, just automatically assume that they will gain weight when they quit smoking because that's what they've heard happens. So they do—it's a self-ful-filling prophecy. Yes, you will probably look to food to replace the mouth satisfaction of cigarettes, but does it have to be fattening junk food that will only cause you more unhappiness? No. There are healthy lean foods that will satisfy your cravings.

When I was thirteen, they were calling me "Twiggy" in school. How-ever, by the time I was sixteen, I was more like the trunk of the tree. I had a few skinny years when my dancing was its most intense, but by the time I was eighteen I was flat-out fat. I took a break from dancing and went to college, took one look at the male population there, and decided to lose weight. I jogged in the middle of winter, I dieted, I started to wage the almighty battle against the college cafeteria fare. I had lost six pounds before I met Randy. We fell madly in love in about ten hours, and spent most of our academic time together . . . not being academic. Randy adored me, but would make the classic male jokes about my "extra padding," or "cushiony tush." I'm sure you've heard numerous variations. I got myself into a reasonable weight range that year, and then, Wham! Randy and I had a big fight and we broke up. Somehow I know you're not surprised. I distinctly remember thinking, "Good, now I can eat. Now I can gain weight, because he's not looking at me, he's not judging me, and he's not touching me. So I pigged out in my misery. The next morning, I woke up, and slightly angry (at him, but also at myself), I said, "I feel horrible. I do not want to be thin for him, my mother, the other girls in the dorm or for anyone else, I want to be thin for myself!" I decided that day that it had nothing to do with anyone else, that I wanted to keep the weight off for myself. That is truly what it is all about—it's for you.

Don't set yourself up to be a victim. Don't buy into everything you read or hear—it might apply to someone else, but it won't necessarily apply to you. Educate yourself and listen to your body. And take respon-sibility for it. My client Charlene goes to lunch every day at the best restaurants. She never sits at a meal and thinks, "What should I have?" Instead she thinks "What do I want, what do I feel like?" She reported to me one day that she had had grapefruit, coffee, and toast for break-fast, felt weak by ten so she had some pineapple and picked at some leftovers. Then she went to lunch at noon, and didn't *feel* like having a salad or another kind of lean lunch, so she just had a German apple pancake. Charlene's problem is that she will constantly indulge herself unless she has someone (like me) dictating her every meal. This goes beyond thinking you're a victim into a complete lack of wanting to take responsibility for oneself.

## Make Sure There's Food for You
## (Taking Care of Yourself)

No one said that fighting off the influence of others or shouldering the responsibility for what you eat is going to be easy. What will make it *easier,* though, is making sure that there are always the right kinds of food available for you to eat. It's hard to turn down junky foods if there is no alternative—that's why you have to make sure that there are alternatives, alternatives that suit your needs. Women especially tend to prepare food for others and not look out for themselves, as if that were selfish. On the contrary, it's not selfish; it's part of getting your priorities straight.

So is incorporating healthy, nonfattening foods into your budget. A very wealthy woman once called me because she wanted to lose weight, especially since there was a charity gala coming up and she had found this fabulous $2,000 dress that she wanted to look good in. When I told her how much my fat-free home delivery food cost she said, "Oh no, that's way too expensive," and hung up. Yet she had no qualms about spending tons of money on a dress! Wouldn't it be better to spend the extra money on the food that goes into your body than to spend it on a dress to hide the fact that you are fat? Another woman wearing a $185 Chanel headband had a similar reaction to the price of my food. When people will spend money on clothes to disguise their bodies' problems or even on potentially dangerous liposuction surgery, but not on the healthy food that will really make a difference in their appearance, their priorities are out of whack. It's not that you have to go out and spend a fortune on food for yourself, but why not spend the extra dollar if it's going to make you feel and look better? The rich woman who called me didn't realize that instead of spending the extra dollar on good food, she'd be spending the extra hundred dollars on a visit to the doctor later on. Food that is healthy may cost an extra cent due to the fact that it is not as highly mass produced (with cheap fillers), but the payoff is priceless.

In a way, if you don't take matters into your own hands—like buying the foods you need—you're simply victimizing yourself. This also means making sure that fattening, unhealthy food is not imposed on you: be prepared with foods of your own. Sometimes it's just a matter of foresight. The best example is bringing your own salad dressing to a restaurant. One client of mine, for instance, said she knew that every time she spent the weekends at her family's beach house that everyone would be snacking all day long on the classics: chips, cheeses, and other fattening munchies. To try to fight the temptation to join in, she would set herself up for a big binge, by sipping coffee or tea all day long, trying to have a piece of fruit, and basically avoiding the fact that she really wanted to eat something substantial. She felt so frustrated by having to hold back that, by the end of the day, her discipline wearing away, she'd start to munch on all those fat-filled foods herself. Then, on to dinner, dessert, and guilt.

Look, I told her, it's fine to munch all day long, and it doesn't have to be on carrot sticks. It also doesn't have to be what the rest of your family is hacking away at. Bring your own bag of groceries. If they have doughnuts, you have a bialy, whole wheat English muffin, bran muffin, or fruit. If they have a sweet for a snack, you have diet hot chocolate and dunk in some fat-free cookies or animal crackers. When they move onto lunch, go for lean proteins like sliced turkey or chicken and some veggies. As they edge into cocktail-hour peanuts, you have your crackers and salsa. Keep yourself oil and fat free at dinner, and then happily munch the popcorn (butter-free) right along with them later that night. You might gain two whole pounds over the weekend—although probably not, because all the foods you're choosing are healthy and burnable, foods that your body can benefit from and won't turn into a lot of fat pounds. When you come back on Monday, clean out, work out a little harder, and know that you got to enjoy your weekend.

Sometimes it's difficult to turn down certain foods without being rude when you're staying at someone else's house. Always let your hosts know you appreciate their cuisine, perhaps indulge in a meal or two, but don't let it destroy you. Once again, and I know I repeat this, if it were a food allergy or religious choice, they would respect your needs. They should also respect the basic way that you eat. Compromise, enjoy some of their foods, but if you are going to be there for a while it's not a bad idea to take a trip to the market on your own and pick up some food that's less fattening than what your hosts have on hand. Or offer to cook so that you can be in control of how much fat is put on the table. Eating foods that are right for you isn't being disrespectful to your hosts, it's just being respectful of yourself.

What's worse than feeling like a prisoner in someone else's home is feeling like a prisoner in your own home. And there's no reason you should. When I was a personal fitness trainer, I would work very closely with my clients on their diets. When I'd go into their kitchens, I'd inevitably find foods that I'd never dream of buying, much less consuming! Time and time again, they'd tell me that the food was for their spouses, children, relatives, ex-relatives, twice-removed aunts, gardeners, dogs, housekeepers, and such. In other words, there was food to please everyone but themselves. They seemed to think it was selfish to have food just for them, yet the pressure to look good, be slim, and be healthy still weighed on their minds.

To avoid being a victim in your own house, it's crucial to make sure your refrigerator and cupboards are stocked with foods that fit into your personal eating style, not just your family's. That's number one. Number two is to make sure that all the meals you eat at home are cooked according to your needs. Jack Sprat and his wife had it down (well, in theory anyway—she was actually fat and he was skinny): He could eat no fat and she could eat no lean but between them both they were able to lick the platter clean. Maybe not the formula for a perfect marriage, but they certainly had the right idea about priorities. In the same vein, not everyone in your family has to give up, say, oil-based salad dressings because you have. Barbecue dinners don't have to be out of the question because you don't eat greasy ribs. All you need to do to meet your own requirements is to look at food preparation from a different angle.

That, you're probably saying to yourself, will require a lot of work. But truly, it takes very little extra effort. And it makes a lot of sense: we all waste a lot of time and energy (sometimes money, too) putting our efforts into various weight loss programs that never do the trick. But ensuring that meals are prepared to your liking will do the trick without the hassle of a diet program. For one thing, meal preparation stays basically the same: it's just minor alterations—a sauce here, no sauce there, a sprinkle of cheese on one portion, a spritz of lemon on the other—that makes the difference. Changing the ground beef to ground turkey, broiling one piece of fish in olive oil, while you broil the other in white wine. Same time, different steps. If you're the one doing the cooking, you'll have no trouble implementing the changes; and if you're not, you should feel comfortable asking whoever is making the meal to try them on your behalf. Once again, you would do this if you had an allergy or illness; think of fat as your health taboo. Considering how easy it is to "tailor" food, asking whoever is cooking to make changes is a small request—and it can result in big health and weight benefits. IT'S WORTH IT!

## Getting Support—Not Flak—from Family and Friends Is Better Incentive Than a Scale

Taking responsibility for the way you eat doesn't mean you don't need input from anyone else. There's no getting around the fact that if you want to accomplish your goals—to lose weight, stay slim, be healthy, whatever—you have to decide on the food rules that are right for you, then stick to them. And you have to do it for yourself, not anyone else. Still, it helps to have some support from friends and family; instead of letting them undermine your efforts, getting them to be your rooting section can be a big help. In fact, support is so essential that many major, nationwide businesses have been built on the idea. Weight Watchers is so successful at it that others like Jenny Craig and The Diet Center have followed in their footsteps. The positive reinforcement they provide works for many people; however, once you stop going, you stop getting the support and guidance that's helped do the trick. The same goes for other people you hire. Private exercise trainers can sometimes be a support, too, although many of them just know about exercise and not much about diet and nutrition.

So how can you create your own support system? Real support, not something you buy or read in a magazine. If you're not getting an iota from your family, look to your friends. Instead of going around the corner for a pizza with your friends, go for a walk. Make a pact to be a support group and meet three times a week to go walking. Pick a course that's at least two miles long and walk it briskly. If you can find a hill to climb, all the better.

When I work out with my friends we use the time to talk about things that are bothering us. Instead of doing something counterproductive like eating to get our feelings out, we do something productive—talking. We share our knowledge of new products and restaurants, ideas on how to keep fattening foods out of our lives. Each time we meet, someone has something to recommend or sometimes we just talk about life. But instead of doing it over lunch, we do it over exercise. We feel better in the end because we've gotten things off our chests while getting some fat off our thighs.

Use time with your support group to confess your food problems, get feedback, and burn calories all at the same time. It's a lot healthier than taking the old misery-loves-company attitude where it becomes easier to accept a friend who's overweight simply to justify your own extra pounds. Knowing that other people share the same struggles with eating that you do can be comforting, but not if you see it as an opportunity to just wallow in misery with someone else. The association is better used to share and compare solutions to common problems, not to mention, a much better method than using the scale as a whipping post.

My girlfriends and I have something we call the "up-and-down system," a method of helping each other deal with our bodies' ebbs and flows. I call the flows (flows of excess pounds, that is) "fat periods." These are times of the year when your weight is up about four or five pounds that just won't seem to budge. Or maybe you just don't even feel like trying to get rid of them. Don't confuse this with the yo-yo dieting syndrome, times when your weight really gets out of hand and you lose and gain in amounts of ten pounds or more over and over again. Rather, fat periods are just relatively normal, small shifts in weigh, four or five extra pounds that warn you to keep an eye on it before it gets out of control.

I have weight swings regularly. During certain months of the year I am just about three to four pounds heavier than I want to be. That may not sound like much, but it's my barometer for weight control. I feel okay to have the extra pounds because they are healthy pounds—I exercise, I eat right. The weight isn't from binging or eating poorly, it's from just eating more. Healthy food, but nonetheless, more food. The fat periods are always connected to stressful or lonely times in my life when I just decide not to worry about how much I'm eating. As long as the four to five pounds come from lean proteins, fresh fruits, vegetables, and other high-carb foods, I know they'll be good for my skin, hair, and general health. If they were pounds of overindulgence or negligence, that would be a different story. That's when you know you have to stop right there and get a handle on it.

I do, though, try to work out a little more during these times so that the extra pounds aren't flabby and don't make me look out of shape. Most important, I don't freak out; I just keep a close watch on it. My husband said to me years ago, "Yolanda, every weekend you eat more than usual, every Sunday you complain that you feel fat, and by Tuesday night you're a rail! Don't you get it? This is your style." He was right, and I learned to relax more about eating more on weekends. The same thing goes for my fat periods—they're simply part of my style. When I gain up to a certain point now, I just cut back my intake to less protein, no starches, and a lot of produce for two to three days. That gets rid of the extra pounds right away.

But back to the up-and-down system. Through all of this, another one of the things that keeps me from browbeating myself for letting things slide—and ensures that I'll get back on track—is the six girlfriends I work out with on a regular basis. Of course, with six women, no one can make it every time, but whoever can does so there are always at least a few of us exercising together. When we exercise, we practice the up-and-down system, which refers to whether we are up or down in pounds. We kind of stumbled on the idea while trying to keep each other's weight—and morale—in check. Here's how it works:

1. You must always be completely honest with the other person; no Mr. Nice Guy.
2. The word *fat* is taboo; *scale* is hardly ever mentioned.
3. Part of the deal is you tell the other women where they're up (and down) and they tell you. It's important to be specific: "Well, you're up slightly here [pointing to the upper thigh], but your stomach is down and your inner thighs look great."
4. You never volunteer this information but, rather, wait until asked— "Am I up?"—or someone starts to complain that they've "really been blowing it lately"; then you offer advice with love.
5. Criticism must be accompanied by concrete advice: "Just do more upper thigh leg lifts today, rep [short for repetition] that area to death and cut out bread for a while." Sometimes someone will say, "Oh, I have a great recipe for no-sugar, no-fat muffins" or "I ate at a Chinese restaurant that served wonderful meals without any oil." The idea is to share information that will help everyone keep her body in shape.
6. To keep hurt feelings at bay, you always point out that you have known the person for years and that she is just going through a fat period and will return to normal shortly. Offer any time you might have to do an extra workout with her so that she might get back on track even sooner.
7. As you exercise, pour out all your woes, raise your heart rate, increase your endorphins, and reduce your stress levels, then go back out into the world a better, healthier person.

The idea here is teamwork. Joint effort and support, which is the opposite of being victimized. All six of my friends and I would be about ten to twenty pounds heavier if we ate oils and other fats and didn't exercise. But as it stands, we're all between the ages of thirty-two and forty-seven and all look good—because WE WORK AT IT. We always laugh at people who are envious. If they only knew!

Don't ever discount that even those who don't look like they struggle with food really do. How many times has a slim, healthy woman walked through a room only to turn the women who are a little overweight green with envy? The thin woman is threatening, she represents the control they feel they don't have. They think she was born that way and never had to work at it. But, in reality, 99.9 percent of the time she watches what she eats and exercises. She probably has her up and down periods just like everyone else. SHE WORKS AT IT! Just like everyone with a healthy relationship, or a functional family, balanced career, or any achievement. They work at it. And working at it . . . works.

Almost every one of us, though, do have fat periods. None of us are perfect; we all just do the best that we can. One day one of the friends in my exercise group called me, terribly upset. Of all of us, she was the one who never weighed herself because she said, "It makes me too neurotic." But one day she did weigh herself and discovered she was eleven pounds over her desired weight. "How could you not tell me!" she asked me. "I had no idea, I kept convincing myself that I didn't look that bad. Help!" Well the truth was, I wasn't doing my job as a support system. I had noticed her rear end was heavy, but just didn't say anything. Most people would think that was being polite, when it really wasn't. My friend works out extremely hard to watch her weight and had just let it slide. It took two months, but she has all of the weight off now, but not before I sat down with her and laid out some dietary changes she'd have to make, then made time to accompany her through more workouts. (She also added a 15-minute run by herself every day.) And I'd expect her to do the same thing for me. That's why I love my friends—even when they tell me I'm up.

# 4

# *Get Your Facts Straight ... and Take* Your *Particular Body into Account*

**T**HESE DAYS, EVERYBODY'S an expert on nutrition— or at least thinks so. Most of the time, though, I find that people have things a little bit mixed up or that they don't understand how to interpret food information as it applies to them personally. Consider, for example, the case for—and against— consuming olive oil. I've appeared on the TV show *A. M. Los Angeles* a number of times and each time I have the same (friendly) argument with (the former) cohost Cristina Ferrare, who admittedly has had a weight problem of her own (you've probably seen her promoting Ultra Slim Fast on TV). Everytime I would mention olive oil Cristina would insist that having at least two tablespoons of olive oil a day is healthy and good for the heart because it lowers cholesterol. "Yes," I would say. "It's healthy, but it is also fattening!"

"But, it's good for the heart," she kept insisting.

Finally, I just laid it out, "Cristina, it is good for your heart, but it makes your butt and thighs fat. FAT, Cristina, FAT!" For her cohost Steve Edwards to have two tablespoons a day, I say fine—he does have a cholesterol problem, but doesn't have a weight problem. But for Cristina, healthy or not, olive oil still has one hundred fat calories per tablespoon and that's more likely to make her rear-end droop than her cholesterol drop. Besides, there are plenty of other foods that lower cholesterol but don't pack a lot of calories and fat.

It's not surprising that Cristina or anyone else is mixed up about how food affects the body. It seems that every day we hear about new studies, surveys, reports, opinions, guides, diets, and health scares all devoted to helping us understand more about food and how it relates to our well-being. But instead of making us wiser about nutrition, all that information just makes us more confused about nutrition. Add that to the fact that, in the nineties, we're already on information overload—by the time you learn to use your new computer, the rest of the world has moved on to an updated model, the phone companies have invented new systems, and even your VCR and CD players have become more technically complex. Result: you've got a very anxious bunch of people on your hands. In other words, it's hard to keep up, and being inundated with nutrition data doesn't help matters much, especially when the information we get on Tuesday usually contradicts what we learned on Monday.

Remember when shrimp was considered a high-cholesterol food? Now we're told it isn't. A few years ago some people tried to pass chocolate and red meat off as healthy because they contain the fat stearic acid, which purportedly also lowers cholesterol. Perhaps, but chocolate and red meat also contain other types of saturated fat—the kind that promotes heart attacks. *New York Times* columnist Russell Baker put it well on the op-ed page a while back: "Almost everything they say is good for you will turn out to be bad for you if you hang around long enough, and almost everything they say is bad for you will turn out not to matter."

Why are there always so many conflicting reports? For one thing, not all studies are conducted properly, and even if they are, the results may just be true for the people they used as guinea pigs and not the population at large. Plus, even if what a study finds is valid, the discovery— say, for instance, that fish oil helps prevent blood from clotting—gets overblown and the next thing you know everyone is downing fish oil capsules, which wasn't what the original study looked at in the first place. Everyone is so overanxious to learn about scientific breakthroughs that we run with any inkling of a breakthrough long before all the facts are in.

With all this information coming at us from every which way we also tend to believe anything "they" say. You know "they" don't you? The mystery people we all rely on so much. Granted, it's important to have regulatory agencies like the Food and Drug Administration (FDA), the U.S. Department of Agriculture (USDA), and the National Academy of Sciences (which issues the RDAs), just as it's important to have university-affiliated researchers looking at the effects of food on our bodies. But they aren't always right. You needn't jump at everything you hear. Take a deep breath and read on.

Let me digress for a second and compare the way that facts about food are presented to us with the way we are taught about religion. While you are growing up, your parents influence your religious views. You receive a lot of information about different religious events and beliefs. However, in the end you believe what you choose to believe. You stay open to information and ideas, but you learn to choose the ones that work for you and edit out the rest.

I think you should do the same with all the daily reports on food, weight loss, and nutrition. I don't mean that you should ignore headlines like "Nitrates Found to Increase Risk of Cancer" just because you've been eating bacon all your life and haven't gotten cancer yet. But in terms of your weight and energy level and your cholesterol level (easily monitored by your doctor), listen to—and look at—your body. If you know the rules that work for your particular body, then you don't have to get neurotic every time there's a news blast exclaiming that what was great for you yesterday is going to kill you today.

## How "Good" Do You Have to Be?

Unfortunately, there is no possible way to maintain a perfectly clean and healthy diet in our society today. Even organic foods, while grown without the aid of pesticides, may be tainted by chemicals in the atmosphere or toxins that simply still remain in the ground from the time they were used forty years ago. Our poultry is more often than not shot up with hormones and raised on questionable, non-nutritious feed. Our dairy products are filled with chemicals and animal by-products to increase their mass. For years grains have been broken down into three different products to create more volume, the nutrient- and fiber-rich bran being sold on its own as an uninspiring health food. What's been done to food in this century is horrifying.

So are we all doomed? I don't think so. They body is an amazing survival machine. It will adapt to almost any circumstance. Think of all the tribes around the world surviving solely on milk, grains, and berries—whatever they can hunt down. Or even all the low-income kids that live on nothing but Coca-Cola, McDonald's hamburgers, and Kentucky Fried Chicken or their equivalents. They survive, perhaps not in the healthiest manner, but they survive. Likewise, we live in areas with incredible air and water pollution and our bodies seem to adapt. The human body adapts and survives in its given environment.

It has been proven that eating *un*healthfully can contribute to cancer and other diseases, and, although eating healthfully is not guaranteed to prevent you from ever becoming ill, it will greatly decrease your odds by limiting the number of chemicals and fats that get into your system, both of which are known to increase the risks of disease. Even if sticking to lean, vitamin- and mineral-rich foods is not a sure thing, that doesn't mean you should junk food your way into senility. Nor should you think that just because you exercise you are doing enough to keep you well and immune to food-related diseases. For some people exercising alone isn't enough to keep them thin either. Day after day I talk to people who have developed a regular exercise program, but still are not happy with the way they look and feel. It's obvious: you have to eat correctly too. Very few athletes or dancers rely on heavy junk food and do well. Even though they are burning many calories per day, junk food just does not provide the necessary energy and nutrients needed to keep things operating properly. Without real food your *machine* or *computer*—words you'll often see me use synonymously with *body*—will survive, but most surely suffer later.

You may not be able to clean up the air and water, but you can clean up your eating habits as best as possible. Learn to listen to the facts that are tried and true and as they apply to you, not other people. Most nutrition and weight loss advice is offered by people who are looking for some kind of answer to food happiness themselves or have found a way that works for them. But what works for them is not necessarily going to work for you. Learn what makes you feel and look wonderful consistently.

I'm not saying that there are no basics truths about nutrition and weight loss. There are many, and that's what you'll find on the pages ahead. What I've done is compile information that is not only widely agreed on by people in the medical and health communities, but that I can vouch for myself, having made a career out of watching how people's eating habits affect their bodies. What I've also done is pare down the facts so that instead of having to wade through pages of iffy health info written in medical lingo—none of which you'll ever remember anyway—you can learn all you really need to know about nutrition and weight loss to make sound food choices. Keep in mind that the information that lies ahead should really just be used as a guideline for helping you make eating rules for yourself. They're not the final word, but truths that I have found to be proven over time, client after client.

## What the Body Does and Doesn't Need to Be Healthy

Everybody knows the basic four food groups, but how they apply to each individual's body is a different matter. Remember that we have evolved as human animals, and we do not need the same diet as our great-grandparents. We are actually a more refined animal. Most times I find that clients think they need more food than they really do. I will repeat this throughout the book: If your body does not "need" it, it will be stored as fat. Your body is telling you loud and clear, "I am not using this much, it's overload!"

Here is a look at what food categories we do and don't need, plus what foods we may not need, but are certain to want and have whether we should or not. There is a world of food in each category, which I go into in detail later in the book. I've just broken the groups down simply to give you some basics for healthy eating.

### *What You Need . . .*

**Complex Carbohydrates.** You've probably heard these words kicked around a lot over the last few years. That's because complex carbs—such as unrefined starches (grain products), fruits, vegetables, and legumes—give you more bang for the buck. That is, they're very satisfying and have few calories, especially compared gram for gram with fat (fat has nine calories per gram, carbohydrates only four). One reason complex carbohydrates are so satisfying is because it takes your system a long time to break them down. On the other hand, "simple" carbohydrates (sugars, which I'll go into later) are burned very quickly by the body. So while both kinds of carbohydrates are sources of glucose—the main fuel of the muscles and brain—complex carbohydrates are a better source because they release the fuel more slowly into the bloodstream.

Look at eating complex carbohydrates as putting a big, thick, slow-burning log into the fire and eating simple carbs as throwing nothing but kindling on the fire: the kindling will light up fast (that burst of energy we feel when we eat sugar), but burn out fast, while the log will last and last. Both kinds of carbs, by the way, mostly get burned and don't usually pile up—that is, get stored by the body as fat. However, keep in mind, that if you're not burning the logs and kindling already on the fire, the new supply will indeed pile up. In other words, eat more carbohydrates than your body is able to burn and it will show up as extra pounds.

Common wisdom has it that complex carbohydrates should make up 60 percent of your total calories, but I believe it's a good idea to eat even more than that, especially in the form of fresh produce. And not just because they're a good source of fuel. Complex carbs are also packed full of vitamins and minerals and they're good sources of fiber. Which brings us to our next subject . . .

**Fiber.** Fiber—and there are several different kinds—comes from the cell walls of plants, so you'll find plenty of fiber in all the complex carbohydrate foods I mentioned above. Unlike other elements of those carbohydrates, fiber does not get broken down in the digestive tract so it takes some getting used to if you haven't been eating enough to begin with. And you would be surprised at how many people's digestive systems are out of shape. When I put my clients who've been eating nothing but fatty, overprocessed foods on a high-produce (and, therefore, high-fiber) diet, they often complain of bloating and gas. I tell them to give their digestive systems two weeks to get into shape; all the symptoms will go away and their bodies will run like clockwork. Which is a delicate way of saying that your bowels will move, the reason many doctors are no longer prescribing laxatives for constipation, but fiber substitutes instead.

If you've always eaten fruits and vegetables, then you've always eaten fiber. But the same is not true if you've always eaten grain products, which although they logically should be, weren't and still aren't always fiber-rich. Visualize it this way: look at a grain (wheat, oats, or rice) almost like a nut. The outer shell—the grain's bran—has been thrown away for years and the inside has been overprocessed into our breads and cereals, leaving our systems literally with nothing to "chew" on. We need that outer shell to be healthy, which is why oat bran and rice bran have been big hits lately.

All the hullabaloo about fiber ("Eat whole bran cereal!" "Have an oat bran muffin!") has to do with some studies showing that fiber can help prevent cancer and can lower cholesterol. Fine, we can digest that. But the fiber issue gets a little complicated because, as it turns out, there are two different kinds of fiber we need to get into our diets. The first is called *soluble fiber* (it's called that because it dissolves in water). Soluble fiber includes pectins and gums (think of the goo that comes from an aloe plant when you break a leaf), which are found in most fruits, vegetables, legumes, and grains. Soluble fiber is the one that's been shown to lower the total amount of cholesterol in the blood, especially the "bad" LDL cholesterol (I'll explain cholesterol lingo later in this chapter).

The cholesterol-lowering soluble fiber you've surely heard the most about is oat bran. What is the truth about oat bran anyway? It is pretty well accepted by the medical community now that oat bran lowers the blood cholesterol levels of people with high cholesterol (if they eat a lot of it). It does seem certain that oat bran on its own is a healthy food. But that doesn't mean you have to start eating it at every meal. I do recommend it for people with high cholesterol in my menu plan on page 132. However, you can also use rice bran (which is a cholesterol lowerer too) or other whole oat and rice products. Just look for healthy bran products—that means foods not overloaded with sugar and fat—and don't get obsessed by it. A good twenty-five-minute cardiovascular workout will probably do more for your cholesterol level than a bowl of oat bran cereal.

Also, consider that there are other good sources of soluble-fiber foods, among them carrots, onions, and cabbage. Beans are another great source of cholesterol-lowering soluble fiber. Remember, though, that, if you're eating oat bran or carrots or whatever to lower your cholesterol, it's not going to work if you are also eating foods that raise cholesterol—like butter on your bread and a bowl of ice cream—every night. Soluble-fiber foods don't work magic by themselves. Unfortunately, most of the new cereals, baked goods, and other products bragging about oat bran on their labels (Beer? Potato chips? Give me a break!) don't contain enough soluble fiber to affect cholesterol levels, and many of them are made with saturated fat. So often manufacturers hear the results of a nutrition study, then try to hop on the bandwagon by adding a small amount of a healthy ingredient to an otherwise unhealthy food. If a, say, bread advertises itself as having oat bran, check the ingredient list on the back to see if the oat bran is listed near the top (ingredients are listed quantitatively—the first ingredient is also the ingredient contained in the highest amount). Also check to see that there is not a lot of fat in the bread.

The other kind of fiber you've undoubtedly been hearing a lot about is *insoluble fiber.* Insoluble fiber is found mainly in whole wheat grains, fruits, and vegetables. By increasing the rate at which food moves though the colon, it helps prevent constipation, diverticulitis (a disease caused by inflammation of the colon wall), and possibly colon cancer, because carcinogenic materials don't spend much time in contact with the colon. Those are all good reasons to get a lot of insoluble fiber into your diet, but also consider that, because insoluble fiber is part of what makes certain foods bulky, those foods tend to keep you fuller longer and that helps you eat less altogether. Plus, insoluble fiber is also thought to control insulin, which is an appetite stimulator.

One company took advantage of these facts and came up with a cookie that they swore was the answer to weight loss. To make it work, you were supposed to eat the cookie (it was packed with every kind of bran you could imagine) and drink two eight-ounce glasses of water before your meals. Well, naturally your stomach was so full of stuff to work on by the time you'd finished, not to mention full of water, that you wouldn't be hungry for hours. Not a bad way to curb your appetite for a while, but the big misconception about this diet program was that you could then eat all (and whatever) you wanted to at meals. That, of course, was crazy especially because you'd be getting the added calories and food value of the cookies. That aside, a small bowl of oatmeal or a bran muffin loaded with extra oat bran and the same amount of water can do the same trick, it doesn't have to be a special cookie. Basically we're talking about foods that stick to your ribs or stay in your digestive system for a while. Once again, never look to one product to be the miracle cure.

So now that you know there are two kinds of fiber you have to get, are you thoroughly confused? Here's an easy way to look at it: in case you didn't notice, many of the foods that contain soluble fiber are also the foods that contain insoluble fiber. If you just base your diet on a variety of complex carbohydrate foods—*fresh fruits and vegetables, whole grains, unprocessed cereals and breads, dried beans*—you should get enough of both kinds of fiber. I'm not going to tell you how many apples to eat per day or the exact amount of fiber grams you should be eating. How would you ever keep track? Simply make sure that you get a good mix of the above foods each day and you'll be fine. Also, when you choose your foods, keep in mind that the more processed a food, the less fiber (both insoluble and soluble) it has. Even juice has a lot less fiber than the whole fruit, a peeled carrot less than an unpeeled one. Cooking also depletes fiber so the more produce you can eat raw, the better.

Bottom line: don't look to one magic bullet fiber product put out by some giant food company to keep you healthy. Simply eat a lot of naturally fibrous foods and you can stop worrying about whether or not you need to buy all those crazy oat bran products.

**Protein.** Before you bite into that big juicy steak, think twice: once because you don't need all the fat it contains and once because you don't need to eat it as a source of protein. Everybody needs protein—it provides the amino acids our bodies are built on—but hardly anybody is protein deficient. We only really need protein to make up 10 to 15 percent of our total calories. Instead of how *much* protein you eat, I think you should concentrate on what *kinds* of protein you eat. While it's not very caloric on its own (four calories per gram), protein is accompanied by fat in many foods. But not all foods. White meat poultry and most forms of seafood are very lean. Nonfat dairy products are nonfat protein sources. Also, not all protein foods are animal foods. All the dried beans—black, white, pinto, kidney, garbanzo, lima, soy—contain a form of protein that is best utilized by the body when it's combined with grains like rice, corn, barley, and oats. When you eat grain foods like pasta and bread on their own, you're getting protein, too.

I happen to eat a lot of protein myself and have come across many people who have been taught that that's not healthy. But if you feel you need a lot of lean protein (that is, you crave it) and you're preparing it correctly (without added fats) then I say "Go for it," especially if it keeps you satisfied.

**Vitamins and Minerals.** Vitamin and mineral deficiencies in this country are very rare, one of the reasons why I'm not an advocate of vitamin popping. Another reason I'm not a big fan of supplements is because people sometimes think of them as a substitute for the real thing. Food is the real thing. I'm not going to give you a listing of the RDAs for each vitamin here. Again, I don't think anyone really knows how to follow those numbers without walking around with a nutrient guide and a calculator. Vitamins and minerals come from good, whole, lean, and natural foods. The worst thing you can do for yourself is to saturate your diet with refined foods that have been stripped of most of their nutrients during processing. The best thing you can do for yourself if you want to get all the nutrients you need is to eat a variety and abundance of fresh produce, frozen produce (it's flash frozen so the vitamins and minerals get locked in), whole grains, and lean protein foods.

Note that *variety* is one of the keywords here: you may not get vitamin A when you eat an orange, but you'll get it when you eat a carrot. You may not get iron from a carrot, but you'll get it from eating kale or spinach. The more types of foods you eat, the easier it will be to cover all your nutritional bases and that means you won't have to be worrying about whether or not you made the RDA for vitamin A or vitamin E or selenium today. Also, be aware that RDA means *Recommended Dietary Allowance,* not *required* daily amounts, and according to the National Academy of Sciences, which issues the RDA guidelines, meeting them over a five- to ten-day span is adequate. So if you are keeping track of those numbers or just know in your head that you should be consuming a certain amount of fruit to get your vitamin C, don't think you're doomed if you don't eat perfectly every day. Just do the best you can and it will all balance out.

There are a few instances when I think supplementing your diet with vitamin and mineral pills might be helpful and that is when you are eating healthfully, but your body is still crying out for help. And it will, if it needs it. The human body is set up to give you signals when it's in need of nutrients. For example, many women feel sluggish and look grayish when they are low in iron. In that situation, it may be wise to take a supplement, especially because it's so difficult to consume enough iron-rich foods on a daily basis. (Red meats are the best sources, but chicken, spinach, beans, raisins, sunflower seeds and tofu all contain iron. Cooking with a cast iron skillet will put some iron into your diet too.)

Women also often have a problem with getting enough calcium to keep their bones strong and prevent osteoporosis. Dairy products have the highest concentration of calcium but, while there are now plenty of non-fat dairy products available, they still contain some cholesterol. I don't believe you have to rely solely on dairy products for the mineral. Cows get calcium from eating grass so it only makes sense that we should be able to get calcium from vegetable sources too. Some vegetable sources, though, are better than others. Spinach, for example, actually contains a lot of calcium, but it's calcium that is not bioavailable—there's another compound in spinach called oxalic acid, which binds up the calcium so the body can't use it. We can only absorb about 5 percent of the calcium in spinach. Kale, on the other hand, gives up about a third of its calcium so we're not eating all vegetable sources in vain. However, how many of us eat kale on a regular basis? And still, whether or not one can get enough calcium from a vegetarian diet is controversial. I think it is good advice for women today to take a mineral supplement because the soils (in which our produce is raised) are so depleted. Also, the monthly menstrual cycle depletes our vitamin and mineral stores, which is why we have so many premenstrual cravings—our bodies crying out, although, no one has yet to figure out how the need for vitamins and minerals turned into a cry for CHOCOLATE! Science still has some mysteries.

The only thing that seems certain, is that nobody is certain about what exactly is the perfect diet. Do, though, try to get as many calcium foods in your diet as possible. Eat nonfat dairy products if you don't have a cholesterol problem. Canned salmon with bones is another calcium source, so are dark green vegetables besides spinach and kale like broccoli; beet, dandelion, and collard greens; and bok choy. Dried beans like soy, kidney, navy, and pinto contain some calcium as does tofu made with calcium sulfate, lime-treated tortillas, and bread with the ingredient calcium carbonate. Most important, note that exercise can help deter bone loss just as calcium does (one can't be substituted for the other—both are important).

I'm not an advocate of pill popping, but I'm not going to tell you *not* to take supplements either. If you're concerned about not getting enough vitamins and minerals, then talk to your doctor about it. Just don't go off and start loading up on supplements—some can actually be toxic if you take too many of them.

## *What You Don't Need . . .*

**Fat.** It's true, the body does need some dietary fat to operate properly. Fatty acids, which make up dietary fat, are responsible for maintaining healthy skin and production of prostaglandins, hormonelike substances that regulate some body functions. Dietary fat also aids in the storage of fat-soluble vitamins like A, D, E, and K. Without dietary fat, the body doesn't store much body fat and, as you probably know, if a woman's body fat level is too low she can develop amenorrhea, that is, she'll stop menstruating, which is very unhealthy.

But—and this is a big but—we get the amount of fat our bodies need to run on just by eating lean, whole, natural foods. It is my belief that foods like poultry and seafood contain all of the natural fat/oils that we need these days. You don't need to melt cheese on your toast, or put butter on your bread, or drink a glass of whole milk, or—Cristina—eat two tablespoons of olive oil—to accomplish your fat requirement for the day. If you have eaten a bowl of cereal with nonfat milk for breakfast; a salad with tuna and oil-free dressing for lunch; plus a slab of swordfish, rice, and veggies for dinner you're not going to wake up the next day with a fat deficiency. You'll be more than fine, you'll be thin and healthy. Frequently include lean poultry and fish in your diet and you will get all the fat you need to keep your body running smoothly. Toss in some healthfully made baked goods (grains contain some fat and most baked goods have at least a little fat/oil in them) and limited low-fat dairy products and you'll be getting exactly what you need.

Most of the recommendations you hear from organizations like the American Heart Association, the American Cancer Society, and the American Dietetic Association stipulate that dietary fat should make up no more than 30 percent of a person's total calorie intake. There they go again, throwing more facts and figures at you. How are you supposed to know if you're eating 30 percent fat on a daily basis? Unless you spend your day calculating every label and keeping score, it's not too feasible.

Besides being complicated, I believe that the 30 percent fat benchmark is too high. The body doesn't need that much fat and there are even lots of nutritional studies now that have found that 10 to 20 percent fat in the diet is quite enough. So why does the recommendation stand at 30 percent? Primarily because Americans eat so much fat now that cutting back to 30 percent total calories is all that most nutrition experts feel they can ask of people. But I believe in asking for more and here's a few reasons why:

▪ A massive, ongoing study being conducted in China has shown that, while the Chinese eat 20 percent more calories than Americans, Americans are 25 percent fatter. That's because Americans eat up to 13.4 percent more fat. Simply put, it seems you are, indeed, what you eat.

▪ Excessive fat intake may up a person's chance of developing cancer and other diseases, including heart disease. On the other hand, cutting back on fat has been shown to help the body defend against disease. Simply put, too much dietary fat is just not healthy. The body is a more efficient machine when it's lean.

▪ Fat calories are much more fattening than carbohydrate and protein calories. A gram of fat, for instance, equals nine calories, while a gram of carbohydrate or protein equals only four. But it's not just the fact that fat is a denser source of energy than the other foods that makes it more fattening. It is also easier for the body to convert dietary fat into body fat than to convert, say carbohydrates into body fat. When carbohydrates are consumed, about 25 percent of the starting calories are burned in the process of converting them into fat. But when fat is consumed, the body only uses up about 3 percent of the calories to convert it, leaving all the more calories available for storing. Some people have bodies predetermined never to gain an ounce, but for most people, you eat fat, you get fat.

I myself don't add any fats to my foods. But even though you don't need to seek fat out, you will inevitably eat some so it's important to know the differences between certain kinds of fats. I'm sure you've already heard all those confusing terms tossed around. Well, what is a good oil, a bad oil, a fattening oil (all of them), a healthy oil, a saturated fat, an unsaturated fat, a polyunsaturated fat, and who saturated it and with what, and how the hell does this apply to what I'm eating? Help, my clients say, just tell me what to eat!

Well let me explain the basics. Dietary fat is really a catchall phrase for several fatty acids, primarily *saturated, monounsaturated,* or *polyunsaturated* fatty acids. Every fat—corn oil, butter, and so on—is composed of a combination of these fatty acids, but it's the predominant fatty acid that counts. Olive oil, for example, is known as a monounsaturate because it has 9.9 grams monounsaturated fatty acids per tablespoon and only 1.8 grams saturated and 1.1 grams polyunsaturated fatty acids.

The body—your computer—reacts differently to each of these fats. *Saturated fats* have been shown to raise serum cholesterol levels even higher than dietary cholesterol, i.e., eating enough foods cooked with palm oil, a highly saturated fat, could potentially raise one's cholesterol higher than eating a well-marbled steak. (More on dietary cholesterol coming up.) Saturated fats include palm oil, palm kernel oil, coconut oil, and animal fats such as butter and lard (which also contain cholesterol so they give you a double whammy); saturated fats are easy to recognize because they're solid at room temperature.

*Polyunsaturated fats,* which include safflower, sunflower, corn, sesame, soybean, and peanut oils, were always thought to be the best kinds of fat, because they lower cholesterol. But recently some research indicates that, besides having the positive effect of lowering LDL (bad) cholesterol levels, they may have the negative effect of lowering HDL (good) cholesterol levels too. (I'll explain the different cholesterol levels shortly.)

One thing to watch out for are *hydrogenated or partially hydrogenated polyunsaturated fats.* The process of hydrogenation is used to convert oils to solid form (to make shortenings and margarines, for example) or to better the texture of processed foods or to increase their shelf life. But hydrogenation also raises the saturated fatty acid level of a fat. For instance, when hydrogenated, soybean oil has a saturated fat level of 17 to 21 percent as opposed to its unprocessed level of 15 percent. A lot of manufacturers are switching from saturated fats to hydrogenated fats so watch out for them—they're a little better, but not the best.

*Monounsaturated fats*—olive and canola oils—are considered the healthiest fats. Diets high in monounsaturates have been found to reduce blood cholesterol levels as much as a low-fat diet does and also improve the ratio of HDL cholesterol to LDL, which can cut the risk of athero-sclerosis (hardening of the arteries).

There is also another beneficial fat: *Omega-3 fatty acids,* which are contained primarily in fish. Fish oil is thought to lower high blood pres-sure and prevent clotting that can lead to heart attack. Fish oil capsules, though, aren't beneficial (the chemistry of a nutrient can change when it is shifted from one form to another). Eating a lot of fish (particularly ones like salmon and mackerel—fattier fish) is the best way to get Omega-3s.

When all of this fat lingo becomes confusing to my clients I like to give them a very simplified visual example of what different fats are like in the body. Try it: take a piece of very cold butter and chop it up into small pieces. It will look like chunks of lard. This is what saturated fat amounts to in your bloodstream. When the body is fed too many saturated fats, "chunks" very much like the butter you diced up start to coagulate in the bloodstream. It has to be deposited somewhere and that somewhere is usually your arteries. So the more saturated fat foods you eat and the bigger the chunks grow, eventually nothing else (like oxygen) is going to get through the old heart valve and, boom, you're dead. That's a pretty clear, if dreary, picture of what high cholesterol amounts to, and it usu-ally has a bigger impact on my clients than the clinical jargon they are used to hearing.

There's also a flip side. I take a healthy monounsaturate like olive or canola oil and show them how smooth and fluid they run—they do not clog up the bloodstream like the chunks of saturated fat. In fact, they attach themselves to the chunks of fat (fiber does this, too) and help speed them through the bloodstream so they don't coagulate. This is why these are considered "good" oils. Of course, looks can be deceiving. As I just explained, not all fluid oils behave the same way in the body. Polyunsaturates may help clean up the nonfluid chunks, but they also clean out other kinds of fat that your body needs for balance. Still, you get the picture—when you do eat fat, stick to the monounsaturates.

No matter how good an oil is, it all comes back to the fact that no one should eat too much fat. Period. And if you're fat, plain old on-the-body fat, you shouldn't eat any fat except what you get in lean fish and poultry, and perhaps some non- or low-fat dairy products. (Nonfat dairy has less than one gram of fat per serving, but still has some fat.) All fats, good and bad, turn into molecules of fat on your body if you can't burn them. Think of the fat in your body like lamp oil—it's a slow-burning fuel, it doesn't flare up and burn quickly. Again, bottom line: if you are trying to lose weight, don't touch any oil. If you have high cholesterol, stick to light, I repeat light, amounts of polyunsaturated and, preferably, monounsaturated fats.

Start to become aware of how much fat you're adding to your diet on a day-to-day basis. Do you add butter or margarine to your foods? Do you drench your salads with dressing? Are you a cheese or even a low-fat yogurt eater? The low-fat brand may be better than the regular kind, but it still contains fat. Do your drinks contain fat? That "health" shake you have every day may in fact be high in dairy. When you keep a food journal, which I'll ask you to do in Chapter 6, write down everything you eat during the week, then take a look at how much fat you're really consuming.

Most people are completely unaware of both how much they eat and the fat content of the foods. Former Beach Boy Brian Wilson is a classic example. He eats very healthfully and counts his calories; however, when I went to his house a while ago, he was eating a popular brand of cereal because he thought he needed some extra fiber. Turning the package, I showed him the label: corn, palm, and coconut oils, and several different sugars! That is exactly what he didn't need.

Take it for granted that fats are added to most things you buy—almost every manufacturer (except the ones I'm going to tell you about in upcoming chapters) tosses some kind of oil into the batter. Most of my clients swear that they have a fat-free diet, yet when I go through their cupboards, I find product after product laden with fat. Now keep in mind that most baked goods—breads, muffins, etc.—have to have a certain amount of oil to be moist. But there are now also fat-free cookies and crackers on the market. When buying the majority of baked products, though, what you want to look for are ones that have a small amount of oil in them. That means they have one type of oil, say canola or safflower, located in the middle or end of the ingredient list. A bran muffin with nuts, palm oil, coconut oil, and butter is equivalent to a junky doughnut.

So check your labels (I'll tell you more about finding hidden fats and label reading in Chapter 5) and make changes: throw out your oily salad dressing and buy an oil-free one. Ask for your foods grilled dry at restaurants from now on. It's like trimming a budget. Cut two cents here, a dollar there—you'll be lopping off five dollars if you just stop eating butter. Clean fats out of your diet as you'd clean out an overcrowded garage. Examine what is going into your mouth. Just by making these few changes you can get your fat intake down below that 30 percent mark without the aid of a calculator. And you'll be surprised at how good it is for your health, energy level, and, of course, weight.

**Cholesterol.** You've already read a little about cholesterol in the fat section and that's because the two are interconnected. Blood cholesterol is a soft, fatlike substance (like other fatty substances, it's known as a lipid) found in the bloodstream. Blood cholesterol can build up in the inner lining of the artery walls over time, narrowing the openings until they eventually close. This keeps oxygen-carrying blood from the heart and generally results in a heart attack. The term plaque, which you may have heard, refers to the buildup of both cholesterol and other substances and is considered the cause of heart disease.

When a blood cholesterol measurement is taken, the number usually refers to the total amount of different kinds of cholesterol in the blood. The most important kinds of cholesterol to know about are lipoproteins, specifically *HDLs (high-density lipoproteins)* and *LDLs (low-density lipoproteins)*. Lipoproteins transport cholesterol and other fats in the bloodstream. LDLs are known as the "bad" cholesterol (like the chunks of butter I described earlier), because they deposit cholesterol on the artery walls. HDLs, known as the "good" cholesterol (like the liquid monounsaturated oils), are thought to carry cholesterol away from the tissues.

To be safe, it's recommended that blood cholesterol levels be no higher than 200 milligrams. There is, though, some controversy in the medical community about whether or not there really is a connection between high blood cholesterol levels and heart disease. Plus, because most of the cholesterol studies are done on middle-aged men, the conclusions drawn from them may not necessarily apply to women and children, particularly because men are more prone to having high cholesterol (although women begin to catch up once they've passed menopause). However, even though the controversy rages and will probably continue for years to come, it seems wise to err on the side of caution. I think we should assume that dietary cholesterol and saturated fats do indeed pose a very real threat to our health. Have your cholesterol checked regularly.

The American Heart Association recommends that a person's diet include no more than 300 milligrams of dietary cholesterol a day. We already know how hard it is to figure out how much that is unless you carry a cholesterol counter with you at all times. So, again as with watching your fat, try to eat as few foods containing cholesterol as possible and you should be fine. If your blood cholesterol level is high, you shouldn't eat *any* high-cholesterol foods. All animal foods contain cholesterol—vegetable products don't—but some have greater amounts than others. Red meats and eggs, for example, have more than poultry; white meat poultry and most fish are relatively low in cholesterol. People with high cholesterol levels also need to watch out for saturated fats (the bad-guy vegetable equivalents like palm and coconut oils)—in fact, especially saturated fats; this is about four times as important for lowering cholesterol as cutting dietary cholesterol.

Even if your cholesterol level checks out, watch what you eat anyway, particularly if anyone else in your family has high cholesterol—you may have a genetic tendency toward it, but it just hasn't registered yet. But genetics, aside, simply eating foods high in dietary cholesterol or saturated fats can *raise* your cholesterol level even if it was okay to begin with. So think of watching what you eat as preventive medicine. Watching your weight can be preventive medicine, too, because losing weight also lowers a person's LDL level, while raising the good cholesterol, HDL, level. And by all means, unless your physician advises otherwise, start a calorie-burning cardiovascular workout that exercises your lungs and heart, and exercise a minimum of three times a week, a minimum of twenty minutes. Most of all, CUT THE FAT—all fats so you keep your weight down, and particularly saturated fats so they don't raise your cholesterol. But also be aware that dietary cholesterol is present in every living animal cell—even the lean part of a steak. So even if you trim away the fat from meat, you're not home free.

## What You Don't Need but Might Want . . .

**Sugar.** First, let me say that sugar is my friend. I love sweet things and I am not going to go to my grave denying myself that love or feeling guilty about it. The first food we're given—breast milk—is sweet. No wonder it's natural to like and crave sweet foods. Some people don't crave sweets and I think that's swell for them. But the majority of us do and there's nothing wrong with that.

Sugar has come to be considered a food "demon" because it's been overused. It's so palatable and cheap that manufacturers put it into everything: breads, cereals, drinks, pasta sauces, jams, even peanut butter. By the time you've had three meals, you're overdosed on sugar—and that's not including dessert. But if you keep your intake of sugar moderate, it's not going to hurt you.

All carbohydrates are made up of sugars. However, the term "sugar" is used to refer to simple sugar molecules: the monosaccharides—glucose, fructose, and galactose (found in milk only)—and the disaccharides—sucrose (table sugar, actually a combination of glucose and fructose), lactose (glucose plus galactose), and maltose (malt sugar). Some of these names you might actually see on food labels. Honey, maple syrup, and corn syrup are other forms of sugar that are found in foods. Sugars all contain or are converted to glucose, our bodies' brain and muscle fuel. However, we don't need to eat any table sugars or have any form of sugar added to our processed foods because we get the sugar we need for brain and muscle fuel from glucose-based complex carbohydrates like fruits and vegetables. Even carrots and beets have sugar in them.

So we don't need excess sugar, but we want sugar. Is that so bad? The only medical problems sugar in excessive amounts has been proven to create are dental cavities. Sugar, for the most part, is not responsible for making people fat. The trouble is that sugary foods are usually fatty foods. Experts who study the sensory appeal of fats often note that what people think of as sugar cravings are really cravings for fat. And it's the fat that causes the weight problem. Sugar has only sixteen calories a teaspoon, and because it's a carbohydrate, the calories are readily utilized by the body—you burn sugar off fast, faster than you burn off fat. One downside of sugar is that it's usually contained in overprocessed foods that have been stripped of nutrients. A candy bar, for instance, offers nothing but empty calories—that is, calories that don't come with many vitamins and minerals in tow. And if you fill up on a lot of sugar foods, you probably won't eat other more vitamin- and mineral-packed foods. But as long as you keep sugar in your diet to a *minimum*—save it for those times you simply must indulge—I believe you won't get into trouble.

Some people can't handle sugar because it causes their moods to swing back and forth. Also, if eaten late at night it can cause sleeplessness. Not everybody gets the sugar blues or sugar hangovers after overindulging, but those who do have all the more reason to avoid OD'ing on sweets. The body is an addictive machine and the more you clean the sugar out of your body, the more you react to it when you eat it again. It's very similar to when a person who never drinks alcohol has one drink and gets tipsy. Even when I do indulge in my low-cal, low-sugar chewy candies, I definitely feel it the next day. It's just that it's worth it sometimes.

As I said in the section on complex carbohydrates, simple carbohydrates like sugar are broken down by the body much more quickly than complex carbohydrates so they can provide somewhat of a rush of energy—but then they'll let you down because the glucose has been used up so fast. If you have somewhere to direct that burst of energy—say, by working it off with intensive exercise—then you probably won't suffer too badly. But, if not, beware the consequences of hitting bottom: you're

FOOD COP

probably going to feel lousy. A good solution is just to allow yourself low-sugar treats (animal crackers, fortune cookies, nonfat frozen yogurt, low-sugar candies, Lifesavers—see Chapter 6 for more suggestions), whether you're sensitive to sugar rushes or not. Even if sugar isn't really all that "bad" for you, there are other better, more nutritious foods you can be eating.

**Artificial Sweeteners.** It always kills me when I see someone have a piece of cherry pie à la mode—and a diet soft drink. It's human nature, I know: "There are so many calories in my dessert, why have them in my soda as well?" Reasonable. But, in reality, what happens, is you use the idea of sugar substitutes to rationalize your poor eating habits. Saving calories by putting Equal in your coffee does not allow you to have a pint of Häagen Dazs. The sugar in your coffee has sixteen calories per teaspoon; the Häagen Dazs is God-only-knows-how-many fat calories per teaspoon. Studies have even shown that using artificial sweeteners encourages people to eat more calories. Another problem with fake sugars is that they let you perpetuate the habit of eating junky foods. Plus, people tend to eat artifically sweetened foods on top of sugar-sweetened foods. It seems that the more sweet foods you eat—whether they're artifically or naturally sweetened—the more you want. If you want to be lean and healthy, you have to get off junk and get into some healthier substitutes for your sweet tooth.

I'm not saying, don't ever have a Diet Coke; I have Equal in my coffee, but not so that I can go on a cookie-eating rampage later. Just don't take sugar substitutes to extremes, not only because it won't help you change your eating habits, but also because I believe the body is not equipped to handle too much of these foreign substances. There are three basic artificial sweeteners on the market: aspartame (NutraSweet), which has nutrients in it and is digested by the body like a protein; saccharin (Sweet 'N Low,) a noncaloric chemical not metabolized by the body; ascesulfame-K (Sunette), also a chemical not metabolized by the body. The FDA believes that they're all safe—and they probably are. However, the catch here is we will only know in time, so my advice USE IN MODERATION!

**Artificial Fats.** There aren't too many facts on this subject yet, but the way food scientists are working, there will be soon. As this book was being written, the first fake fat was introduced: NutraSweet's Simplesse. It was first used in a frozen dessert product called Simple Pleasures and is planned for use in products like mayonnaise, sour cream, dips, cheeses, and salad dressings; it's made of egg white and milk proteins and contains about one to two calories per gram. The FDA readily approved Simplesse because it's made from real food derivatives and is considered safe (even by the Center for Science in the Public Interest, a well-respected watchdog organization in Washington, D.C.).

So maybe Simplesse isn't the worst thing you can eat. And perhaps Sealtest Fat Free nonfat ice cream, which is made with cellulose gel instead of butterfat, won't hurt you either. But there are more frightening kinds of artificial fats on the way. Procter & Gamble is close to getting approval for Olestra, a mix of sucrose and oil molecules that the body is unable to break down—it passes right through your system, and so do the calories—and which in one study has been shown to increase tumor growth in animals. There is the possibility that cheeses, ice cream, mayonnaise, and salad dressings will be one day made with Olestra and that it will be used to deep-fry foods. Frito-Lay, Arco Chemical Company, and Best Foods are all also experimenting with their own versions of fake fats.

Just think, if your body doesn't digest something (fiber excluded because it not only has its own benefits, but comes in the company of vitamins and minerals) *then it's not food.* Real fat can be unhealthy in excessive amounts, but at least it has food value; it contains nutrients. Common sense should tell you that eating nonfoods can't be too good for you.

Food science in combination with food marketing can be scary. The goal seems to be to satisfy the mass's cravings for the overprocessed foods they've become addicted to, trick them into thinking what they're eating is healthy, and make tons of money in the process! The facts on fake fat aren't all in yet, and they may, indeed, prove to be harmful, even if they do end up having FDA approval (initially so did things like cyclamates and carcinogenic red dyes). My fear is that these quasi foods won't be scrutinized well enough and that's objectionable.

But even more objectionable is that fake fats, just like artificial sweeteners, let people go on overeating all that junk they shouldn't be eating in the first place. Even if foods like Simple Pleasures and Sealtest Fat Free are safe, they're still packed with sugar. Yet, nonetheless, fake fats can easily give you a false notion that you're eating healthfully. If you want to have some of the fake-fat foods once in a while, fine. But don't think you can live off fake fats and be healthy—or that you'll necessarily be slim. To do that, you have to eat nutritious whole foods, not nonnutritive junk foods.

**Salt.** Sodium is an essential mineral for maintaining the fluid balance in the body. Too much of it can upset the fluid balance, which is why some people get bloated when they eat a lot of salty foods. Sodium can contribute to high blood pressure (hypertension), which in turn ups the risk of heart attack and stroke. But not all people are sensitive to salt and there is even some controversy about whether or not it helps to cut back on sodium if you have high blood pressure. Still, it's probably a good idea.

Once again, the answer is balance and understanding your own body. If you have high blood pressure, then salt is your enemy and you are well advised to try to completely cut it out of your diet. Even if you don't, there's no sense in overdoing it if salt can even potentially create a health problem for you (which it might if you have a family history of hypertension). The American Heart Association recommends consuming not more than 1,000 milligrams sodium per 1,000 calories not to exceed 3,000 milligrams per day. But who's got time to count every gram of sodium she or he eats? Take the easy way out. For every product on the supermarket shelves loaded with sodium, there is one marked low/no sodium right next to it. Go for those. Cut down on sodas, crackers, spreads, cereals, condiments, baked goods, and snack foods that are high in sodium. Read the labels: any ingredient with sodium, Na (its chemical symbol), or sodium in the title—e.g., sodium chloride (table salt), monosodium glutamate (MSG), sodium benzoate, sodium hydroxide, sodium nitrite—means salt. That alone will help you reduce your salt intake. If you have a habit of salting everything on your plate, stop and consider what really needs the salty flavor. Most likely it's the vegetables or starch—so salt them, but sprinkle only half of what you normally would. The best thing you can do is to start using the many new seasonings without salt on the market today (see the cravings sections of Chapter 6) and you can use lemon juice, garlic, and dry wines to replace the saltiness in foods as you are cooking as well.

Sodium is something that, once you become aware of all the products it's contained in, is easy to cut back on without carrying a calculator. Plus, while salt is one of the flavors people crave most, studies at the Monell Chemical Senses Center in Philadelphia have shown that people lose their taste for salt once they reduce their sodium intake. The taste for salt may be natural, but so is the taste for limited amounts. In other words, you can create or destroy the habit. Cutting back may seem difficult at first, yet try the new seasonings and low/no-sodium products and you'll find your salt habit diminishing quickly.

## What the Body Does and Doesn't Need to Lose Weight

One of the most important things to remember when you're trying to lose weight is that the body is primed for survival. So if you stop feeding it it's going to do its best to survive regardless. That translates into this familiar scenario: You go on a very low calorie diet. Initially, you lose weight fairly fast because you are losing water; when the body doesn't receive adequate fuel in the form of carbohydrates, it breaks down muscle tissue (protein), a process that causes the kidneys to excrete water. Next, the pounds stop coming off as quickly because your body, thinking it's faced with starvation, starts to conserve energy by slowing down the rate at which it burns food. Low-calorie dieting can reduce your metabolism as much as 15 to 30 percent within two days. What's worse is that the more often you go on starvation-type diets, the slower your metabolism will become. This is what is referred to as yo-yo dieting because, when you go off the diet, your metabolism will stay lower than it was when you started just in case your body is subject to what it perceives as starvation again. Inevitably, this will make you regain and cause you to diet once more. Back and forth, back and forth. And the effects are cumulative. Each time you go on and off a diet, your metabolism will slow down even further.

Here's another way to think of it. Say your body is like a house and that body fat is like canned goods in a store room, tucked away for you to live off in case of an emergency. If the big earthquake should hit, your body will live happily off those canned goods, while skinny over there will bite the dust because she has nothing stored. So any time some extra canned goods enter the house, the body stores them away, storing, storing until its literally bursting at the seams with canned goods. In other words, you're fat. You might try and stop eating—that is, stop bringing in canned goods and use up the ones you have—to get back down to size, but the body is going to ration out those remaining canned goods bit by bit. And if the store rooms get low, it's going to give you cravings that will eventually make you fill them up again.

This is the reason so many low-calorie diets are frustrating. When you stop eating, you are changing the program your body has come to know and it's going to fight you tooth and nail. Is it hopeless, then, to even try and lose weight? No, not at all. It's hopeless, though, if you try to do it by eating practically nothing so that your body shuts down. On the contrary, you can lose weight if you give your body reasonable amounts of burnable fuel (that is lean protein and complex carbohydrates). And if you exercise. For one thing, exercise will burn off some of those "canned goods" you've got stored away. For another, exercise can boost your metabolism and help counteract the slowdown that comes from eating less. Exercise also builds muscle and muscle tissue requires more energy to maintain than fat tissue. That is, you'll burn off more calories just sitting there if your body composition is heavy on the muscle, light on body fat. In some ways, it's as if muscle is more alive than fat.

As I said earlier in the section on fat, the one sure way to lose weight is to cut out the dietary fat from your diet. If you don't eat fat, you won't be fat, pure and simple. You can stop buttering your bread, you can lay off the ice cream, you can switch to nonfat milk. But you must also do more than just the obvious. There is fat hidden in so many of the foods we eat. Do you realize that a Ritz Cracker is almost 50 percent fat? Or that the ladleful of Ragú spaghetti sauce you put on your pasta is more than one-third fat? Later on in this book is a section that will teach you what to look for on a food label so that you're not duped into buying foods that might seem healthy, but are really loaded with fat. And, really, that's the key to losing weight and keeping it off: not going on a diet for a week here, a week there but, rather, learning what foods you can eat for life.

The best advice I can give you is not to jump on every gimmicky diet bandwagon or get caught up in every new weight loss fad. Learn to know yourself, learn about food, and then stop the nonsense and begin eating as it's right for your, not anybody else's, life.

## What Dos and Don'ts Mean in Terms of Real Food

Nobody really thinks "I want some fat" or "I should have some complex carbs" when they eat, they think about—well—they think about food. Here, I've summed up what our bodies need—or at least will be best off with—in terms of what we really consume.

**Fruits and Vegetables.** These complex carbohydrates contain tons of fiber, plus tons of the vitamins and minerals essential to the human body. They are not and never will be fattening in their natural state (with perhaps the exception of avocados). Produce is very "burnable": your body uses what it needs and throws the rest away. To become fat on produce alone, you would have to overeat a tremendous amount and barely move. I encourage you to try different kinds of produce and eat as much and as many kinds of fruits and veggies you want, at whatever hour you want.

**Poultry.** Chicken (meat without the skin is best if you are trying to lose weight or to lower your cholesterol, and white is less fatty than dark) is lean and healthy—just take that extra step and ask your butcher about the farms the chicken has been raised on. Do they raise the animals without hormones? Feed them organic feed? Most farms that do take those extra steps make a point of saying so either on the label or in a little booklet. Those are the healthiest kinds of chickens—they may cost a few cents more than mass-produced poultry, but just deduct it from your medical bills. Turkey is even leaner than chicken and becoming a supermarket staple. You can find turkey cut up into sections at the market now as regularly as chicken parts. Ground turkey has become the best replacement for ground beef. Remove the skin, as you would with chicken for special diets. Although turkey sausages and cold cuts are less fatty than their beef and pork counterparts, they still contain a fair amount of fat. Don't make a habit of them. Also note that ground turkey is sometimes ground with dark meat and skin, which ups its fat content. The best kind is ground turkey breast that you ask the butcher to grind for you.

**Seafood.** All forms of shellfish and seafood are lean and healthy. The only problem is that they sometimes come from polluted waters. The safest fish are those from deep waters, because they aren't exposed to near-shore pollution; the riskiest are those from fresh water, which is often contaminated with pesticides from agriculture runoff. It's not a pleasant bit of information, but it doesn't mean that you have to give up seafood. Just ask the person at the fish counter about the origin of the fish and don't trust any fish that is frozen with preservatives, mass produced, or preseasoned. Also, be aware that fatty fish, besides having more fat calories (see page 240), carry more contaminants. Despite all this, I still consider seafood to be the healthiest and leanest of foods, and I think it will become more of a staple of our diets in the future.

**Red Meat.** The way we've evolved as human animals does not lend itself to eating meat—we just don't digest it as well as we used to. Most red meat in this country is so poorly raised that it is barely edible food by the time it gets to the market. The meat industry has suffered the blows of bad press (especially due to the American Heart Association) and, therefore, many more companies are taking efforts to raise lean, clean, healthy animals. Meat in it's natural state is not a killer generally (however, recent reports have linked it to colon cancer). If you want to have red meat once in a while, fine, but ask your butcher for the leanest cuts, raised on healthy farms, or choose ones marked "Choice," the leanest grade. And of course, cut off all the excess fat.

**Dairy Products.** Milk and milk products are not necessarily unhealthy, but they are high in fat and cholesterol (skim milk products are fairly low in cholesterol, but they still have it) so naturally, too many of them can be unhealthy. There is no reason to eat anything but low-fat or nonfat dairy products—whether you're an adult or a child. They may taste lackluster the first few times, but believe me, after a while, it's the whole milk products you won't want to have—they'll seem too rich. And if you start your kids out on the lower fat products, they'll never even know the difference. They have even come out with "light milk" now, which is lighter in milk fat—just another sign that food in our lives is really changing.

**Whole Grains.** The key word here is *whole,* not the grain that has been separated into three to five different parts and made into seventy-something different products. You want to get the bran layers with your grains. Whole grain products contain many more vitamins and minerals and fiber than the processed and bleached kind. This category is also important because it includes possible cholesterol lowerers like oat bran and rice bran. Whole grains are under the category of complex carbohydrates so they're not really fattening, but if you do eat an overabundance of them, you will need to burn them off or you will gain weight. Moderate them throughout your diet, and make sure they don't have a lot of fat added in.

**Legumes.** Beans and peas are an excellent source of protein, fiber, vitamins, and minerals—try to eat them as often as you can. Normally the problem with legumes is that they are prepared with other products that are fatty so, as always, watch what they're mixed with. Seeds and nuts are also legumes and if you can afford the fat calories, fine. But if you can't, watch out for them, since they're very fattening and some contain saturated fat.

**Chemical Additives and Preservatives.** Yes, these are part of our food system too—and a part we don't need. You can't avoid them entirely, but you can really try to keep them to a minimum in your life. For instance, I don't buy diet sodas, because I like them and will drink them if they're available. Once in a while, though, I will have one when I'm out, but *only* when I'm out—that is one way I minimize the amount of chemicals I ingest. It is obvious that we don't want them in our foods, but the fact is that they are there and you need to make an effort to avoid them as much as possible. The good news is that the food industry is changing fast, and preservatives and other unhealthy additives are being edged out.

## The Best Foods for Your Body Type

Now I'm going to get a little more specific. How much of the above foods you can eat and what exactly within each of those food groups should and shouldn't be part of *your* diet will depend on your body type— specifically your weight and cholesterol concerns. And it differs from person to person. Take the fictitious family described below. The members fall into varying body-type categories, one of which you probably fall into too. Under each category is a set of dietary recommendations designed to serve as guidelines for making rules that also take your lifestyle, wants, and needs into account. In the final evaluation, every member of this family will probably eat differently from all the others—but that doesn't mean they need a separate chef to serve every person! This family can all sit down to eat at the same table—easily—because, although the differences are major in regard to their health and efforts to stay fit, the differences in preparation are minor (see "Meals for Mixed Needs" in Chapter 8).

One guideline for everyone to keep in mind: eating overprocessed, chemical-infused junk food will be to your detriment no matter what your body type! Give it up! Drugs are out, smoking is out, so for the most part is junk food. Now meet the Drapers . . .

*Mr. Draper, 46.* He's very slender, has never had a weight problem, but has high cholesterol. Overworked, he's a typical case of a heart attack in the making. But because there's no visual eyesore—fat— it's hard to understand that there's trouble traveling through his veins.

*Mrs. Draper, 42.* She is always about 15–20 pounds overweight, always going on and off unreasonable-rule diets, and has low cholesterol.

She's just beginning to walk for exercise, but is also beginning to think there's no way she'll ever get those extra pounds off.

*Adam Draper, 23.* Adam is very slender, has low cholesterol, exercises regularly, and wants to eat healthfully. He thinks being "buff" is hip. Yet he probably has his father's genes and if he eats the same way Dad always did, he's going to develop cholesterol problems later on. He doesn't need to count calories, but he needs, and wants, to eat real food.

*Amanda Draper, 12.* She is a growing child, with no weight or cholesterol problems, and doesn't want to have problems in the future. And she won't if she isn't given the leeway to eat whatever she pleases just because she's a child. She has a higher capacity to burn junk food because she is growing, but she still shouldn't overdo it.

*Grandma Draper, 66.* Grandma has always had a weight problem and now has high cholesterol too. She's the classic case of someone who's known little else besides this century's overprocessed foods. It's hard for her to understand foods that are not Hamburger Helper or Rice-A-Roni. Her tastebuds are highly conditioned to salt and sugar.

*Aunt Victoria Draper, 34.* She is a single professional, always trying to lose 5 to 7 pounds, who has no cholesterol problem. She's hip to all the current workout programs, tries to eat well but can never seem to get those last few pounds off or figure out how to get the right food into her busy, stressful life.

The Drapers all fit into one of the four body-type categories. Here's where they fall, plus the "rules"—guidelines, actually—that work for each one.

### *Gains Weight Easily/Low Cholesterol*

Both Mrs. Draper and Victoria—and 85 percent of American women—fall into this category.

1. NO ADDED FATS (OILS, BUTTER, OR MARGARINE) OF ANY KIND! You are allergic to oil.
2. No nuts or seeds.       } Anything you can make oil
3. No avocados or olives.  } from contains oil.
4. Limited nonfat dairy products.
5. Limited lean red meats.

6. Unlimited lean proteins: all seafood and chicken and turkey (both skinless white meat only).
7. Limited eggs and caviar.
8. Limited rice, potatoes, breads, pasta, and whole grains, prepared without butter or oil (once you lower your weight you can eat more of these).
9. Unlimited fruits, vegetables, and legumes, prepared without butter or oil.
10. Limited sugar/sweets.

## Gains Weight Easily/High Cholesterol

Grandma Draper represents a large portion of Americans who, after a lifetime of processed, chemical-filled junk food, have developed taste buds that only respond to heavy amounts of salt, sugar, and fat. The rules get tough here . . . but they'll work.

1. NO ADDED FATS (OILS, BUTTER, OR MARGARINE) OF ANY KIND!
2. No nuts or seeds.        ⎫ Anything you can make oil
3. No avocados or olives.  ⎬ from contains oil.
4. No dairy products.
5. No red or organ meats.
6. Unlimited lean proteins: nonfatty fish only and chicken and turkey (both skinless white meat only).
7. No eggs or caviar.
8. Limited rice, potatoes, breads, pasta, and whole grains, prepared without butter or oil (once you've lowered your weight you can eat more of these).
9. Plenty of oat, rice, and other brans, prepared without butter or oil.
10. Unlimited fruits, vegetables, and legumes, eaten without butter or oil.
11. Limited sugar/sweets.

## Doesn't Gain Weight Easily/High Cholesterol

Mr. Draper belongs to this group and so probably will Adam Draper if he doesn't start educating himself about food right now. It's easy for people in this category to be fooled by their thin bodies into thinking they can eat whatever they want. Not so. You may not see the evidence on the outside until you drop from a heart attack. You have to watch what you eat—there're no two ways about it.

1. NO DAIRY PRODUCTS, ESPECIALLY BUTTER!
2. No nuts or nut oils (like peanut or walnut oil).
3. Go for seeds and seed oils (like sunflower).
4. Yes to olive and canola oils.
5. No red or organ meats.
6. Unlimited lean proteins: nonfatty fish only and chicken and turkey (both skinless white meat only).
7. Unlimited soy and tofu foods.
8. No egg yolks or caviar.
9. Plenty of rice, potatoes, bread, pasta, and whole grains, prepared without butter.
10. Plenty of oat, rice, and other brans, prepared without butter.
11. Unlimited fruits, vegetables, and legumes, eaten without butter.
12. Limited sugar/sweets.

## *Doesn't Gain Weight Easily/Low Cholesterol*

Amanda Draper belongs in this group (so does Adam, but he's better off eating more like his father in case his cholesterol level jumps). Most of us were in this group as children and are now fighting the damage that can happen with an "I can eat anything I want" mentality. You may never be fat or have high cholesterol, but if you don't eat healthfully, it will catch up with you one day. So even if you can get away with more indulgences than those with other body types, don't go overboard.

1. Choose nonsaturated vegetable oils and margarine over saturated fats like butter.
2. Don't condition your taste buds to foods that are highly salted, greasy, or sweetened.
3. Nonfat dairy products, when possible.
4. Limited red meats.
5. Plenty of rice, potatoes, pasta, and whole grains.
6. Unlimited fruits, vegetables, and legumes (people in this group often neglect to eat produce—try to eat dishes like vegetarian lasagna, fruit salads, steamed veggies).
7. Limited sugar/sweets.
8. Be kind to those around you who can't indulge and not pay for it or you'll end up eating alone!

# 5

# *Throw Out the Junk: How to Make Over Your Refrigerator and Cupboards*

"**G**ROW UP!" THAT'S what I told my client Dr. Fletcher when I found a tub of peanut butter in his refrigerator. No, I wasn't trying to do a Joan Rivers imitation, I was making a point.

At Dr. Fletcher's request to "put him on a diet," I arrived at his house one Saturday afternoon and was confronted with his personal trainer as well as his chef—they were there to learn what I had to say so they could also help Dr. Fletcher in his quest to lose weight. The trainer was very open to ideas because he had many other clients he hoped to help slim down. The chef was nervous.

I proceeded to ask Dr. Fletcher just what exactly he had been eating lately. When he was halfway through his report, I got up and walked to the refrigerator. From all the consultations I've done I've learned that while a client might "forget" what they've eaten, his or her refrigerator and cupboards never lie. As I opened Dr. Fletcher's refrigerator my eyes scanned the creamy Italian salad dressings, smoked turkey, Kraft cheese, then landed directly on the jar of Skippy. When I asked him why he had all these fattening products in the fridge he rambled off a list of the other people that lived in the house and said they were for them. But when it came to the Skippy he confessed. "It's mine, I get up at about two or three in the morning and I come down to the kitchen and eat peanut butter." "How old are you?" I asked. He said forty-something. "If you're a man who is fat and over forty," I said, "you don't get Skippy. It's for kids—and not even that healthy for them. It's a fattening product. There is no way around it: If you eat Skippy or any other peanut butter, you will be fat. Make your choice! There comes a time when you have to grow up." The trainer's eyes popped and the chef lit his third cigarette. I tossed the peanut butter into the garbage can. Dr. Fletcher was a little shocked, but appreciated my direct approach and we proceeded to get rid of the other products that were ruining his diet. The next day I returned to his house with bags of groceries that made more sense. Small bowls of Sans Sucre Sugar Free Chocolate Mousse, a less fatty alternative for midnight snacking, for example.

Nobody said it was fair that Dr. Fletcher can't eat peanut butter . . . who said life is fair? If you are overweight, it's not that you can't have high-fat foods like peanut butter ever again, it's just that you should know right now that you can't continue to eat them on a regular basis and expect to be a slender person. Quite simply, there are certain foods that you just can't have. This is the "get-real" approach to eating. Which is why I rely on the allergy excuse. Some foods give some people hives, or headaches, well, fatty foods give you fat cells. Determine your "allergies" and avoid foods that exacerbate them.

One of the first things I do during client consultations is go through the foods in the refrigerator and cupboards, then describe to them just what those foods they're keeping around are doing to their bodies. Nine out of ten clients have nothing but junky, fattening food in their kitchens and, maybe, a couple of pieces of fruit. The others have botched attempts at processed diet foods (packages of Lean Cuisine) or an array of unopened products from that one trip to the health food store they made last year. And most of the time they have foods for everybody except themselves. They buy products they think they should or are conditioned to buy, either because they've been eating them since day one or because they've been influenced by the advertising. They buy products they know nothing about and don't realize are unhealthy and/or fattening.

Or they buy nothing at all and eat out all the time. The bottom line is that the food (or nonfood) in their cupboards and refrigerators is not working for them, yet they wonder why they are fat and unhealthy.

If you go to the market and look at what's in people's shopping carts I think you'll see what I mean. This is where the truth comes out. Look at the person, then check out the products in his or her cart. Every single time I see people with a basketful of Weight Watchers or Lean Cuisine, they are always overweight, probably because either they're just beginning to try and lose weight or, just as likely, those diet foods aren't working. Look at the amount of fresh produce in their carts—usually, it's not much. What you put in your shopping cart is going into your cupboards and refrigerator, and eventually into your body. That's why in helping you to figure out what to eat, I'm going to start in the supermarket aisles.

## Fables on Labels

One of the best things you can do in terms of keeping your body lean and healthy is to become a sharp, informed label reader, not an easy job considering that most labels are now full of health-hype lingo nobody quite understands. Product manufacturers who make nutritional claims on packaging, though, are required by law to provide just about all the information you really need to know. It's just a matter of wading through the lies and exaggerations to get to the truth about a food's nutritional status.

The process of labeling products has gone through many changes in the last fifty years. Requirements for ingredient labeling were minimal at first. Then, as the demand for more information grew, so did the rules and regulations. The problem is that the regulatory agencies—the USDA regulates beef and poultry, the FDA regulates all other foods—don't have rules for every term used on the label and not all nutritional aspects of a food must be noted.

One of the most frustrating things I run up against in my work is helping clients read past the big "FIBER," "OAT BRAN," "NO CHO-LESTEROL," "LOW SUGAR," "THIS WILL IMPROVE YOUR SEX LIFE" sales gimmicks on the package. When a health claim is made, the manufacturer must, by law, back it up with nutritional information (i.e., if the words *fat free* appear on the box, the back must give details about, not only fat per serving, but carbohydrate, protein, and sodium per serving; the percentages of the U.S. RDA of protein, five vitamins, and two minerals; additional minerals; and cholesterol). This would seem to make things clear, but the fact is that current regulations require ingredients to be itemized in descending order by weight, which can be misleading. By listing the various types of sweeteners separately, for instance, some cereals conceal the fact that sugar is their main ingredient.

Even if manufacturers are required to reveal the fat content of their product in certain instances, there are *no* regulations requiring to them specify exactly what kinds of fats their product contains. So while a label may shout "no cholesterol" and, in fact, the product doesn't contain any animal fats (the only foods that do contain cholesterol), a food made with saturated fat—*which can raise blood cholesterol levels*—may nonetheless be lurking.

During the time I was writing this book, *fat free* suddenly became the buzzwords of the moment. But when I went to investigate, I found that some of those supposedly fat-free products—one salad dressing, in particular—actually contained oil. So who's to say what *fat free* means? At this point, the FDA has not established standards so it could mean almost anything. No good fat? No bad fat? No fat from a different, artificial source? Look for the words *oil free* to be on the safe side, but I do not recommend that you make the fat-free version of any food a regular part of your diet as it is still junk food. It is much better to use products such as nonfat natural frozen yogurt or sorbets to satisfy your dessert cravings than "fat-free" products that have lots of sugar and chemicals in them. Plus, fat-free foods will not help you train your palate so that you begin to prefer healthier foods. Some of them, I will admit, are legitimate. Health Valley, for example, has fat-free muffins and other baked goods out now and I'm sure other reputable companies will follow. But, for the most part, to me, the more commercial fat-free junk foods are sort of like smoking filtered cigarettes. You're still smoking.

This reminds me of a parody of a cigarette ad I recently heard on a New York City radio station. "No cholesterol—never had it, never will," the "spokesperson" said, trying to get people to buy his brand. Of course, cigarettes don't have cholesterol—but they'll kill you anyway. This is the same fashion in which a lot of food is marketed. Does it really matter that Crisco doesn't have cholesterol? It's pure fat, and hydrogenated fat at that. Next thing you know they'll be pasting "no cholesterol" labels on Coca-Cola cans.

Ultimately, it's often too easy for food manufacturers to twist the lingo in order to sell their products. Even Health and Human Services Secretary Louis W. Sullivan, M.D., addressing the 1990 National Food Policy Conference, said, "The grocery store has become a Tower of Babel, and consumers need to be linguists, scientists, and mind readers to understand the many labels they encounter."

In fact, there are all kinds of things manufacturers can do to fool the consumer. For instance, a very famous soup company has always listed the amount of sodium per serving on its label. Not too long ago, they simply changed what constituted a serving—there had previously been two servings per can, with the change it became two and a half servings per can. Naturally, the smaller servings contained less sodium (and less of everything else), but sensing a good marketing scam, the company announced that the soup was now a "reduced-sodium" product. Sure, but who's going to eat such small servings (everybody always eats the whole can anyway!) plus it was technically a lie: the company did not reduce the amount of sodium in the can. Without legal limits, manufacturers can make false health claims and contort the variety of "rules" to meet their selling needs. Serving size, in particular, is a something to consider carefully: A product might appear to be low calorie until you look at how big the serving actually is—probably about half the amount you're going to eat.

Here's another good example that was sited in an issue of the *Tufts Diet and Nutrition Newsletter* and that is enough to make you dizzy: Featherweight Whipped Topping (by SandozNutrition) has a label that says that it contains four calories per tablespoon and that it contains zero grams of fat, protein, and carbohydrate per serving. So how can a product have none of the above and yet still have calories? And if not fat, protein, or carbohydrate calories, calories of what? Here's the trick: Protein, fat, and carbohydrates make up a food's total calories, but by law they may be rounded off to the nearest gram. So in this case it means that one serving provides less than half a gram each of these nutrients, which allows the manufacturer to list them at zero. But either there really are some protein, fat, and carbohydrates in the whipped cream or there is something nonnatural occurring in there. Four calories, even if it's fat, isn't going to kill anyone, but you've got to wonder why the labeling is so complicated. Spend your day figuring that one out!

The reduced-sodium soup and whipped topping are just two examples of how confusing and deceptive labels can be. *Sodium,* just like *cholesterol* and *light,* is a modern-day buzzword designed to catch the public's attention. I talked about this in Chapter 4 and I'll say it again, it's really important to hold your ground when the media are pumping the hell out of some supposed superstar food or food compound like vitamin C or oat bran. In some ways, we are the same people crowded around the stagecoach, mesmerized by the medicine man selling the great miracle cure in a bottle. The one bottle that cures it all, helps all ills. Well, the story hasn't changed: the man always takes off with the cash and you are left with a bottle of nothing too terrific.

As this book was being written, the FDA at the behest of Dr. Sullivan was looking into changing the rules governing labels. Among other things, revisions would require that information about saturated fat, fiber, cholesterol content, and calories from fat all be mandatory on labels and that serving sizes be standardized (no more sodium tricks from soup companies). Presently undefined phrases like *low fat, fat free,* and *high fiber* would also be defined so that consumers would know what they're getting. But until the time these proposals are put into effect, companies will continually find a way to slap on an eye-catching label, even if it's misleading. We all have to be wary.

The most offensive "health" claim may be the term *light.* Light? Or is it lite? And lighter in what? Sugar, salt, fat, price? It's very hard to say, you see, because no one ever defined *light* as it applies to a food product. Most consumers assume that it means the product has fewer calories—fewer, maybe, but they are by no means light in calories—as many "light" foods on the market now prove. Consider the following:

1. *Light Olive Oil.* Lighter in color but same food, fat, and calorie content.
2. *Sara Lee Lights Cheesecake.* Lighter in texture, still pretty heavy in calories.
3. *Doritos Light.* Take some fat and grease out and call it light, it's still junk food to me.
4. *Jones Light Links.* Take a greasy pork sausage, add some cheap bleached rice to it for bulk, so you have less greasy pork fat per sausage, but it's still the same rotten sausage. This one made me mad.
5. *Lite canned fruits.* It usually means syrups with less sugar, but fruit doesn't need *any* syrup. You want the ones that are canned in their own juices.
6. *Lite or fat-free desserts.* Much of the baked goods industry—labels like Entenmann's and Hostess—are now putting out the same old bad products under light labels. Look what's in Entenmann's Fat-Free Chocolate Loaf Cake: **sugar, bleached flour, egg whites, water, nonfat milk, cocoa, fructose, natural & artificial flavors, modified cornstarch, modified food starch, mono and diglycerides, baking powder, (baking soda, sodium aluminum phosphate), oat fiber, salt, potassium sorbate, dextrose,**

**maltodextrin, xanthan gum, guar gum, sorbitan monostear- ate, polysorbate 60.**

Yes, they took out some of the animal fats and high-cholesterol oils, but sugar is still the number one ingredient. This product is still fattening and unhealthy. Not to mention that you will probably eat twice as much because you think it's less fattening. Many of these manufacturers put in so many questionable substitutes to try and achieve the same texture or taste as the original product, that they just end up making another junk food. Remember, a food can be "light" because it has fewer calories than similar products, but a large percentage of those calories may still be fat (see "Deciphering Meat and Poultry Labels," below, to learn how to calculate the amount of fat calories in a food).

I think by now I've made my point. You can't always take every word on a label at face value. First, consider what is required by law on a label, then learn what else above and beyond you need to look for to find out the truth about what's in a food.

**Light/Lite.** This term may refer to a food's color, taste, really any- thing—there's no regulation to determine its definition (except for meat and poultry products—see below). However, if light/lite refers to any food's calorie content, then the manufacturer is obligated to provide nu- trition information to back it up—read the fine print on the back of the box.

**Low Calorie.** When this claim is on a label, the product by law may not contain more than forty calories per serving. Remember, check out the serving size—if it's so minuscule you're likely to eat five helpings, then the forty calories a serving doesn't really help you.

**Reduced Calorie.** A reduced-calorie food must by law be at least one- third lower in calories than the food to which it is compared, for example, if potato chips have 160 calories per one-ounce serving, reduced-calorie potato chips must have 107 or fewer calories per ounce. Note that re- duced *calories* doesn't necessarily mean reduced *fat*.

**Diet/Dietetic.** These labels mean that the food must meet the require- ments of either low- or reduced-calorie foods or a clear explanation must be given of how they are useful for special dietary purposes.

**Sugar Free/Sugarless.** A sugar-free food cannot by law contain table sugar, fructose, or corn syrup. It may be sweetened, though—look to see if aspartame (NutraSweet) or saccharin is in the ingredient list. Also note that sugar by any other name is still sugar: sucrose (table sugar), malt, maltose, lactose, fructose, corn syrup, honey, maple syrup, dextrose, dextrin, manitol, sorbitol, and molasses are all sugars.

**Sodium Free/Low Sodium/Reduced Sodium.** Sodium free means a food may not have more than 5 milligrams of sodium per serving, low-sodium may not have more than 140 milligrams, and reduced sodium must have at least 75 percent less sodium than the regular version of the food. To put this in context, remember that the American Heart Association recommends no more than 1,000 mg. sodium per 1,000 calories per day. As you check labels for salt content, be aware that anything with the word *sodium* in it—sodium nitrate, sodium phosphate, sodium bicarbonate (baking soda), monosodium glutamate (MSG), sodium saccharin, sodium caseinate, sodium citrate—translates as salt.

**Enriched.** When flour is refined it loses up to 80 percent of its nutrients. Enriched means they put the iron, niacin, thiamine, and riboflavin back in, but not all of the other minerals or the fiber. Essentially, you are not getting the healthiest possible product.

**Fortified.** When a food is fortified, it is bolstered with vitamins or minerals it never had to begin with. Orange juice, for instance, does not naturally have calcium, but at least one producer fortifies its product with the mineral. It's not necessarily bad (and may even be good), but it's not necessarily a reason to buy a product either.

**Low/No Cholesterol.** If a product is touted as cholesterol free it by law can have no more than two milligrams cholesterol per serving. Low cholesterol means twenty milligrams or less per serving; reduced cholesterol means that the product has 75 or more percent less cholesterol than the regular version. (Again, remember that the AHA recommends a cholesterol intake of no more than 300 milligrams per day.) As I said before, cholesterol is only contained in animal foods so when you see a can of vegetables that says, "no cholesterol", say, "no kidding." It's no great feat; vegetables have never had cholesterol. Manufacturers are trying to capitalize on that all the time. One of the biggest label fads these days is pasting a "NO CHOLESTEROL!" banner across a package. And you see this on every form of junk food from chips to cookies to sausage. What they won't tell you though is that a product contains saturated fat, which is just as bad, if not worse. Watch out for hydrogenated vegetable, palm, and coconut oils on labels—they're all saturated fats.

**No Saturated Fats.** Realizing we're getting hip to their tricks, some manufacturers are going beyond "no cholesterol" and actually getting rid of saturated fats. Of course, you want to pick up a box of Hydrox cookies and a bag of Doritos made without saturated fats, stuff them down and believe that they are doing you good. Fat chance. Literally. The products are still loaded with so much garbage that the minor change in the oils the manufacturers are using doesn't really make a difference and it certainly doesn't qualify the product as nonfattening or good for your body. Remember, your body is not digesting the words on the label, it has to deal with everything contained in that product, break it down and do something with it. It *is* a step in the right direction, and thirteen major food companies have made the switch from tropical oils to less-saturated oils. Sunshine Biscuits, Kellogg's, Pepperidge Farm, Keebler, General Mills, Ralston Purina, Borden, Quaker Oats, Pillsbury, Procter & Gamble, Heinz U.S.A., Nabisco, and General Foods (except for their Cool Whip) are all now using healthier oils in their products—and slapping the sales pitch on their packaging as soon as possible. But it's a good sign that the major food companies realize they had better give us healthier foods or they will be out of business. Their goal isn't to protect your health—they would have gone into medicine—it's to protect their assets. Yet in the end, if protecting your health protects profits, then we all win.

## Deciphering Meat and Poultry Labels

Meat and poultry are monitored by the USDA, rather than the FDA, and are governed by their own unique regulations. What's most important to know when choosing beef is what the grades mean: *Select* marks the leanest and least-marbled cuts, *Choice* means moderately lean, and *Prime* (a term usually used by restaurants on the menu) indicates that a cut is the fattiest, most marbled kind available.

Unlike with processed foods, there are regulations governing the use of the terms Light and Lite when applied to beef and poultry. *Light, Lite, Leaner,* and *Lower Fat* mean that the product must be at least 25 percent lower in fat than comparable products. A *Lean* or *Low Fat* label can only be attached if the meat or poultry is no more than 10 percent fat by weight; *Extralean* means no more than 5 percent fat by weight. Meat and poultry products with these claims must also have the total grams of fat on the label. (The exception is ground beef—labeling standards don't apply to it and the fat content can vary.)

One thing you have to watch out for when buying meat and poultry products is that "fat by weight" is a lot more than it sounds. If a product is advertised as 80 percent fat free—that is it has 20 percent fat—don't be fooled into thinking that it's necessarily lean. Percent fat *by weight* is not the same as percent fat *of calories*. A while back, Louis Rich Turkey Franks sported a label claiming they were 80 percent fat free. But in the final analysis, it turned out that the product may have only been 20 percent fat by weight, but 80 percent of its calories were from fat. To be sure about a claim do some calculations. Say a food has 120 calories and five grams of fat. Convert the grams of fat into calories (one gram fat = 9 calories), then divide the total number of calories into the number of fat calories:

$$5 \text{ grams fat} \times 9 \text{ calories} = 45 \text{ calories fat}$$
$$45 \text{ calories fat} \div 120 \text{ total calories} = 0.375$$
$$0.375 \times 100 = 37.5 \text{ percent fat calories}$$

## Unfamiliar Words You *Don't* Have to Worry About

Yes, believe it or not, there are some long words on those labels that sound strange, but are actually good for you or at least harmless. As the world of food science expands, more and more research is being done to find natural ways to enhance our food products (usually with thickening and emulsifying agents) and extend their shelf life (with stabilizers). I'm just going to list a few of the most common additives (to do every current additive on the market would require a whole other book) you needn't worry about when you see them on the label.

*Acetic Acid.* Present naturally in vinegar, cheese, wine, apples, and tart-tasting fruits, it is a flavoring agent and used to control the pH factor (acidity) in many foods.

*Algae (Seaweeds).* There are many varieties of seaweed that are used for thickening, stabilizing, and emulsifying (keeping ingredients from separating). The most common names are carrageenan, dulse, agar-agar, and kelp. There is some controversy about whether or not these additives are safe; obviously, if the waters are polluted, so is the seaweed. Trust the health-food industry manufacturers to utilize algae from the safest waters possible.

*Amino Acids (Cysteine, Glycine, Lysine, Methione).* These organic compounds form the basic constituent of proteins and are needed by the body for the repair and replacement of tissue. They are used in various ways to enhance texture and flavor.

*Annato.* A natural yellow food coloring from the seeds of a tropical tree.

*Bicarbonates and Carbonates.* These are found naturally in tissues and fluids in the body. In foods they are used as leavening agents and to neutralize acidity.

*Carotenes (Beta-Carotene).* A yellow-orange pigment occurring naturally in fruits and vegetables, especially prevalent in carrots, spinach, turnips, and beet greens. Carotenes, which the body converts into vitamin A, are thought to help guard against cancer.

*Dextrose.* A food sweetener obtained from corn sugar; a form of glucose.

*Fructose.* Fruit sugar.

*Gelatin.* An extract of collagen, it is a major protein in the connective tissue of the body. The kind used as food additives usually comes from pigs or cattle and is used to thicken and gel.

*Glucose.* Corn syrup, used as a sweetener, is a natural constituent in the body, but is a form of sugar, like dextrose.

*Glycerine (Glycerol).* This clear, thick, sweet liquid is an alcohol found in all fats. It's used in foods to maintain water content so they remain moist.

*Guar Gum.* A complex sugar gum that is the extract from seeds of the guar plant. It's used in food processing as a stabilizer, thickening agent, and texture modifier.

*Lactose.* Milk sugar, this is the main carbohydrate in milk and dairy products. It is used to improve flavor, texture, color, and aroma.

*Lecithin.* Commonly occurring in plants and animals, it is usually extracted from soybeans and added to foods as an emulsifier and antioxidant (a rancidity retardant).

*Pectin.* Occurring naturally in most plants, pectin strengthens the cell's walls. Citrus peels and apples are high in pectin and are used by food producers to thicken, gel, and help blend foods.

*Xanthum Gum.* From cabbage leaves, this is used to thicken and stabilize foods.

If you're still completely confused about reading labels, my best advice is to stay away from the major food companies who come out with new products and labels every time a health claim is made. If the company is serving the masses and making megabucks, you can almost be sure theirs is not a truly healthy product. Do not buy the big word on the label, turn the box around and read the fine print.

## The Big Kitchen Cleanup

If you're serious about wanting to change your eating habits, I suggest that you not wait until you've finished all the unhealthy or fattening foods you have in the house right now, but that you throw them all out and restock your kitchen with decent edibles. Get out a big bag and go through your cupboards and refrigerator, then take the tossables to a soup kitchen or shelter for the homeless. I realize this begs the question, "Why should I give to someone else what I wouldn't eat myself," but I don't have the answer to that or any other question about social inequities. It just seems better to give the food away and let people decide for themselves whether or not they want to eat it.

Okay, you say, but now Yolanda, help! What do you actually buy, how do you shop, and what if you can't get the best products in the area you live in? Are there any alternatives? Obviously, I can't walk down the aisles of every single supermarket and go through every single product, but what I've compiled here is a very comprehensive list of the best (and the worst) foods on the market today. And if you're under the impression that only big cities carry these innovative items, get out and look around. Yes, it's true that there are more of the new food products available in the bigger cities, but I spent some time traveling through the states while writing this book and I was pleasantly surprised. I found a world of healthy, nonfattening foods, even in one of the smallest towns in Florida.

The entire food industry is making the switch to better ingredients, just as the whole country is beginning to be aware of recycling. Eighty percent of the products I buy in Los Angeles are also available in smaller towns. All you have to do is put on a different pair of eyes when you shop, take a risk and try the new products. Keep in mind the foods on my WORST list are there because, to my mind, they are, for the most part, overprocessed, have chemicals/preservatives/ additives, little or no food value, or are just plain bad for your body. There are always controversial foods like peanut butter, which falls into the healthy category, but only when it has no added salt or sugar and is not eaten (even by children) on a regular basis because it's almost completely fat. But mostly what I am going to lay out is a list of the real junk, the best possible replacement, and the next best thing if you can't get the ideal product. Of course, all of this is with the understanding that you have read the preceding chapters about cravings and rules, and have a pretty good idea of the kinds of foods that suit your personal needs.

Most of the products I consider the WORST are what I call food from the fifties, the "it's quick and it tastes good" line of foods. Many of the products I consider the BEST are those created by the natural foods industry and even some of the bigger companies. They imitate highly flavored, convenient fifties foods, but are made with only healthy ingredients. The best example is Hain's box fettucine mix. My daughter loves it and I don't have to worry about it making her fat or clogging her arteries (I make it with skim milk and nonfat cheese) like I would if she were eating the Stouffer's version. And, yes, it is as easy to prepare. I see new items that have been created to take the place of junk foods on a daily basis. If you give these foods a chance you may miss the old punch of MSG, heavy salt, and other strong flavors for a while, but as you continue eating more healthfully your body will adapt to its new clean state and you won't miss or crave the old junk anymore.

The following lists primarily name the manufacturer brand names that can be relied on to have healthy ingredients and those that can't, but you'll also find the names of generic foods on these lists, which unless otherwise specified, are generally healthy products no matter who puts them out. Of course, it would be *impossible* to name every brand or food, new and old, under the sun, but I've tried to include as many of the most widely available ones as possible. They are all foods that can be found at stores just about every town has access to: one is the local supermarket, the other is a health food/natural food store. (Don't let that scare you. The old health food market of small, dusty isles filled with nuts, seeds, a lot of brown items, and ten rows of vitamins is a thing of the past.) If you can't find the BEST brand names locally, ask your store's manager to order them—you'd be surprised at how compliant stores can be. I know I'm being repetitive, but the world is changing its attitudes toward recycling, the pollution of the earth, and the pollution of food.

At the bottom of my lists of the BEST and WORST foods, you'll find THE NEXT BEST THING. I hate to say this, because I wish it weren't true, but it is extremely hard to stay away from all chemically processed foods. I have tried to make a list of products that are not too obscure; however, if you absolutely, unconditionally cannot find the BEST products go for second best. Unfortunately, I find myself beginning to sound like a hypocrite as I make the list because I can't really say I recommend these foods. But I will say that they are a better choice than the WORST foods. And if you feel they may satisfy you a little more than the BEST, then the answer is, yes, go for them, but don't delude yourself into thinking you're eating as healthfully as you can.

Note that the lists cover a variety of foods, but to figure out whether they're right for your particular body type, refer to the chart at the end of this chapter. Remember, healthy is not necessarily slimming. Learn what is right for you and what is right for your family.

Now, let's go shopping!

I'll start with the lean proteins I talk so much about. They are a necessary and healthy part of every diet when prepared correctly.

## *Poultry*

Because poultry is generally lean (and leanest without the skin and when the meat is white), it's also generally healthy. Unfortunately, a lot of poultry farmers use hormones. When you can, it's best to buy free-range poultry or check the label (or ask the butcher) to make sure the farm the poultry comes from does not use additives or hormones. The word *natural* on a label is not enough either—that only means that nothing unnatural has been added during processing, not necessarily during the feeding process. Also, be aware that many brands of chicken/turkey cold cuts and wieners are still loaded with chemicals, preservatives, salt, fat, and sugar. The manufacturers haven't changed anything but the fact that it's not beef or pork, and you still don't know what parts of the poultry they used to make up these products. The only brand of poultry cold cuts I've found to be healthy is Shelton Farms, available in the frozen food section (they're frozen because they don't have preservatives) at natural food stores. As for ground turkey, it can be lean or not so lean, depending on whether it was ground with the skin and dark meat. The best, least fatty kind is that which the butcher personally grinds for you.

Cornish game hens are another good poultry choice if you're not trying to lose weight—it's hard to get the skin, and thus the fat, off of them. Duck, on the other hand, is fatty through and through as well as high in cholesterol.

| BEST | WORST |
|---|---|
| **Miscellaneous Poultry** | |
| Cornish game hens | Duck |
| **Chicken** | |
| Skinless boneless breasts | Smoked Chicken |
| Skinless boneless thighs | Prepared chicken |
| Whole chickens, roasted | Fried Chicken |

| BEST | WORST |
|---|---|
| Chicken gizzards | Chicken bologna |
| Drumsticks | Chicken roll |
| Thighs | Frozen fried or precooked chicken |
| Livers | |
| Ground | |
| Chicken dogs, frozen health store variety | Chicken dogs |
| Chicken bologna, frozen health store variety | |
| Any Shelton Farms product | |
| **Turkey** | |
| Breasts | Smoked turkey |
| Tenderloins | Turkey roll |
| Breast slices | Turkey bologna/salami |
| Ground | Turkey dogs |
| Thighs | Turkey cold cuts |
| Drumsticks | Turkey sausage with nitrates |
| Whole roasted turkey | |
| Turkey sausage, frozen health store variety | |
| Turkey dogs, frozen health store variety | |
| Turkey bologna/salami, frozen health store variety | |
| Any Shelton Farms product | |

**THE NEXT BEST THING**

You should be able to get the BEST kinds of chicken/turkey anywhere. If you cannot find the healthy chicken/turkey dogs sold in health food stores, then opt for the chicken/turkey dogs sold at regular markets over pork or beef. They will at least be lower in fat. If you can't find the natural turkey bologna/salami, then you might want to get the new 95 percent fat-free meat cold cuts sold at all markets (they now occupy more space than the traditional varieties); however, don't make them a regular part of your or your children's diet.

## *Seafood*

It is my belief that food from the sea (nonpolluted waters) is good for you and that, unless you bread and fry them to death, fish and shellfish are lean and healthy. I think that the sea is untapped as far as its potential as a food source, and we will be finding more about what is edible in the next century. When choosing fish, consider that some are fattier than others so make sure you check the body chart for the best fish to eat when you are trying to lose weight (and see the fish chart on page 240 for calorie and fat listings). Personally, I eat fish five nights of the week and would like to see more people eat fish as often as they currently eat red meat. One cautionary note: try to vary the kinds of fish you eat. Fattier fish and freshwater fish tend to harbor more toxins, but experts advise that you can eat them as long as you don't, for instance, have fresh tuna or lake trout every night.

| BEST | WORST |
|---|---|
| **Fresh Fish** | |
| Swordfish | Fried fish |
| Halibut | Any frozen preprepared fish |
| Flounder | Imitation crabmeat |
| Sole | Fish sticks |
| Trout | Mrs. Paul's |
| Sea bass | Van de Kamp's |
| Butterfish | Weaver |
| Bluefish | Banquet |
| Salmon | Gorton's |
| Yellowtail | Taste o' the Sea |
| Catfish | Tyson |
| Black cod | Singleton |
| Whitefish | |
| Shark | |
| Orange roughy | |
| Tuna | |
| Red snapper | |
| Tilapia | |
| Mahi mahi | |
| Whaoo ono | |
| Cod | |
| Scrod | |
| Squid | |
| | |
| **Fresh Shellfish** | |
| Shrimp (even frozen without sauce) | |
| Scallops | Any fried, preprepared shellfish |
| Crab | Any frozen shellfish with sauces or |
| Lobster | seasonings |
| Oysters | |
| Clams | |

## THE NEXT BEST THING

If you cannot get fresh fish on a year-round basis, then look for fish that is sold frozen, but without anything added to it. Make sure that you rinse it after it has thawed because most frozen fish is dipped in a preservative solution before freezing.

# *Red Meat*

Basically, as I've said before, I believe that humans are evolving away from the consumption of red meat. Our bodies no longer digest it as well as they did sixty to seventy years ago. As our world changes so do the computers that we live in (our bodies). I am not against anyone having red meat on occasion, but make sure you are getting it from butchers who know their suppliers—preferably farmers who have raised their cows without hormones—and that the meat is free of coloring, flavorings, and other additives. Look for cuts that have loin or round in the name (e.g., sirloin and top round). They are the leanest. Prepare them without heavy fats and cut away any fat around the rim and there is nothing wrong with having red meat.

Unfortunately, any red meat served at a restaurant is bound to be treated, unless you are informed that it's meat from cows raised naturally, so you risk feeling sluggish the next day if you order it. However, if a big juicy steak is what you would absolutely die for once in a while, I say go for it—as long as it's not a regular thing. Make sure you drink a lot of water and have a good salad to aid in its digestion.

| BEST | WORST |
|------|-------|
| Lean cuts of beef marked Choice or Select | Bacon |
| Veal | Ham |
| | Beef/pork cold cuts and wieners |
| | Any smoked red meat |
| | Any presauced, pretreated red meat |

## THE NEXT BEST THING

Use ground turkey to replace ground beef and ground chicken for veal, look for soy-based bacon bits for bacon flavor. If you're craving ham, there are butchers who smoke it naturally.

## *Cheese, Butter, Margarine, Eggs*

Cheese is a natural and healthy product unless processed with chemical additives (orange cheeses are colored either artificially or with a natural food coloring such as annato) or high levels of salt. But cheese is also full of fat and dietary cholesterol, both of which can be hard on your heart. *And* cheese is extremely fattening. There is no way that I can list the hundreds of types of cheese, so the following list was designed to show you some of the new products. The cheeses on the BEST list are based on nonfat milk or are the lowest fat cheeses available. For instance, this is how a healthy cottage cheese label (this one is Alta-Dena low-fat cottage cheese) reads: **Grade A pasteurized cultured nonfat milk, cream, milk protein, salt** (cottage cheese almost always has salt—you can excuse it in this case). This is how all your cottage cheese labels should read, no added preservatives or fillers. Obviously this is not a choice food for people with high cholesterol, but is still a healthy product.

But eating any cheese made from milk—even nonfat and low-fat cheese—is not ideal if you have high cholesterol. Many manufacturers are now making cheeses from soy. However, note that these cheeses are more fattening than the nonfat and low-fat cheeses because the milk fat is replaced with a lot of cholesterol-free oil. It is my belief that you should keep all kinds of cheese to a minimum in any diet. For children, the calcium is good, especially if you do not give your children milk to drink at every meal. However, I suggest you give your children the lower fat dairy products, so they won't have a problem later. I am a cheese lover, but save my cravings for Wisconsin Cheddar, Brie, and Camembert on special occasions, eat the nonfat cheeses more often and use a little Parmesan in my cooking.

Butter is a food we'd all do well to live without. It's fattening and contains a lot of cholesterol. But don't think that butter substitutes are all that much better. Because it's made with vegetable oils, margarine has less cholesterol than butter (although it may contain some cholesterol-raising saturated fat), yet many brands contain chemicals and preservatives and are overprocessed . . . and are still fattening. The same goes for most of the "butter-substitutes." Stick with margarines that are nonadulterated and not overprocessed (ask at the health food store).

I've also added eggs onto this chart. Eggs are not particularly fattening (if you don't cook them in pounds of butter) and are a good source of protein. Again, they are high in cholesterol so eat as few as possible (and don't forget they're contained in baked goods) or just go for the whites, which are cholesterol-free.

| BEST | WORST |
|------|-------|
| **Eggs** | **Egg substitutes** |
| **Cheese** | |
| Cabot Vitalait | Borden |
| Lifetime | Kraft |
| New Holland | Nucoa Heart Beat |
| Frigo string cheese/mozzarella | Any processed cheese spread |
| Nu Tofu cheese spread | Any cheese containing chemicals, |
| Soyco—makes a great American | artificial colorings/perservatives, or |
| sliced cheese—or Soya Kaas | MSG |
| Zausner's natural cream cheese | Kraft Philadelphia cream cheese |
| Any kind of part skim-milk mozzarella, | Any powdered cheese product that |
| regular Parmesan or Romano and | comes in a cardboard box on the |
| nonfat cottage cheeses; ricotta, | dry shelf |
| pot, and farmer cheeses (the last | Any bottled, canned, or spray cheeses |
| three contain less fat than other | Velveeta |
| cheeses) | |

## THE NEXT BEST THING

There are a variety of diet cheeses available like Weight Watchers, Dorman's Lo-Chol, Lite-line, and many others, which are lower in fat, but also overprocessed. Remember that when a product is mostly processed/artificial your body cannot use it as a wholesome food source and burn it as effectively as the real thing. If you have to have cream cheese on bagels every Sunday then, yes, it is better to have the new "Lite" version. The dairy industry has been quick to put out lite versions of everything; just don't eat the alternatives often.

| **Margarines** | |
|------|-------|
| Hollywood safflower margarine | Parkay, Fleischmann's, Heart Beat, |
| Lecithin spread (soy-based) | Imperial, Country Morning Blend, |
| | Shedd's Spread, Blue Bonnet, or |
| | any other processed margarine with |
| | questionable additives |
| | I Can't Believe It's Not Butter! |
| | Weight Watchers |
| | Le Slim Cow |

**THE NEXT BEST THING**

Learn to live without butter and margarine and you will be better off. If you have to have an alternative you might try a product called A Touch of Butter (I know I said butter substitutes are bad, but we're talking last-ditch alternatives). They do go into your body as fat, though, so make sure you're exercising to burn any butter/margarine product off.

## *Yogurts*

Throw out any yogurt with labels indicating high amounts of sugar or NutraSweet (aspartame). Yogurt is a natural, healthy product and delicious without sugar. You'll be seeing some of the new light yogurts around, but while they use nonfat milk instead of low-fat, some also contain cornstarch for more body and NutraSweet instead of sugar. Stick to the real thing. The best yogurts have basic ingredients: milk derivatives, natural fruit sweeteners—and no added salt, sugar, gelatins, or stabilizers. One way to make sure you're getting a healthy and nonfattening yogurt is to buy nonfat plain yogurt and mix in a teaspoon of two of sugar-free jam or add in some fresh fruit. There are many brands of yogurts, but first I would like to show you a label of a healthy nonfat yogurt versus a less-healthy brand of yogurt. Then, look for the BEST brand names on the list in your market and avoid the WORST.

Healthy: Alta-Dena Nonfat Yogurt, Mixed Berries
**Ingredients: Cultured Grade A Pasteurized non-fat milk, sweetened with natural fruit juice concentrate, strawberries, blueberries, raspberries, blackberries, carrageenan, natural flavors, lemon juice, color solely from blueberries and blackberries.**

Less-Healthy: R. W. Knudsen Family Lemon Flavor
**Ingredients: Cultured Grade A Pasteurized Milk and Nonfat Milk, sugar, water, food starch modified, lemon puree to insure freshness, kosher gelatin, natural flavor, lemon juice concentrate, with sodium benzoate and potassium sorbate as preservatives, turmeric. With active yogurt cultures.**

A note on sour cream: In my travels I found two products that are replacements for sour cream. One is called Formagg, which is a play on the French product *fromagge,* which is a very rich cream. The basis of this product, like the butter substitutes, is soybean oil, corn syrup solids, and a long list of additives. It's a perfect example of diet junk food. Use it in a pinch, but don't think that it is the miracle ingredient you can now use in all your cream sauce recipes. Stick to working with plain, nonfat yogurt and tofu. There is also a similar product by King, which has a big cholesterol-free label. It may not clog your heart, but won't benefit your body or your health either.

| BEST | WORST |
|------|-------|
| Alta-Dena | R. W. Knudsen Family |
| Continental | Yoplait |
| Brown Cow Farm | Weight Watchers |
| Dannon | Bon Lait |
| Breyers | Johnston's |
| | Kissle |
| | Dairi Fresh |

**THE NEXT BEST THING**

When push comes to shove, look for Dannon Light, Polly-O Lite or Yoplait Light, which seem to be the best of the diet yogurts. Always opt for nonfat, low fat if you can't find it. When you choose a yogurt that *does* contain sugar, just make sure the sweetener is low on the ingredient list.

# *Breads*

Everyone is aware by now that bleached, processed white bread has no nutritional value. To make white flour, the manufacturers have to remove the wheat kernel's endosperm, germ, and bran—the parts of the plant that contain all the fiber and nutrients. The best breads, for both their fiber and vitamin content, are whole wheat, whole grain, stone-ground kinds, and breads with sprouted wheat and wheat berries. However, many manufacturers add just a small amount of whole wheat flour to the same basic low-fiber batter as white breads and try to pass it off as healthy. Don't just check the label, check the ingredient list: *Whole wheat* flour should be the first (and preferably the only) wheat flour ingredient, meaning it makes up the bulk of the bread. *Wheat flour* can mean white flour—*whole* is the operative word.

Breads made with rye flour (rye and pumpernickel—the latter contains caramel or molasses for color and flavor and is still pretty nutritious) are healthier than white too. *Healthier* is the key word. Although most white breads are made from processed/bleached flour, they are not un-healthy if they have no chemicals or preservatives. A good loaf of sour-dough, French, or Italian bread is still a healthy food. Try, though, to find the loaves made from unbleached flour.

For sandwiches and such, go for the whole grain breads when possible and search out the healthy hamburger and hot dog buns and dinner rolls that are now available. There are as many (if not more) healthy whole grain breads on the market today as there are unhealthy breads. The brand names in your area may differ, but you should be able to find healthy whole grain breads available everywhere. What to avoid, what to look for:

A typical junk food whole wheat bread label: Home Pride Wheat
**Ingredients: Enriched flour [barley malt, iron (ferrous sulfate) niacin (a "B" vitamin) thiamine mononitrate ($B_1$), riboflavin, ($B_2$)], water, corn syrup, wheat bran, whole wheat flour, contains 2% or less of: sugar, wheat gluten, yeast, salt, whey, soyflour, butter, honey, vegetable oil, (contains one or more of canola oil, corn oil, cottonseed oil, soybean oil), dough conditioners, (contains one or more of sodium stearoyl lactylate, mono- and diglycerides, ethoxylated mono- and diglycerides, mono- or dicalcium phosphate), calcium sulfate, calcium caseinate, potassium bromate.**

This is barely a food product, and spongy enough to mop a floor.

A typical lean and healthy bread label: Goodstuff Oat Bran Bread
**Ingredients: Oat bran, unbleached wheat flour, water, honey, oat fiber, oatmeal, yeast, vital wheat gluten, soybean oil, sea salt, molasses, raisin paste, ascorbic acid.**

This is obviously a real food product.

It's in situations like this that I really emphasize: don't compare calories. Even though the lighter junk food bread may have fewer calories, the healthier bread will ultimately be used by your body more efficiently and the fiber will help lower your cholesterol.

| BEST | WORST |
|------|-------|
| Goodstuff | Wonder |
| Pritikin | Sunshine |
| Food for Life | Pepperidge Farm |
| Alvarado St. Bakery | Millbrook |
| Healthtime | Roman Meal |
| Golden Harvest | Thomas' |
| Oasis | Weber's |
| Oroweat | White |
|  | Olympic Meal |
|  | Sun-Maid |
|  | Home Pride |
|  | Pioneer |
|  | DiCarlo |
|  | Francisco |
|  | Kings |
|  | Country French |
|  | Van de Kamp's |

**THE NEXT BEST THING**

There really is no excuse for eating junk bread anymore, as every store stocks more than one healthy whole wheat bread.

## *Muffins*

Just because something is called a bran muffin (or oat bran muffin) doesn't mean it's healthy or nonfattening. If you are trying to lose weight, make sure you find a fat-free muffin with no raisins or nuts, or one with the oil at the very end of the ingredient list. Same old story: many companies are putting a minimum of bran in a processed muffin and making them out to be really healthy. Muffins are sweet enough from the fruit added to them or can be sweetened well with fruit juice concentrates. And they don't need a ton of oil to be moist either.

| BEST | WORST |
|------|-------|
| Wendy & Toby's | Your local supermarket's bakery |
| The No Muffin | muffin (made from a mix) |
| Zen Bakery | Entenmann's |
| Your local health food store's muffin | Van de Kamp's |
| Check with your local bakery to see | Any donut shop, i.e., Winchells, |
| what ingredients they use | Dunkin' Donuts |

**THE NEXT BEST THING**

Ask the local supermarket how they make their bran muffins or just make your own. Take some time on the weekend and make a big batch and freeze them. Many health food stores carry mixes for bran muffins, and you can add the blueberries or *a few* raisins.

## *Pitas, Tortillas, Bagels*

Pita bread does not need to be made with oil to taste good. Look for whole wheat ones without lard, oil, or preservatives. Likewise, opt for tortillas made without lard and preservatives. The healthiest tortillas are corn tortillas, which are made with lime and water and no fat. Flour tortilla recipes call for fat, but it can be vegetable oil instead of lard. Many of them are made without lard and preservatives these days. Also you can buy whole wheat flour tortillas now, another good option. If they appear dry just steam them for a second to soften.

Bagels, by definition—flour, yeast, and water—are a healthy food. Therefore if you are buying one loaded with chemicals, fat, sugar, and salt you are being gypped out of the real thing. One thing to be aware of is that bagels are fairly high in calories: most calorie books list them at about 164 calories, but those are the small kind—big deli-style bagels can be over 300 calories.

You really have to check your local bakeries and read your labels on these products.

| BEST | WORST |
|------|-------|
| Garden of Eatin' tortillas/pita | Mission tortillas |
| Bialys (from any bakery) | Van de Kamp's bagels |
| Goodstuff pita | International bagels |
| Fresh, local bagel-shop bagels | |
| Lender's bagels | |

**THE NEXT BEST THING**

There are different bakeries in each town or county that produce bagels, breads, etc. Make the effort to scout out the ones that don't overprocess their products. I know the Pritikin products are sold nationally.

## Crackers

Crackers are one of the most polluted products on the market; if I were to write about all of the junk food crackers, it would take up a whole chapter. This is where manufacturers really lay on the fat—often saturated fat—salt and sugar.

Take a look at this Wheat Thins label:
> **Ingredients: Whole wheat flour, enriched wheat flour (niacin, reduced iron, thiamine monoitrate, riboflavin), vegetable shortening (partially hydrogenated soybean oil), sugar, salt, high fructose, corn syrup, malted barley flour, vegetable colors (anatto extract), turmeric, paprika oleoresin.**

The fat content of Wheat Thins is very high (hydrogenating saturates fat and makes it even unhealthier) and the vitamin listings mean that the flour was so well stripped of all its nutrients that chemical vitamins had to be added back in. In other words, when you get these vitamins from this product, you don't get them naturally. Also note that the next three largest ingredients beside flour and fat are sugar, more sugar (high-fructose corn syrup) and salt. Not the optimum in good nutrition.

But with intense flavorings like those, it's no wonder the country is hooked on munchies. There are, however, also loads of healthy munchy, crunchy-type crackers around. Again, look for products that have fats listed toward the end of the ingredient label and preservative and artificial flavorings not listed at all.

| BEST | WORST |
|---|---|
| Health Valley | Nabisco |
| California Grain | Sunshine |
| Edward & Sons | Pepperidge Farm |
| Kavli Crisps | Kellogg's |
| Barbara's | Ralston Purina |
| Hol-Grain | Old London |
| Lifestream Krispbread | Keebler |
| Wasa Crispbread | |
| Manischewitz Whole Wheat Matzos | |
| Stone Ground Wheat Thins | |
| Pacific Rice Crackers | |
| Hain | |

**THE NEXT BEST THING**

Harvest Crisps, Wheatsworth, or even saltines are a good substitute when you're stuck at a corner store. You can also usually find a crispbread, stone ground wheat thins, or a lighter cracker. Carr's Table Water Crackers are another a good alternative and low in fat. Check the labels and buy the ones with the simplest ingredients.

## *Other Munchies*

At one time, your munchy choices were just about limited to potato chips, corn chips, and cheese puffs. These salty, fried foods were some of the first to be recognized as just plain rotten for you, not to mention very fattening and addictive—really a thorn in the side of people trying to shed extra pounds. Fortunately, there are other, healthier options now and even dips to go with them. The dry dip mixes can be mixed with tofu, or nonfat yogurt. Hain has even put out a canned dip that is made without lard or hydrogenated fats. The best dip for someone trying to lose weight is fresh salsa, which you can usually find in the refrigerator section of the market (or buy the bottled kind). Check the label, as some contain preservatives and some contain oil—skip those. You can also use your favorite diet salad dressing to dip low-fat munchies in.

I've also included some other healthy snacks on this list. What I left out—but are worth looking for—are the many soy products now in the deli section, good alternatives to commercially packaged salads like potato, macaroni, and cole slaw. Keep in mind, though, that while they are healthy, they usually contain soy oil (to replace dairy), so they can also be fattening. The same goes for some of the other snacks listed on the chart (e.g., granola bars, nuts, and seeds) so check the body chart to see if they're right for your body type. Now read this wonderful BEST list and munch away!

| BEST | WORST |
|---|---|
| **Crunchy Snacks** | |
| Hain Mini Rice Cakes (seven flavors) | Frito-Lay |
| California Grain—risotto and polenta | Laura Scudder |
|    chips (five or six flavors) | Pringles |
| American Grain rice bites | Chee-tos |
| Barbara's baked cheese puffs | Lays |
| Pritikin Rice Cakes | Ruffles |
| Quaker Rice and Popcorn Cakes | Doritos |
| Westbrae Natural oat bran chips | Eagle |
| Garden of Eatin' corn chips | Bell |

| BEST | WORST |
|------|-------|
| Fromage Sticks (Select Harvest) | Mission |
| Skinny Haven Munchies | Wheat Nuts |
| Lapidus popcorn | Any potato chip, corn chip, cheese |
| Kettlechips | puff |
| Barbara's whole wheat pretzels and sesame sticks | |
| Bell's natural chips | |
| Dutch-style and regular pretzels | |

## THE NEXT BEST THING

Obviously, there are a slew of "lite" products out now by the manufacturers on the WORST list. I strongly recommend that you only fall back on things like light Doritos when faced with starvation or a really tough sticky situation. These products are still fattening and bad for your health.

### Extras

| | |
|------|-------|
| Dip mixes by Hain | Canned commercial dip |
| Sophisticated Nibbles dips | Package dips to be mixed with sour |
| Fresh salsas | cream or mayonnaise |
| Enrico's bottled salsas | |
| Pace bottled salsas | |

## THE NEXT BEST THING

If you are stuck making a dip with one of the packaged dips, then at least mix it with a blend of tofu and nonfat plain yogurt. If you can't get the tofu, then stick to just plain nonfat yogurt. I don't care what anyone says, I say the reduced or lite mayonnaise is still lethal for your health and shape, and should be eliminated altogether.

### Miscellaneous Snacks

| | |
|------|-------|
| Cosmic Cukes pickles | Pickles bottled with preservatives |
| New Morning pickles | |
| Cascadian Farm pickles | |
| Shelton Farms turkey jerky | Beef jerky |
| Barbara's apple snacks | |
| Superior Products Lite munchies | |
| Granola bars: Health Valley—regular and fat free; Nature's Choice; Barbara's Lite | |
| Natures Choice fruit leather | Fruit leathers made with sugar |
| Nature's Warehouse Pastry Poppers | Pop Tarts |
| Dried fruit (without sulfites) | Dried fruit (with sulfites) |
| Nuts/seeds (plain) | Nuts/seeds roasted in oil |
| Natural applesauce | Applesauce with sugar or corn syrup |

# Cereals

There is absolutely no need for manufacturers to add junk—a lot of oil, sugar, corn syrup, an overabundance of sodium, preservatives—to cereal. By itself, cereal is a natural and healthy product. Consider what ingredients make up Healthy Times Crispy Graham Flakes, a delicious healthy alternative to junk cereals for kids: **Graham flour, 100% Organically grown whole wheat flour, cornmeal, apple & grape juice concentrate, unsulphured molasses, wheat gluten, sprouted barley, soy oil, whey.**

The most important thing to watch for on cereal boxes are health claims like "lowers cholesterol." Be wary of the big health claims big companies put on their cereal labels on the *front of the box.* Also be aware that most granolas contain tons of fat (sometimes saturated) as well as nuts, raisins, honey, and more. In other words, they're fattening. I have listed cereals only by brand name because to list each cereal on the market would take pages. Not to mention the fact that cereals change constantly. They seem to go with whatever the current trend of cartoons running, everything from the Trix Rabbit to the newest Ninja Turtles Cereal. By the same token, cereal manufacturers are the first to slap every star ingredient of the moment on the front of their product's box. One of my favorites is Cheerios. The label on the front says "For nearly 50 years / Excellent Source of OAT BRAN." Turn the box to the side and read the ingredients: **Whole oat flour (includes the oat bran), wheat starch, sugar, salt, calcium carbonate (provides calcium) trisodium phosphate, vitamin C (sodium ascorbate), Iron (a mineral nutrient), a B vitamin (Niacin), vitamin A (palminate), vitamin $B_6$ (pyridoxine hydrochloride), vitamin B2 (riboflavin), vitamin $B_1$ (thiamin mononitrate), a B vitamin (folic acid) and vitamin D.** I know that you see a lot of "vitamins" on this label, but they are chemicals added to the batter, they do not come from the ingredients.

On the other hand you have Nabisco's new version of Shredded Wheat with Oat Bran, which claims that the ingredients are *Nothing but whole wheat and oat bran.* But further down they mention that BHT has been added as a preservative, which is what keeps the product out of health food stores. However, I consider this a much better alternative to the other cereals that go on with paragraphs of excuses to cover the fact that they are still . . . junk. Again, check those labels!

| BEST* | WORST |
|---|---|
| Health Valley | Kellogg's |
| Barbara's | Nabisco |
| Erewhon | Ralston (some hot cereals are fine) |
| Arrowhead Mills | General Mills |
| Nature's Path | Post |
| Familia | Carnation |
| Perky's | Quaker (some hot cereals are fine) |
| New Morning | |
| Golden Temple | |
| Healthy Times | |
| Kashi | |

## THE NEXT BEST THING

Post Grape-nuts, Nabisco Shredded Wheat, Kellogg's Nutri-Grain, General Mills Fiber One, Quaker Puffed Wheat, Rice, or Corn.

# *Soups*

Soup is basically a healthy food—as long as it's not cream filled or packed with salt and preservatives. Believe me when I tell you that for every canned, dry, or instant soup mix that is 90 percent chemical crap there are ones that are healthy and lean—and here they are.

| BEST | WORST |
|---|---|
| Hain canned and dry soup mixes | Campbell's |
| Pritikin | Progresso |
| Health Valley | Gourmet Pride |
| Fantastic Foods soup in a cup | Lipton's Cup-a-Soup |
| Nile Spice soup in a cup | Top Ramen |
| Westbrae Natural Ramen soups | |

## THE NEXT BEST THING

Because soup is by nature, a mixture of ingredients, you have to read that label carefully. Campbell's or Progresso's minestrone, vegetable, or variations thereof

*If you are trying to lose weight just make sure you don't pick one of the varieties with raisins or nuts, but buy one of the plain flakes or puffed ones instead.

. . . . . . . . . . . . . . . . . . . . . . . . . . . . . . . . . . . . . . . . . . . . . . . . . . . . . . . . . . . . . . . . . .

**FOOD COP**

have a lot of healthful ingredients (along with a few not so healthy) and are fine for a quick meal. If you are trying to keep your weight down, stick to the soups without oil and look for the lowest calorie counts.

## *Canned Goods*

There are some good chilies and beans in a can, but when it comes to produce I prefer fresh or frozen. However, if you must buy fruit or vegetables in a can, just be sure they contain no preservatives, artificial flavorings, sugar, or salt (it's hard to find brands that don't use some salt, but buy them when you can). Instead, look for ones like Whole Earth baked beans. Here's what's on the label: **Navy beans, tomato puree, apple juice, apple cider vinegar, sea salt, tamari soy sauce (soy beans, sea salt), guar gum, onion powder, kelp, cinnamon, dill herb, ground nutmeg, cayenne, cloves.**

| BEST | WORST |
| --- | --- |
| NutraDiet canned fruits and veggies | S&W |
| Hain | Green Giant |
| Health Valley | Del Monte |
| Whole Earth | Libby's |
| Water chestnuts—all brands | Springfield |
| Hearts of palm—all brands (not in oil) | |
| Artichoke hearts—all brands (not in oil) | |
| Whole Earth beans and chili | Heinz |
| Goya beans | Hormel |
| | B&M |
| | Chef Boyardee |
| | Campbell's |
| | Van Camp's |
| | Rosarita |
| | Hunt's |
| | Bush's |
| | Dennison's |

**THE NEXT BEST THING**

Frozen vegetables (on page 118) as long as they're not loaded with sauces, additives or other goop.

# Rice, Grains, Sides

Rice is a nutritious food by nature—until it is processed and bleached. Always look for brown rice and natural grains instead of white rice. Most of the grains sold in your local health food market are healthy. Virtually all of the rice mixes sold in your local supermarket are not. There are grains in their natural state—the ones to buy—and then there are grains that are prepackaged flavored mixes—the ones you don't want. Once again, the natural foods industry has borrowed the idea of preflavored mixes, but done them in a healthy manner. If you are using one of the natural rice mixes, and are on a weight loss program, just replace the oil required in the recipe with chicken broth, wine or, if it's just required to keep the grain from sticking, Pam cooking spray.

| BEST | WORST |
|---|---|
| Hain grain side dishes | Rice-A-Roni |
| Arrowhead Mills | Uncle Ben's |
| Lundberg | MJB |
| Fantastic Foods | |
| From the health-food store bins: | Suzi Wan |
|   Wild rice | Minute Rice |
|   Basmati rice | Comet |
|   Whole grain brown rice | Knorr |
|   Couscous | Reese |
|   Quinoa | Hamburger Helper |
|   Risotto | Stove Top Stuffing |
|   Pasta | Any instant potato mix |
|   Millet | Vigo |
|   Barley | Velveeta |
| | Betty Crocker |
| | Quaker |
| | Lipton |

**THE NEXT BEST THING**

Every market has a natural and healthy array of rices and grains, as easy and delicious as the instant versions.

# Frozen Vegetables, Frozen Dinners

Surprisingly, frozen vegetables are sometimes even healthier than fresh vegetables. While frozen veggies are frozen immediately after they've been picked so all the vitamins and minerals get locked in, fresh produce, often sits around on the shelf, losing more and more nutrients by day. Also, frozen vegetables do not need to be treated with anything to stay fresh. Most companies, like Green Giant, sell plain frozen vegetables (the one exception being potatoes, which are always loaded with oil, salt, and preservatives) as well as presauced and seasoned ones with a nice dose of MSG. A perfect example of where to go wrong is to buy frozen potatoes. I never found one that was not processed into junk, so my answer is to get a real potato! That is one source of produce that is always available, and anyone can cook (at least microwave) a potato.

The products that upset me the most are frozen dinners. This has been a novelty item since the forties. Yes, it's a convenient answer to the stressful lives we lead, but they really are the worst kind of foods you can serve yourself or your family. The level of convenience makes people conditioned to being lazy. It's just as easy (well, almost) to boil some pasta and make a healthy sauce as it is to heat one of these dinners. If you must go for frozen dinners, look for the healthy brands of frozen dinners in the BEST column. Here's an example of one good choice: Oven Poppers Crab & Stuffed Sole: **Sole, red potatoes, broccoli, onions, seasoned cracker crumbs, butter, crabmeat, herbs & spices, salt free seasonings.** Due to the butter, this meal is not great for your cholesterol and it won't help you lose weight, but is still a fairly healthy food item, especially in comparison to the others out on the market. It is the type of food item that I might serve my child, if caught in a rush, since butter isn't often part of her diet.

| BEST | WORST |
| --- | --- |
| Oven Poppers | Swanson |
| Jaclyn's | OreIda |
| Soypreme dinners and pizzas | Healthy Choice |
| Legume | Oh Boy |
| Vans | Mrs. Paul's |
| Amy's | Banquet |
| Shelton Farms—pot pies, meats | Van de Kamp's |
| | Campbell's |
| | Chun King |
| | Hot Pockets |
| | Pitaria |
| | Celentano |
| | Golden Tiger |
| | Royal Dragon |
| | Le Menu |

| BEST | WORST |
|------|-------|
|  | Stouffer's |
|  | Tyson |
|  | Celeste |
|  | Pillsbury |
|  | Jenos |
|  | Golden |
|  | Wilton Farms |
|  | Kraft |
|  | Mrs. Smith's |
|  | Marie Callender |
|  | Sara Lee |
|  | Pepperidge Farm |
|  | Kellogg's |
|  | Weaver |
|  | Singleton |
|  | Bryan |
|  | Pita Stuffs |
|  | Jones |
|  | The Budget Gourmet |
|  | The Budget Gourmet Light |

## THE NEXT BEST THING

I really tried to find a decent product in the frozen food prepared food section. I couldn't, with good conscience, recommend any. The plain frozen vegetables and fruit are fine. Avoid the rest and get out of the habit of fast-food frozen dinners. Look for the new bags of frozen vegetables and pasta, usually under different name brands and, once again, check for any added sauces.

## Condiments, Marinades, Salad Dressings

It's very difficult to make a good bottled dressing without oil; the oil is what gives the dressing body and makes it cling to the salad. However many natural food companies are starting to use xanthum gum, carrageenan, and other natural food products to stabilize dressings and give them bulk so they don't need oil. There are still a lot of marinades, barbecue sauces, and condiments rife with sugar and oils on the market, so be on the look out. As always, be a label reader. The following are listed by brand name, as each company has a line of several different kinds of products. The asterisk indicates manufacturers who make healthy salad dressings.

| BEST | WORST |
|---|---|
| Enrico's | Heinz |
| Hain* | Hunt's |
| Uncle Dave's | Wish-Bone |
| Robbies | Bernsteins |
| Premier Japan | HiddenValley |
| San'J | Kraft |
| Uncle Bum's | Lawry's |
| Cook's* | Springfield |
| Duggans* | Seven Seas |
| Emerald Valley | Oriental Chef |
| Erewhon | Weight Watchers |
| The Wizards | Reese |
| Sonoma* | Chris & Pits |
| Paula's* | |
| Marin Brand | Bull's-Eye |
| Cardini's* | Best Foods |
| The Source* | Sharwoods |
| Scotty's salsas | K. C. Masterpiece |
| Pritikin* | |

## THE NEXT BEST THING

Holland House has four great marinades out that are oil free; although they also contain some sugar and preservatives; they're not fattening. Cattlebaron has an oil-free barbecue sauce, which also has some sugar and additives and is likewise nonfattening. Good salad dressing alternatives are Henri's Light, Kraft Fat-Free, Walden Farms, and Herb Magic.

## *Pasta Sauces*

You do not need masses of salt and sugar (it's often in the form of corn syrup in sauces) in your pasta sauce. If you are trying to lose weight, note that I have put an asterisk by the sauces with no oil.

| BEST | WORST |
|---|---|
| Health Valley | Ragú (except for the natural) |
| Ci'Bella* | Newman's Own |
| Mama Coco's | Chef Boyardee |
| Pritikin* | Prego |
| Robbies | Classico di Bologna |

| BEST | WORST |
| --- | --- |
| Enrico's | Tommy Lasorda's |
| Tree of Life | Hunt's |
| Classico | Contadina |
| | Buitoni |

## THE NEXT BEST THING

Make your own. Take some time and make a big batch on your day off; it will last for quite a while. Otherwise, try Weight Watchers Spaghetti Sauce Flavored with Meat, Hunt's Spaghetti Sauce with Mushrooms, or Newman's Own Spaghetti Sauce Flavored with Mushrooms.

# *Oils*

Basically every oil has to go through some process to become an oil, but many times it goes through *over*processing to become an oil. Overprocessing simply strips a food of almost everything nutritious; think of the way bleach strips hair and leaves it for dead. I prefer to stick to the health food industry brand names, because I trust the processing they're using is natural. All oils are fattening, and even if they are good for your cholesterol, like canola and olive oil, I still avoid the companies that mass produce.

| BEST | WORST |
| --- | --- |
| Hain | Puritan |
| Spectrum | Wesson |
| Hollywood | Crisco |
| Olive oil | Mazola |
| Canola Oil | |

## THE NEXT BEST THING

Take the time to find one from the BEST list. Olive oil, especially, is everywhere now.

## Mayonnaises and Spreads

Remember: all have oil and all are fattening. The following list is for the healthy versus nonhealthy. Again, the question here is the processing methods of the companies who only make healthy changes when the trends demand it. I believe mayonnaise to be one of the unhealthiest products you can consume.

| BEST | WORST |
|------|-------|
| Nayonnaise | Best Foods |
| Hain | Springfield |
| Hollywood | Kraft |
| Spectrum Naturals | Weight Watchers |
| Westbrae Natural | |

**THE NEXT BEST THING**

Look for soy-based products that emulate mayonnaise. The best solution is to look at page 198 for my version of mayonnaise (which I once called Yolonnaise). It is based on tofu and nonfat yogurt, with added seasonings. I still make it in batches for my friends. It is not as creamy as real mayonnaise, but it's even more delicious.

## Herbs and Spices

Most spices are nonfattening and healthy. The ones you have to watch out for are those loaded with chemicals, artificial flavors, sugar, salt, MSG, or added oils. Once again a little sugar and salt aren't going to kill you, but you want to make sure that they are low on the list of ingredients. Spices usually come from manufacturers who create a whole line of different herbs and spices or mixes. I am going to list the manufacturers by name as it would take forever to list every spice they make. The spices on the WORST list are made by manufacturers who, not always, but very often spike their products with MSG, chemicals, sugar, and all the other things you want to avoid. Even if they are selling you a low-sodium sign on the label, the rest of the product may be unhealthy. Or consider Butter Buds, which is a nonfat substitute for butter. Sure, it has no fat, but look at what it does have: maltodextrin (sugar) and salt.

The spices on the BEST list are natural (nonchemical), low to no sodium, and sugar free. Having these herbs, spices, and mixes is essential to creative, healthy cooking. Changing your diet can just be a matter of throwing out that old favorite salty garlic bottle of, say, Lawry's seasoning salt and replacing it with Parsley Patch's Garlic saltless seasoning. (Note: this list does not include the plain, natural herbs and spices found in every market, i.e., Schilling's tarragon, oregano, basil, etc., which are all good choices.)

| BEST | WORST |
|---|---|
| Parsley Patch | Lawry's mixes |
| Sun Isles | Schilling mixes |
| Nile Spice | Butter Buds and other substitutes |
| Health Valley | Salt substitutes |
| Modern Products | McCormick mixes |
| Sea Seasonings | |
| Bioforce | |
| Paula's | |
| Capello's | |
| Chef Paul Prudhomme's | |
| Hain | |

## THE NEXT BEST THING

Most of the manufacturers on the WORST list have a few products in their line that aren't so bad. For instance Lawry's has a garlic powder that is coarse ground with parsley. Ingredients: **garlic, partially hydrogenated vegetable oil (cottonseed, soybean), and parsley.** Obviously not a health food item, but it isn't going to hurt you to have it once in a while.

## *Juices and Sodas*

Juice is naturally sweet and doesn't need sugar of any kind. Look for sodas made of fruit juice and mineral water, which are fast catching up with the flavored mineral water market. Some of the WORST companies have begun to make a few healthy versions. How good is their processing—who knows? All together now . . . "Read the label!"

Gatorade and other products that claim to quench thirst are selling you a false healthful image by tying them into athletics. These products are nothing but sugar, salt, and junk. Knudsen, however, makes a healthy version called Recharge, which contains **water, white grape juice concentrate, orange extract, and sea salt.** Also, very important, if the product is called *drink,* as in tropical drink, cranberry cocktail drink, or orange drink, it has sugar and additives! Avoid that word on your juice products and stick to juice only.

| BEST | WORST |
|------|-------|
| Crystal Geyser | Diet and regular: |
| Calistoga | Coca Cola |
| Knudsen | Pepsi |
| Hansens | Shasta |
| Sundance | Seven-Up |
| Martinellis | Dr Pepper |
| After the Fall | Capri Sun |
| L & A | Hi-C |
| Treetop | Tang |
| Mott's | Gatorade |
| | Welch's |
| | Kern's |
| | Ocean Spray |
| | Springfield |

## THE NEXT BEST THING

Once again, many of the juice manufacturers, like Mott's, will have one line of natural juice, and then another line of junk juices. Some brand names to look for their healthy products: Mott's, Ocean Spray, Welch's, Minute Maid, or a local brand name.

## *Cookies and Cakes*

It is my opinion that a little sugar is not going to kill you, but that products that contain a load of sugar along with a load of chemicals and fats will hurt you. Most cookie and cake products made by big companies have always contained tropical oils, although now many manufacturers have switched to healthier oils—and are slapping heart-healthy and no-cholesterol signs on their labels as fast as they can. Even so, it is my feeling that neither the mainstream food scientists or the natural foods industry have found how to make a completely healthy product that will satisfy the longing for wonderfully rich and sweet desserts. The food scientists just keep coming up with more chemical answers, and although the fruit juice concentrates that the natural foods industry uses are wonderful, sometimes they just don't make the grade. This really becomes a matter of your own taste. Try to satisfy your sugar cravings with the healthiest sweets you can find at least the majority of the time, then go for the decadent dessert you desire on occasion.

| BEST | WORST |
|------|-------|
| Natures Choice | Nabisco (most of cookies on market) |
| Health Valley | Pepperidge Farm |
| Marin Brand | Mothers |
| Natures Warehouse | Entenmenn's |
| Barbara's | Van de Kamp's |
| Westbrae Natural | Duncan Hines |
| Nanakars | Keebler |
| El Molino Mills | Sunshine |
| | Peek Freans |
| | Delicious |
| | Candita |
| | Archway |
| | Lu |
| | Pogen |
| | Delacre |
| | Carr's |
| | Stella D'oro |

## THE NEXT BEST THING

Fat-free products from the junk producers like Entenmann's and Hostess are probably second best. But I'll repeat myself, they are second best and not healthy.

Dry cake mixes are notoriously full of chemicals. However, the natural food industry has come out with a few healthy contenders:

| BEST | WORST |
|------|-------|
| Fearn | Betty Crocker |
| Arrowhead Mills | Duncan Hines |
| Amaranth | Pillsbury |
| | "Jiffy" |

## *Frozen Desserts*

Ice cream in its "natural form" is basically cream, sugar, salt, ice, and flavorings (e.g., chocolate and vanilla). So it's also basically fattening and not very healthy to begin with. Plus, most commercial ice creams (on the WORST list) also contain chemicals and preservatives, like formaldehyde, to extend not only their shelf life, but to extend the time before they melt in your bowl. A lot of the companies who make these ice creams now make light or diet versions, which may mean that they changed one of a few things: low-fat or nonfat milk instead of cream, a sugar substitute instead of real sugar. And they may have even added other chemicals or additives to make the product more like real ice cream.

Now, ice cream is one of our favorite delights, but the sad news is that if you have high cholesterol, ice cream—any dairy, for that matter—is out. And even if you don't have high cholesterol, real ice cream should only be an occasional treat—and if you're trying to shed some pounds, I mean *very* occasional. Diet junk food take-offs on ice cream, which usually contain nonfat milk and a sugar substitute, may ease your pain at having to turn down a Häagen Dazs cone, but this doesn't mean that you can eat them whenever you want, or as often as you might feel like it: They're not calorie-less, and eating them constantly won't help you break habits that made you fat in the first place.

Sorbets, fruit glacés, and ices are generally made up of ice, fruit, and sugar and are another alternative to ice cream. Sometimes, though, they contain milk or cream, too, which makes them almost as bad as real ice cream. But if they're plain, great—once again, the sugar calories are easily burned, and it won't hurt your cholesterol.

Nonfat frozen yogurt is a healthier alternative as well. Just don't abuse it. For a while, every time an exercise studio opened up in LA, a frozen yogurt joint opened next to it, and I swear, knowing the low amount of calories the yogurt contained per ounce, woman were eating twice as much as they could burn off in their exercise classes. Nonfat frozen yogurt should be considered a treat—it's still dairy-based.

The natural foods industry has attempted to come up with some less-fatty frozen dessert entries of its own—and with more success than it has had with cookies and cakes. One is called Ice Bean, and the basic ingredients are **Water, soybeans, honey, corn oil, vanilla extract, soy lecithin, carob bean, guar, and salt.** Another, similar product to look for is called Rice Dream. The ingredients vary according to the flavor, of course, but most of these are still fattening. However, these products are better than ice cream if you have high cholesterol and a good choice for kids who don't have a weight problem.

What if real ice cream is your passion? Have it once in a while, then eat the healthiest substitutes you can find more often (but still in moderation). Remember what I said earlier about fat-free foods. This holds for the Sealtest new fat-free line and all new "plastic" products—like Simplesse—based on fat substitutes.

| BEST | WORST |
|---|---|
| Stars frozen yogurt | Dreyers |
| Rice Dream | Breyers |
| Garden of Eatin' fruit glace | Carnation |
| Nouvelle Sorbet | Jell-O brand |
| Cafe Glace Light | Johnstons |
| Alta-Dena | Knudsen |
| | Mocha Mix |
| | Welch's |
| | Dove bars |
| | Crystal Light |
| | Fudgesicle |
| | Ben & Jerry's |
| | Steve's |
| | Häagen Dazs |

## THE NEXT BEST THING

There are always things like Weight Watchers diet fudge bars and the new fat-free and fat-substitute ice creams that I discussed on page 126.

## *Diet Junk Foods*

When I say "diet junk food" I'm not just referring to diet candies or slenderizing milk shakes. I'm talking about things like Lean Cuisine Glazed Chicken with Vegetable Rice and Weight Watchers Southern Fried Chicken Patty. These are foods that, while they may have a low-calorie tag, are always about 75 percent fats, oils, sugar, salt, MSG, and Lord knows what else to try to give a dieter the taste of the real thing. But the flavor appeal lasts only for about four bites. Then the dieter is left hungry, deprived, and still making fat cells out of the ingredients.

Remember, when you are learning to make weight control a permanent part of your life, you have to learn to wean yourself from foods loaded with fat, salt, and sugar. The majority of diet foods on the market not only contain ingredients that are not healthy, but they just reinforce the desire for junk. Check out some of these labels on these pasta and chicken dinners (normally lean foods) and you'll see what I mean.

Healthy Choice Fettucini Alfredo
> **Cooked Fettucini Noodles (flour, water, eggs), water, Parmesan cheese (milk and milk fat, salt, cheese cultures, en-**

zymes), soybean oil, modified food starch, alfredo cheese blend (cultured cream, Parmesan cheese, milkfat and nonfat milk, salt, cheese cultures, enzymes), whey, partially hydrogenated soybean oil, nonfat dry milk, salt, garlic, spices, parsley, natural flavor, citric acid, sodium phosphate, dried sweet cream, sugar, salt flavorings, spice, corn syrup solids, milk and cream solids, whey.

Give me a break! For one thing, if you are watching your weight you should be eating pasta with a nonoily red sauce. That's the way you have to learn to eat. Creamy fettucini dishes should not be on your agenda and even if they are you certainly don't need food prepared with hydrogenated oil, sugar, and corn syrup.

The Budget Gourmet Light French Recipe Chicken and Vegetables Ingredients:

Chicken broth, potatoes, celery, chicken breast, carrots, onions, pearl onions, water, wine, peas, mushrooms, butter, beef base (beef, hydrolyzed plant protein, salt, beef extract, yeast extract, chicken fat, natural flavorings), bacon fat, modified food starch, tomato paste, spices including paprika, salt, dried garlic, sugar, milk protein hydrolysate.

HELP! This product is called light, but it contains butter and chicken fat. The reason many of these dishes have only a few calories is because the portions are TINY! Wouldn't you rather have a big hearty meal of nonfatty foods than a dollop of chicken in cream? And how about this one . . .

Weight Watchers Chicken Kiev

Chicken breast with rib meat, cooked white rice, water, broccoli, cauliflower, carrots, bread crumbs, cooked wild rice, corn flour, margarine, onions, modified food starch, salt, bleached wheat flour, partially hydrogenated soybean oil, natural (extractives of vegetable oils) and artificial flavors, chicken meat including natural chicken juices, sugar, sodium phosphate, locust and guar gums, leavening (sodium acid pyrophosphate, sodium bicarbonate), corn oil, hydrolyzed vegetable protein, granulated onion, spices, monosodium glutamate, xanthan gum, granulated

**garlic, vinegar, dehydrated chives, dried whey, reconstituted skim milk, flavorings, dehydrated onions, beta carotene, eggs, turmeric color, lemon oil.**

In case you weren't counting, there are five sources of sodium in this dish, which can mean water retention for whoever eats it—and there's nothing worse than retaining water when you're trying to lose weight. The dinner also contains margarine, soybean oil, corn oil, eggs—in other words, a lot of fat. The bottom line is that this dish contains 10 grams of fat, close to 40 percent of its 230 calories, and that's just too much.

There really is no BEST list for diet foods as far as I'm concerned. By now—from things I've already pointed out in this and in previous chapters, you know what exactly constitutes a lean food. The following is just a WORST list—and a big slap to the manufacturers of these products:

**WORST**

Weight Watchers frozen dinners
Stouffer's Lean Cuisine frozen dinners
The Budget Gourmet Light frozen dinners
Le Menu frozen dinners
Armour frozen dinners
Healthy Choice frozen dinners (may be better for your cholesterol, but are still processed and unhealthy)
Butter Buds seasoning
Richard Simmons salad dressings
Sego drinks
Estee diet products—really for diabetics, not weight loss
Carnation Slender drinks
Figurines*
Fibar*

When you are trying to lose weight stick to the real foods that your body will burn for energy. Just a reminder of the basics:

Fresh produce
Lean proteins
Whole grains
Limited nonfat dairy
NO OILS/FATS!

*There is no one bar that takes the place of a healthy, lean meal.

So stock your house full of products from these BEST lists and sleep well knowing that you are feeding yourself and your family the right foods. If you have to fall back on THE NEXT BEST THING list make sure it is a small 10 to 15 percent of what is in your home and in your diet. You will find yourself moving away from junk food in a matter of months as your body will become as addicted to eating well as it was to eating poorly. To narrow it down even further—the healthiest food for every body type—see the following chart.

## Shopping By Your Body Type

Now that you have a general idea of the BEST foods, let's get down to the nitty-gritty details. The following chart further breaks down the shopping list so you know what's healthy for your specific body. While I haven't included every item from the preceding lists, there are enough here to give you the right idea.

The Key   [Y-Yes   N-No   L-Limited]

**BF/LC: Body Fat with Low Cholesterol.** No cholesterol problem, but wants to lose weight.

**LBF/HC; Low Body Fat with High Cholesterol.** Doesn't need to lose weight, but needs to lower cholesterol.

**BF/HC: Body Fat with High Cholesterol.** Better watch out, you have to be really careful about what goes into your mouth.

**NOR: Normal.** Or rather the person everyone loves to hate. Keep in mind that if you're "normal" you must start or continue to eat the kinds of foods listed here or you could very easily become a BF/HC.

| PRODUCT | BF/LC | LBF/HC | BF/HC | NOR |
|---|---|---|---|---|
| **Chicken** | | | | |
| Breasts, skinless | Y | Y | Y | Y |
| Thighs, skinless | Y | Y | Y | Y |
| Whole roasted chicken | without skin | without skin | without skin | Y |
| Chicken gizzards | Y | N | N | Y |
| | without | N | N | Y |

130

| PRODUCT | BF/LC | LBF/HC | BF/HC | NOR |
|---|---|---|---|---|
| Drumsticks | skin | | | |
| Livers | Y | N | N | Y |
| Ground chicken | Y | Y | Y | Y |
| Chicken dogs (from health food store) | Y | Y | Y | Y |
| **Turkey** | | | | |
| Breasts | Y | Y | Y | Y |
| Tenderloins | Y | Y | Y | Y |
| Ground | Y | Y | Y | Y |
| Thighs | Y | Y | Y | Y |
| Drumsticks | without skin | without skin | without skin | Y |
| Whole roasted turkey | without skin | without skin | without skin | Y |
| Turkey sausage (from health food store) | N | N | N | Y |
| Turkey dogs | Y | Y | Y | Y |

**All seafood is a yes for everyone, prepared without fats for BF/LC and BF/HC**

| PRODUCT | BF/LC | LBF/HC | BF/HC | NOR |
|---|---|---|---|---|
| **Cheeses** | | | | |
| Cabot Vitalait | Y | N | N | Y |
| Lifetime | Y | N | N | Y |
| New Holland | Y | N | N | Y |
| Frigo string cheese | N | N | N | Y |
| Nu Tofu cheese/spread | N | Y | N | Y |
| SoyCo | N | Y | N | Y |
| Soya Kaas | N | Y | N | Y |
| Zausner's natural cream cheese | N | N | N | Y |
| Mozzarella | N | N | N | Y |
| Parmesan | Y | N | N | Y |
| Romano | Y | N | N | Y |
| Alta-Dena | N | N | N | Y |
| Eggs | Y | white only | white only | Y |

| PRODUCT | BF/LC | LBF/HC | BF/HC | NOR |
|---|---|---|---|---|
| **Other Dairy Products** | | | | |
| Hollywood margarine | N | Y | N | Y |
| Lecithin spread | N | Y | N | Y |
| Nonfat yogurts | limited | N | N | Y |
| Nonfat cottage cheese | limited | N | N | Y |
| Nonfat milk | limited | N | N | Y |
| **Breads/Crackers** | | | | |
| Whole wheat sliced bread | limited | Y | limited | Y |
| Bran muffin without nuts or raisins | limited | Y | limited | Y |
| Bran muffin with nuts or raisins | N | N | N | Y |
| Bran muffin without nuts | N | Y | N | Y |
| Fat-free bran muffin | Y | Y | Y | Y |
| Pritikin English muffin | Y | Y | Y | Y |
| Whole wheat fat-free pita | Y | Y | Y | Y |
| Corn fat-free tortilla | Y | Y | Y | Y |
| Bagel | limited | Y | limited | Y |
| Health Valley crackers | N | Y | N | Y |
| California Grain | N | Y | N | Y |
| Edward & Sons | Y | Y | Y | Y |
| Kavli Crisps | Y | Y | Y | Y |
| Barbara's | N | Y | N | Y |
| Hol-Grain | Y | Y | Y | Y |
| Krispbread | Y | Y | Y | Y |
| Wasa Crispbread | Y | Y | Y | Y |
| Manischewitz Whole Wheat Matzo | Y | Y | Y | Y |
| Stone ground wheat thins | N | Y | N | Y |
| **Munchies** | | | | |
| Hain Mini Rice Cakes: | | | | |
| Apple Cinnamon | Y | Y | Y | Y |
| Teriyaki | Y | Y | Y | Y |
| Other flavors | N | Y | N | Y |
| Risotto chips | limited | Y | N | Y |
| Polenta chips | limited | Y | N | Y |

| PRODUCT | BF/LC | LBF/HC | BF/HC | NOR |
|---|---|---|---|---|
| Rices Bites | limited | Y | N | Y |
| Baked cheese puffs | limited | Y | N | Y |
| Pritikin Rice Cakes | Y | Y | Y | Y |
| Quaker Rice Cakes | Y | Y | Y | Y |
| Popcorn cakes | limited | Y | limited | Y |
| Oat Bran potato chips | N | Y | N | Y |
| Garden of Eatin' corn chips | N | Y | N | Y |
| Fromage Sticks | N | Y | N | Y |
| Skinny Haven Munchies | Y | Y | Y | Y |
| Lapidus Popcorn | airpopped | Y | airpopped | Y |
| Kettlechips | N | Y | N | Y |
| Pacific Rice Crackers | Y | Y | Y | Y |
| Whole wheat pretzels | limited | Y | limited | Y |
| Bell's natural potato chips | N | N | N | Y |
| Pickles—salt free | Y | Y | Y | Y |
| Turkey jerky | N | Y | N | Y |
| Barbara's light granola bars | Y | Y | Y | Y |
| Light Munchies | Y | Y | Y | Y |
| Healthy granola bars/no nuts | N | Y | N | Y |
| Healthy granola bars/all | N | N | N | Y |
| Raisins (dried fruits) | N | Y | N | Y |
| Applesauce—sugar free | Y | Y | Y | Y |

**Soups**

| | | | | |
|---|---|---|---|---|
| All healthy labels | N | Y | N | Y |
| Pritikin | Y | Y | Y | Y |
| Any without oil (i.e., tomato) | Y | Y | Y | Y |
| Fantastic Foods soup in a cup | N | Y | N | Y |
| Nile Spice soup in a cup | limited | Y | limited | Y |
| Westbrae Ramen soups | Y | Y | N | Y |

**Canned Goods**

| | | | | |
|---|---|---|---|---|
| Nutradiet fruits/veggies | Y | Y | Y | Y |
| Whole Earth beans/chili | N | Y | N | Y |
| Hearts of palm | Y | Y | Y | Y |
| Artichoke hearts | Y | Y | Y | Y |
| Baby corns | Y | Y | Y | Y |

| PRODUCT | BF/LC | LBF/HC | BF/HC | NOR |
|---|---|---|---|---|
| Water chestnuts | Y | Y | Y | Y |
| Any veggies without oil/salt | Y | Y | Y | Y |
| **Cereal** | | | | |
| All healthy brands—no nuts/fruits | limited | Y | N | Y |
| All healthy brands—puffed | Y | Y | Y | Y |
| Oatmeal—plain | Y | Y | Y | Y |
| Hot grain cereals—plain | Y | Y | Y | Y |
| Added nuts or fruits | N | N | N | Y |
| **Cookies/Cakes** | | | | |
| All healthy brands—no nuts/butter | N | Y | N | Y |
| All healthy brands nuts | N | N | N | Y |
| Graham crackers | limited | Y | N | Y |
| Animal crackers | limited | Y | limited | Y |
| Plain oatmeal | limited | Y | N | Y |
| Ginger snaps | limited | Y | N | Y |
| **Dressings/Condiments** | | | | |
| Enrico's ketchup | Y | Y | Y | Y |
| Hain ketchup | Y | Y | Y | Y |
| Robbie's no-oil products | Y | Y | Y | Y |
| Premier Japan | N | Y | N | Y |
| Uncle Dave's ketchup | Y | Y | Y | Y |
| San'J light soy | Y | Y | Y | Y |
| San'J marinades | N | Y | N | Y |
| Uncle Bum's | N | Y | N | Y |
| Uncle Bum's no-oil products | Y | Y | Y | Y |
| Cook's salad dressings | N | Y | N | Y |
| Cook's Garlic Gusto—oil free | Y | Y | Y | Y |
| Duggans oil free marinades | Y | Y | Y | Y |
| Duggans salad dressings | N | Y | N | Y |
| Emerald Valley marinades | N | Y | N | Y |
| Erewhon sauces | N | Y | N | Y |
| The Wizard sauces—oil free | Y | Y | Y | Y |

| PRODUCT | BF/LC | LBF/HC | BF/HC | NOR |
|---|---|---|---|---|
| Sonoma dressings | N | Y | N | Y |
| Paula's vinegars | Y | Y | Y | Y |
| Paula's dressings | N | Y | N | Y |
| Marin Brand sauces | N | Y | N | Y |
| Cardini's dressings | N | Y | N | Y |
| The Source dressings | N | Y | N | Y |
| Hain dry mixes | N | Y | N | Y |
| Hain dry no-oil mixes | Y | Y | Y | Y |
| Pritikin dressings | Y | Y | Y | Y |
| Herb Magic | Y | Y | Y | Y |
| **Pasta Sauces** | | | | |
| Health Valley | N | Y | N | Y |
| Ci'Bella | N | Y | N | Y |
| Ci'Bella no oil | Y | Y | Y | Y |
| Mama Coco's | N | Y | N | Y |
| Pritikin | Y | Y | Y | Y |
| Robbies | N | Y | N | Y |
| Robbie's no oil | Y | Y | Y | Y |
| Enrico's | N | Y | N | Y |
| Tree of Life | N | Y | N | Y |
| **Oils—No Saturated or Hydrogenated Oils/All Cholesterol Free** | | | | |
| Hain | N | Y | N | Y |
| Spectrum | N | Y | N | Y |
| Hollywood | N | Y | N | Y |
| **Mayonnaises/Spreads** | | | | |
| Nayonnaise | N | Y | N | Y |
| Hain | N | Y | N | Y |
| Hollywood | N | Y | N | Y |
| Spectrum Naturals | N | Y | N | Y |
| Westbrae Natural | N | Y | N | Y |

### Juices/Sodas

All natural juices should be cut in half with mineral water for the person trying to lose body fat. Although healthy, those natural sugar calories can add up, and you might even be more satisfied having an actual piece of fruit. Remember sugar calories are burnable, but if you have too many that's all the more you have to work at burning off.

| PRODUCT | BF/LC | LBF/HC | BF/HC | NOR |
|---|---|---|---|---|
| Crystal Geyser sodas | Y | Y | Y | Y |
| Calistoga mineral waters | Y | Y | Y | Y |
| Knudsen juices/sodas | limited | Y | limited | Y |
| Hansens sodas | N | Y | N | Y |
| Sundance | limited | Y | limited | Y |
| Martinellis | N | Y | N | Y |
| **Rices/Grains/Sides** | | | | |
| Hain side dishes | limited | Y | limited | Y |
| Arrowhead Mills plain rice | Y | Y | limited | Y |
| Arrowhead Mills mixes | limited | Y | limited | Y |
| Lundberg plain grains | Y | Y | limited | Y |
| Fantastic Food mixes | limited | Y | limited | Y |
| Wild rice | Y | Y | Y | Y |
| Basmati rice | Y | Y | Y | Y |
| Whole grain brown rice | Y | Y | Y | Y |
| **Frozen Foods** | | | | |
| Oven Poppers dinners | N | N | N | Y |
| Jaclyn's | N | Y | N | Y |
| Soypreme | N | Y | N | Y |
| Legume | N | Y | N | Y |
| Van's | N | Y | N | Y |
| Amy's | N | Y | N | Y |
| Shelton Farms | N | N | N | Y |
| **Frozen Desserts** | | | | |
| Stars | N | N | N | Y |
| Rice Dream | N | Y | N | Y |
| Garden of Eatin' glacé | Y | Y | limited | Y |
| Nouvelle sorbet | Y | Y | limited | Y |
| Cafe Glace light | Y | Y | Y | Y |
| Alta-Dena ice creams | N | N | N | Y |
| Frozen Yogurt—nonfat | limited | N | limited | Y |

## Diet Junk Food

If you are cutting back on calories to lose weight and need a "fix," go ahead and use some Sweet 'N Low or some of other diet products such as a diet soda or Butter Buds. If you feel they're going to save you from going on a binge on the real thing, just do it. However, once again, don't make consuming these products a habit. In other words, "take only as needed."

# 6

# Put It to Work: Now It's Time to Eat

**I**F THE PRECEDING chapters have made any impact at all, you should now have a "clean" kitchen filled with nutritious, nonfattening foods. You should know your rules and have pledged to take responsibility for what goes into your mouth (and thereby onto your hips and stomach). "So, okay," you say, "I've got the idea, but I still need to know how to tie all those bits of information together day to day. I'm still a little confused about what it all means." In other words, Yolanda, tell me what to eat.

By now you know that I'm not going to write a prescribed "do it my way" diet for you. But I also realize that the popularity of all those diet books and programs lies in the fact that people really do want someone to guide them step-by-step. My philosophy is that you have to guide yourself: By having enough knowledge about food as well as insight into your body's needs and wants, you will also have what it takes to make the right choices. This ability, though, isn't going to come to you overnight, so let's compromise: I'll give you an example of what I think is a week's worth of healthy eating and you use it as a menu to help you get started. Follow it to a tee if you want, or just use it to give you some ideas of what to eat at home or order when you're dining out.

# First Things First: Taking a Long Look at What You're Eating Now

Before I give you a week's worth of menus, I think it's important to cast a critical eye on what you're already eating. The best thing you can do is take three to seven days and keep a food journal of everything that goes into your mouth (excluding toothpaste). This is how I get started with every client, and it's very revealing. Sometimes they're doing better than they think and only need to make a few adjustments here and there. Sometimes their diets are a complete disaster. I think that by writing down what you eat you can get a better overview of what your total day looks like, and that in turn should help you balance your meals and snacks better. It will also give you the opportunity to really think about what satisfies you, what doesn't, what you eat simply out of habit and what—based on what you have learned about food and your body in this book—just shouldn't be a part of your eating lifestyle anymore. The point of keeping a food journal is to see where you're slipping up in the course of your day, but haven't really noticed it. Perhaps you just grab a few handfuls of trail mix when you get home from exercise class without even thinking about it—you'll think about it when you see it on paper, though, and I hope you'll realize that you could be adding up to 500 fat and sugar calories to your day, therefore negating all the work you just did in class.

The reason I'm asking you to look at your daily intake now instead of in the beginning of this book—it is, after all, the first assignment I give my clients—is that I wanted you to first have the knowledge needed to accurately assess your journal. Since I can't personally peruse your diary, you have to act as your own nutrition counselor. And as I said before, if you've read this far you've learned how to shop and read labels; you are a food scholar! Now put that information to use.

The following is my client Beth's seven-day food diary. Along with what she ate and how much, I asked her to fill in where she ate it and what she was doing at the time. The "where you eat" and "what you are doing at the time" are the keys to finding out what your emotional needs for food really are. For instance, maybe you are eating lunch with your girlfriends and ordering food that you don't care about just to feel part of the scene when you'd really much rather skip it and have frozen yogurt with your child at 3:30. Or perhaps you have a situation like my client Anne, a very successful political consultant whose lunches, always tied into business, were her biggest meals and the ones she cared about the most. Anne would have those great lunches, then go home and eat the same dinner as her family, not because she was still hungry, but because her husband had gone to the trouble of making it himself. Later on, she learned to sit with the family at night and have a very light dinner and keep her lunches as the main meal.

*Where* you eat often connects to what you eat and why you're eating it. Think in terms of ambiance. You choose certain restaurants over others because the ambiance suits your mood. The same goes for other places you eat. If you're hiding out eating in a closet—not a very pleasant place—you're probably not in a pleasant mood and not being very pleasant to your body, that is, not giving it nutritious foods. If you're standing in front of the refrigerator eating, you're most likely in a lazy mood—and you're probably at that moment being just as lazy about maintaining a healthy diet. If you're eating in the dingy cafeteria at work, you probably don't care what you're going to eat (you just want to get out of there) and so just toss something—most likely something fattening—down. If going outside for a walk during lunch is what it takes to get you to eat more healthfully, then by all means get out there and do it. Use your food journal to prod you into thinking about where you're eating, why you're eating it, and how you can make some changes.

Along with Beth's diary, are my comments, plus a discussion of her dietary "bloopers." I hope by reading about her mistakes, it will help you understand what you, too, are doing wrong or, perhaps, doing right. Also, once you have your own food journal in hand, you can, I hope, see the areas—that is, specific meals—where you need help. *Then* look at the planned menus, which follow later in this chapter, and let them guide you. For instance, if your food journal makes it plain that lunch is your biggest problem, plug one of the healthier lunches from my menus—like nonfat pasta salad primavera or chicken dogs—into yours. Assess your diet, assess mine, then combine the best aspects of both.

## Beth's Case History

Beth, in her early forties, is married and works at home writing. She loves food and has quite a gourmet palate, which of course means she likes lots of olive oil. When you read Beth's journals keep in mind that she needed to lose 40 pounds. You can see where she has attempted to eat "healthfully" or make stabs at cutting back. One of the biggest problems is that she did not exercise in the least. So before I even started in on her diet, we talked about beginning a walking program. This will usually knock off the first few pounds just by kicking up the metabolism.

**DAILY FOOD JOURNAL**

Name _Beth_                                                                     Date _April 5, 1990_

| Time eaten | Food eaten | Quantity | Where did you eat? | What were you doing? |
|---|---|---|---|---|
| 8:30 A.M. | cereal (Nutri-Grain wheat) (1) dried apricots fresh strawberries nonfat milk | medium cereal (Oon!- lots of dried apricots) | kitchen table | reading the paper |
| 12:30 P.M. | chicken sandwich on wheat roll w/ tomato onions + sprouts - Crystal Lt geyser water | 1 small sandwich + 1 drink mayo? | at deli | reading a book |
| 3:30 P.M. | choc. chip cookie (1) | 1 medium | at shopping mall | shopping w/ daughter |
| 6:30 P.M. | salad of chicken (2) + black beans, lettuce in taco shell | medium large portion of salad - small bits of taco shell | restaurant | after shopping |
| 10:00 P.M. | shortbread + iced tea | 2 pieces | in bedroom | watching TV |
|  | Have plain chicken w/ no bread more veggies + fruits |  |  |  |

\* plus slice sourdough bread + 2 large glasses of iced tea.

Obviously i! one is overweight one does not get cookies!

too many carbohydrates for one day w/o exercise

# Day 1: April 5
## Beth's Bloopers/Yolanda's Corrections

**Breakfast.** First of all Nutri-Grain is one of those typical cereals that has a nutritious-looking picture and healthy-sounding words on the label, but is nonetheless an overprocessed product—it's not the worst cereal on the market, but she could do a lot better. Beth also has made the old mistake of thinking that if a food is relatively healthy, it must be nonfattening, too. She would be better off with a small bowl of puffed wheat (rice or corn) with nonfat milk and fresh fruit instead of dried apricots. Dried apricots not only are fattening because they're high in fruit sugar calories, they often have sulfites, which have been known to cause dizziness, cramps, breathing problems, and other adverse reactions in many people. (If you must eat dried fruit, look for the kinds that are sulfite-free.) As you'll see when you look at the rest of Beth's week, she's constantly downing dried apricots. Instead, she should be grabbing some grapes or berries or other type of fruit.

**Afternoon Snack.** Chocolate chip cookies! Once again, if you are fat and you don't want to be fat, then don't eat chocolate chip cookies just because your child is! By the time Beth has her 3:30 cookie, she has already had a sufficient lunch and lots of complex carbohydrates at breakfast and lunch, but she hasn't done much to burn those carbs. If she has a late afternoon sugar low, then she should have a cappuccino (made with skim or low-fat milk) or a few Lifesavers rather than a fat-filled chocolate chip cookie. Even a tea biscuit would be better than the cookie. If the cookie is all she lives for and having it at the mall will make her keep the rest of her diet clean, then she should make it her one treat and consider herself indulged.

**Dinner.** Keeping in mind that Beth is trying to lose a lot of weight, she did not order a proper dinner. Between the bread and the salad's taco shell, plus its oily salad dressing, she probably *gained*, not lost on that day. As she edges into dessert—shortbread cookies, because they are packed with butter and oil, are a terrible choice—a weight gain is almost certain. What Beth should have done was brought her own dressing or made her own at the table (see Chapter 9 on restaurant eating), asked for no beans (at restaurants, they're usually made with added fat), and skipped both the bread and taco shell—she already had a good amount of carbs during the day. Not knowing the menu of the restaurant she went to, I can't say what else she might have ordered, but for future reference (yours and hers), plain chicken is a better choice than smoked, because smoking requires that oils be added to the meat. Of course, Beth should also change her nighttime cookie snack to fruit or at least to animal crackers (which are low fat) if that's the time she needs a cookie break the most.

### Day 2: April 6
### Beth's Bloopers/Yolanda's Corrections

**Lunch.** Since Beth already had toast for breakfast, she didn't need a roll for lunch. Don't have bread at every meal. Have a great big salad with an oil-free dressing. This is the time to get those vitamins and minerals from produce.

**Afternoon Snack.** Cookies again? Her first choice should be fruit. If she had not had grain products at every other meal, then some flavored rice cakes or rice crackers, a few Lifesavers, or diet candies would be fine. Again, if she really needs a cookie at this hour, then she should try some fat-free or low-calorie oat bran cookies—her body will burn these calories more readily because they're not *fat* calories. Even a nonfat frozen yogurt or yogurt in a cup would be a better choice.

**Dinner.** I wish I had a nickel for every time I have and will say "OIL IS FATTENING!" Beth's dinner would have been a great meal if it weren't for the olive oil. Next time, sauté chard in wine, sherry, or Pam . . . read the upcoming recipe chapter for more low-fat cooking solutions.

### Day 3: April 7
### Beth's Bloopers/Yolanda's Corrections

**Lunch.** Because Beth knew she was going out to dinner, she should have planned to have a lighter lunch, not pasta with oily sauce—and, oh, there are those cookies again. This is a perfect example of how you can make plans so as not to fall victim to circumstance—think ahead, set up your

## DAILY FOOD JOURNAL

Name _Beth_    Date _April 6, 1990_

| Time eaten | Food eaten | Quantity | Where did you eat? | What were you doing? |
|---|---|---|---|---|
| 9:15 A.M. | (dried apricots) | small handful | running out the door | (being late!) |
| 10:30 A.M. | whole wheat toast + sugarless jam | 2 slices | kitchen table | reading |
| 12:30 P.M. | chicken sandwich on wheat roll w/ tomatoes, sprouts + onions — Crystal Geyser water | 1 small sandwich + 1 drink | at deli | eating lunch w/ husband |
| 3:15 P.M. | (apricot jam filled cookies) | 4 | walking around the house | (stressing out) |
| 8:00 P.M. | grilled tuna steak w/ papaya salsa (stir-fried w/ olive oil) 1 sm. slice bread | small portions of everything | kitchen table | eating dinner w/ husband |
| | 1/2 glass white wine | | | |

Switch cookies to flavored rice cakes or fruit          too many carbs          no oil!

**DAILY FOOD JOURNAL**

Name _Beth_   Date _April 7, 1990_
(Saturday)

| Time eaten | Food eaten | Quantity | Where did you eat? | What were you doing? |
|---|---|---|---|---|
| 9:30 A.M. | whole wheat toast w/ sugarless jam & tea | 1½ slices | kitchen table | reading newspaper |
| 2:00 P.M. | pasta w/ spicy red pepper sauce (classico) + rye cookies + iced tea | ~3 oz. pasta w/ ~3/4 c. sauce 2 cookies | kitchen table | reading magazine |
| 7:00 P.M. | whole wheat bread sticks + glass white wine | 3 thin sticks small glass wine | living room | entertaining friends |
| 8:30 P.M. | tapas, paella, red wine, flan — french bread | generous portions of tapas + paella 1 glass wine — ½ g small flan | restaurant | entertaining friends |
|  |  |  |  |  |
|  |  |  |  |  |

→ You're better off eating more pre-dinner munchies than eating a heavy dinner. Learn to "order it your way."

day, save your calories for the time (like Beth, when you'll be entertaining friends for cocktails, then dining out) you'll want them most. To prepare for her restaurant meal, Beth would have been better off sticking to fruits, vegetables, and lean proteins during the day.

**Cocktail Hour.** While she had the right idea of sticking to nonfat foods during the cocktail hour, something like hearts of palm, crudité, or rice crackers with fresh salsa rather than more bread calories would have better rounded out her day (don't forget how vital the vitamins and minerals from vegetables are).

**Dinner.** This may have been one of Beth's favorite restaurants, but if it wasn't a place that dazzled her, she should have ordered some dishes prepared without oil and, most important, passed on the greasy tapas. (Again, see Chapter 9 for good restaurant dining tips.)

## Day 4: April 8
### Beth's Bloopers/Yolanda's Corrections

**The Whole Day.** This day had pretty much the same problems as the others. Nothing but grain products all day, more oily pasta sauce, then into the dried apricots again. Considering that Beth had already packed in a lot of calories by dinner time, her cold saved the day. Get more fruits and vetetables into your diet, I told her, and perhaps you wouldn't have a cold.

## Day 5: April 9
### Beth's Bloopers/Yolanda's Corrections

**Breakfast.** The corn muffin she ate was loaded with fat and additives. I had her switch to a healthier fat-free, low-calorie bran muffin. And have more fluids, starting first thing, to nurse that cold.

**Afternoon and Evening Snacks.** One muffin a day is enough. I recommended that Beth have some oranges instead of tortillas and breadsticks (again, she's eating as if she's carb-loading for a 26k race). Sliced red peppers would also be a good snack because they're loaded with vitamin C. As long as she's trying to lose weight it is okay to take advantage of her loss of appetite and not have dinner—but it would have been much healthier if she had varied her intake during the day and eaten more vitamin- and mineral-packed foods.

# DAILY FOOD JOURNAL

Name __Beth__

Date __April 8, 1990__
(Sunday)

| Time eaten | Food eaten | Quantity | Where did you eat? | What were you doing? |
|---|---|---|---|---|
| 1:15 P.M. | whole wheat bagels + no-sugar jam + tea | 1½ bagels | Kitchen table | reading newspaper |
| 1:45 P.M. | (angel hair pasta w/ Classico di Roma spicy red pepper sauce + iced tea) | 2 oz pasta w/ ½ cup sauce | Kitchen table | reading a book |
| 4:30 P.M. | 3 corn tortillas with no-oil salsa iced tea | → | family room | watching TV |
| 7:00 P.M. | * (dried apricots) | medium handful | kitchen | cooking for husband |
| | (* didn't eat dinner because had bad cold- nothing tasted good!) | | | |
| | | | | |

# DAILY FOOD JOURNAL

Name _Beth_   Date _April 9, 1990_

| Time eaten | Food eaten | Quantity | Where did you eat? | What were you doing? |
|---|---|---|---|---|
| 8:00 A.M. | Pepperidge Farm Corn Muffin + grapes | 1 muffin ~ 1 cup grapes | Kitchen | fixing breakfast for family |
| noon | Loo Rick Turkey Frank on pita - grilled red onion - mustard | 1 hot dog - ½ pita | Kitchen table | reading magazine |
| 3:30 P.M. | 1 Sugarnes "Morning Glorious Muffin" + iced tea | 1 muffin (tho fairly large) | family room | watching TV |
| 6:00 P.M. | 2 corn tostilada w/several tablespoons of no-oil salsa → | → | family room | reading |
| 7:30 P.M. | 6 thin whole wheat bread sticks → | → | Kitchen table | Keeping husband company while he had dinner |
| | | | | ✓(still not much appetite at night due to cold) |

too many carbs

# Day 6: April 10
## Beth's Bloopers/Yolanda's Corrections

**The Whole Day.** If by chance Beth lost a pound or two during her cold, she probably put it back on double today. As I wrote at the bottom of her sheet, "Nothing but dough in your stomach all day!" There should be more fruits, veggies, lean proteins, and nonfat dairy throughout this day. For instance:

7:30 A.M.: ½ dry bagel (not 1 and ½) with no-sugar jam and one thick slice of cantaloupe (a good compromise—she gets her bread, but fills up on fruit).

11:30 A.M.: One salad with lettuce, tomato, green peppers, scallions (any raw veggie), one small can of water-packed tuna, and one hard-boiled egg, with oil-free dressing or balsamic vinegar.

4:00 P.M.: 10–15 mini teriyaki rice cakes and one piece fruit OR one 4-ounce nonfat frozen yogurt with fresh fruit topping.

5:30 P.M.: 10–15 baked rice snaps OR one lunch-size bag of baked low-cal cheese puffs to satisfy her cravings for carbs.

7:30 P.M.: Grilled chicken or fish (no oil), steamed broccoli, brown rice, and a sliced cucumber salad; the wine was okay.

9:30 P.M.: 10 animal crackers and a banana (much less fat here than in shortbread).

Now, these are just suggestions for Beth or you—but there's also a whole shopping chapter preceding this one of other alternatives to choose from.

# Day 7: April 11
## Beth's Bloopers/Yolanda's Corrections

**Breakfast:** Because Beth knew she would be attending a birthday party—one of those "give it up" situations where she'd have little control over what she ate (more on these situations in the following chapter)—she should have known it didn't mean she could pig out the whole day. Having just tea for breakfast would have been fine and going for a walk that morning would have been good fat-prevention.

**Lunch.** I'd say she did the right thing: Enjoyed the luncheon.

# DAILY FOOD JOURNAL

Name _Beth_

Date _April 10, 1990_

| Time eaten | Food eaten | Quantity | Where did you eat? | What were you doing? |
|---|---|---|---|---|
| 7:30 A.M. | bagel + no-sugar jam + tea | 1½ bagels | kitchen table | reading newspaper |
| 1:30 P.M. | 2 oz pasta → with ½ cup of Classico spicy red pepper sauce + iced tea | | kitchen table | reading magazine |
| 4:00 P.M. | 1 Oatmeal, choc. chip cookie | | walking downtown | walking from one appointment to another |
| 5:30 P.M. | 1 bagel w/no-sugar jam and iced tea | | family room | watching TV news |
| 7:30 P.M. | pasta w/mushrooms + parmesan cheese — (~3 oz pasta) + 1 glass red wine | | kitchen table | dinner w/husband |
| 9:30 P.M | 2 shortbread cookies | | kitchen | finishing dinner dishes |

Nothing but dough in your stomach all day!
Need more protein/veggies/fruits/fiber

# DAILY FOOD JOURNAL

Name __Beth__    Date __April 11, 1990__

| Time eaten | Food eaten | Quantity | Where did you eat? | What were you doing? |
|---|---|---|---|---|
| 7:30 A.M. | 1 bagel with sugarless ** jam + tea | | kitchen table | reading paper |
| 2:45 P.M. | *sorrel soup – fresh tomato tart – fresh asparagus – cheese bread – Pavlova dessert (small piece) (meringue, cream & strawberries | | friend's dining room | attending a luncheon |
| 4:30 P.M. | handful of dried apricots | | kitchen | starting dinner preparations |
| 7:30 P.M. | assorted roast vegetables + sautéed polenta (with cheese) french bread – white wine | | dining room | eating |
| 9:30 P.M. | two molasses Crisp cookies (Pepperidge Farm) | | family room | watching TV |
| | | | | |

* Birthday luncheon for a close friend – in a private home – a very rare occurrence – I seldom do "ladies-who-lunch" – when I do it's usually at a restaurant where I have more control.

** If you know you have this kind of lunch – skip breakfast + walk instead. Overload!

**Dinner.** But here's where she slipped up again. A predinner walk would have been smart, and if she hopes to drop weight, there was no need to have such an elaborate dinner with cookies for dessert—especially because, if she thought about it, she probably wasn't that hungry considering she'd had a big lunch. Beth, next time, go for a light dinner and have fruit for a snack.

This should give you the basic idea of how you should analyze your own food journal. Most of the time you could be eating a lot lighter at meals that aren't important to your emotional needs and saving the goodies for the times when you crave them the most.

## What Does One Week's Worth of Healthy Eating Look Like?

Far be it from me to give you a "diet" plan or prescription, but I do think it might help you answer that persistent question What should I eat? if you have a week's menu to give you some ideas. I completely understand the need to have steps laid out for you to begin the journey of reshaping your eating lifestyle. Yet, once again, use this week's worth of menus as a *guideline* only to creating menus that fit in with your own rules.

The following is a diet based on healthy, chemical-free foods for a person with no weight or cholesterol problems who has a regular (i.e., three times a week) exercise program. There are special instructions for those who are trying to lose or control their weight (WC) and those trying to lower their cholesterol (LC), but not their weight. If you have both a weight problem and a cholesterol problem, follow both the WC and the LC suggestions. The asterisks mark dishes for which recipes are included in this book.

Singer/actor Rick Springfield is the perfect example of someone for whom this basic menu is right. Very tall and naturally slender, no cholesterol problem, the guy can eat what he wants, not to mention that he runs four miles every day. However, Rick is adamant about eating only healthy food. He loves a well-balanced and all-natural diet. So think about him (now that's a pleasant task) when you read the basic menu, then read the notes for your own adjustments.

One way of working with these menus might be to read them, then make a week plan for yourself based on those suggestions you find appealing, plus the things you know already work for you. At the end of the seven days, look at your projected week plan and note where you felt you couldn't stick to it, where you needed more, less, and anything else that comes to mind. Make strong notes about the cravings you have and any sticky situations you found yourself caught in, as they are usually what will have tripped you up. We'll address those problems later in this chapter and in the following chapter too.

*RECIPES FOR STARRED ITEMS APPEAR IN CHAPTER 8.

## SUNDAY

### Breakfast
- Cinnamon-Vanilla French Toast* with Knudsen sugar-free fruit syrups or sugar-free jam
- Turkey sausage or patties
- Melon
- Juice
- Coffee

WC: Skip the sausage and have a choice of juice or melon.
LC: Skip the sausage.

### Lunch
- Halibits*
- Fruit salad
- Green salad with whole wheat roll (and without butter)

WC: No-oil dressing, and make sure the Halibits are sautéed in Pam.
LC: Make sure you use oat bran on the Halibits and that the oil is canola or olive.

### Dinner
- Roast Turkey Breast with Mustard Sauce*
- Zucchini and carrots steamed with tarragon and parsley
- Baked potato with nonfat yogurt and chopped scallions (or chives)
- Apple Tart* with frozen yogurt or sorbet

WC: Use the mustard sauce from the turkey instead of yogurt on your baked potato, have sugar-free sorbet or fruit instead of frozen yogurt.
LC: Have sorbet instead of frozen yogurt, and soy-based margarine on the potato instead of yogurt.

# MONDAY

## Breakfast
- Low-fat muffin with sugar-free jam
- Two eggs, poached or scrambled with Pam
- Fresh berries
- Juice
- Coffee

WC: One egg poached on whole wheat toast or no toast and a muffin (fat-free) instead; either berries or juice, not both.
LC: No eggs, make sure muffin is oat bran, and have extra fruit.

## Lunch
- Cajun Quesadilla*
- Fresh salsa
- Apple

WC: Make sure the cheese is the Lifetime or other low-fat variety, and that everything is sautéed in Pam.
LC: No cheese on the quesadilla.

## Dinner
- Orange Roughy with Ginger Sesame Sauce*
- Brown rice—or Hain Oriental rice side dish
- Yellow squash, julienned and steamed, sprinkled with garlic seasoning and Parmesan cheese
- Frozen yogurt and oatmeal cookies

WC: Cook the rice without oil and go lightly on the Parmesan. Always opt for fruit as a dessert first. If you want something more, then have only a small amount of nonfat frozen yogurt and no cookies.
LC: Use Soyco's Parmesan, no frozen yogurt. Have sorbet or Tofutti.

# TUESDAY

## Breakfast
- Oatmeal or natural cereal with fruit or nuts and low-fat or nonfat milk
- Grapefruit
- Juice
- Coffee

WC: Have a puffed or low-fat flake cereal with nonfat milk, plain oatmeal with choice of juice or fruit, not both.

LC: Opt for the oatmeal or a health bran cereal with oat bran, nonfat milk.

## Lunch
- Fantastic Foods soup in a cup (choice of variety) or a healthy version of canned vegetable soup
- Turkey Burger* on whole wheat roll with sliced lettuce, tomato, mustard, ketchup or soy mayonnaise
- Banana

WC: Make one of Westbrae's miso noodle soups (also instant) or any of the Pritikin soups; have the Turkey Burger plain—no bread, no mayo.

LC: Make sure your choice of soup does not have any cheese or other ingredients that affect cholesterol.

## Dinner
- Grilled Lime Chicken with Two Salsas*
- Steamed baby new potatoes
- Steamed broccoli with grated nonfat cheddar
- Whole wheat roll
- Baked Apple* with sorbet

WC: Have either the roll or the potatoes, not both, and skip the sorbet; just have the Baked Apple.

LC: Use Soyco's grated Cheddar cheese.

## WEDNESDAY

## Breakfast
- Whole wheat English muffin with (soy-based) margarine and sugar-free jam
- Plain nonfat yogurt with fruits and nuts
- Melon
- Juice
- Coffee

WC: No margarine, plain or fruit nonfat yogurt, choice of melon or juice.

LC: No yogurt; try scrambling beaten egg whites with some grated Soyco cheese in the middle.

## Lunch
- **Shrimp Pasta Salad Primavera** (See "How to Fill Your Refrigerator with Food for One Week" in Chapter 8)
- **Fruit**

WC: Use an oil-free dressing.
LC: Use oat bran pasta.

## Dinner
- **Turkey Scallopini\* over pasta with Parmesan cheese**
- **Steamed baby carrots**
- **Chopped spinach sprinkled with balsamic vinegar**
- **Healthy brand cookies and Ice Bean**

WC: Make sure your scallopini is sautéed without any oil and go easy on the cheese. Have either apple cinnamon rice cakes for dessert or a Weight Watchers popsicle, but always opt for fruit first.
LC: Make sure your scallopini is sautéed in olive oil, or canola oil. Use the Soyco Parmesan and make sure your cookies have bran. Have sorbet or Tofutti rather than Ice Bean.

## THURSDAY

## Breakfast
- **Oat bran waffles (available frozen in your health food store), or oat bran pancakes, and sugar-free fruit syrup**
- **Fruit**
- **Juice**
- **Coffee**

WC: Only have one waffle or pancake, and either fruit or juice, not both. Eat more fruit than you would waffle or pancake (which should be cooked with Pam).
LC: Go for it.

## Lunch
- **Shelton Farms chicken or turkey dogs on whole wheat buns with mustard and sauerkraut**
- **Healthy no-salt corn chips**
- **Orange**

WC: Have the chicken or turkey dog with lots of mustard and sauerkraut.

Have pickles instead of chips, or a few rice snaps and some carrot or celery sticks.

LC: Make sure the corn chips are made with a heart-healthy oil, or look for oat puffs, which contain oat bran.

## Dinner
- **Cha Cha Cha Chicken***
- **Brown rice**
- **Salad with Oil-Free Vinaigrette***
- **Kiwi and papaya (look for frozen berries if the fresh is not in season)**
- **Rice Dream—any flavor**

WC: Sauté the chicken according to recipe in white wine and broth. Choose a Weight Watchers ice cream bar or a low-fat cookie.

LC: Add 2 Tbs. oat bran to rice.

## FRIDAY

### Breakfast
- **Scrambled eggs with whole wheat toast**
- **Fruit salad (mix any fresh fruits)**
- **Juice**
- **Coffee**

WC: Scramble the eggs in Pam, dry toast, choose fruit or juice.

LC: Have an egg-white omelette with Soyco cheese, cooked in Pam.

### Lunch
- **Shelton Farms chicken bologna sandwich with pickles and corn chips**
- **Grapes**
- **Low-fat cottage cheese (not more than 1 cup)**

WC: Chicken bologna alone wrapped in Boston lettuce (instead of bread) with mustard or some tofu mayonnaise (on page 198). Skip the corn chips and have Skinny Munchies, low-fat style chips.

LC: No cottage cheese, and make sure your bread has oat bran.

### Dinner
- **Spaghetti with marinara and Parmesan**
- **Hearts of palm salad with balsamic vinegar**

- Whole wheat roll
- Apple Tart* with sorbet, or Ice Dream

WC: Use an oil-free pasta sauce and very little Parmesan, no roll as you are having plenty of carbs with the pasta, and choose either the Apple Tart or the sorbet.
LC: Use the Soyco Parmesan, and have only the Apple Tart. Toss your spaghetti in olive oil after it comes out of the water.

## SATURDAY

### Breakfast
- Buckwheat pancakes with the sugar-free fruit syrups (every health food store has a great mix for whole wheat or buck wheat pancakes)
- Any fresh fruit
- Juice
- Coffee

WC: Have one pancake with syrup, and a lot of fruit, or skip the juice.
LC: Go for it.

### Lunch
- Tacos*
- Fresh salsa with salt-free corn chips
- Jicama Salad*

WC: The tacos according to my recipe are fine, have extra salsa and no chips, and jicama salad.
LC: Make sure the chips are cooked in a nonsaturated or nonhydrogenated oil, and skip the cheese on the tacos.

### Dinner
- Stuffed Trout Provencal*
- Frozen or fresh green beans tossed with margarine and Romano cheese
- Wild rice with peas
- Corn on the cob
- Rice Dream, oatmeal cookies

WC: Use plain herbs on the vegetables, you will have sauce from the trout to pour over them. No butter on the corn, if you have to have something, then sprinkle herbs or a little fat-free dressing on it. Have fruit for dessert.

LC: Add 2 Tbs. oat bran to rice and make sure the margarine is soy based. Skip the cheese. Have sorbet instead of Rice Dream.

You probably noticed almost every dinner on this menu plan calls for steamed vegetables and you're probably thinking, boring, boring, boring! But really, they're not; no one hates bland food more than I do. Sprinkle seasoning mixes on those veggies, pep them up with fresh herbs, drizzle a tiny bit of cheese on top for flavor. They will not taste boring and you will be getting lots of fiber, vitamins, and minerals. Plus, they'll fill you up. Get in the habit of eating steamed veggies often.

. . . . . . . . . .

## Coping With "Bad" Food Cravings

You might very well have just read the preceding menus and said to yourself, "I could follow those easily—until my daily craving for potato chips . . . or m&m's . . . or a chocolate croissant kicked in." One reason I believe so many structured diet programs fail is because we are all subject, and somewhat enslaved, to our food cravings. Most of the time we attribute them to some deep-seated childhood problem or simply a lack of being in control, stable, and responsible, a sure sign of failure in a world of thin successes. Cravings creep up on you from nowhere, alien to your best endeavors as a healthy eater, fully in control.

The good news is that cravings are not something from the *Twilight Zone*. They are real, they are valid, and the more you learn to listen to and interpret your cravings, the more successful you'll be at getting and staying thin and healthy. The bad news is that does not mean indulging in every single craving that hits. It is obvious from Beth's food journal that she craved nothing but carbohydrates, the carbs we know as cookies, bread, and pasta, not the unadulterated vegetable kind (they're complex carbohydrates too). Fine, they're healthy, but as I described in Chapter 4, eat too many of them and you're not going to burn them off. In the book *Eat to Win*, the author emphasizes an extra-high-carbohydrate diet. Swell, he's a marathon runner, but Beth is not. In fact, when we started she didn't have an exercise program, so her body really packed away that extra fuel as, alas, fat.

The worst thing you can do is pretend that you're not going to have cravings just because you're trying to lose weight and eat more healthfully. If anything, they'll get worse and you'll become all the more aware of them. Everything you sweep under the carpet is bound to come out sometime. The smartest approach is to identify what your personal "bad" food cravings (anything from chocolate to a greasy burger to creamy Camembert cheese) are, when they most often hit, and under what circumstances. Then develop a strategy to handle them. And when I say handle them, I mean even giving in to them if you have to, letting it go at that and not feel that you've blown it. Accepting your own cravings and weaknesses without thinking they will get the better of you.

For some people, I know, giving into a craving can trigger a full-scale binge—the old "no one can eat just one" syndrome. One woman I know of buys a pint of ice cream, takes one or two bites, then immerses the carton in hot water to melt the rest. Otherwise she would eat the whole pint. Know what food does that to you. For me it's cookies. Once I start, I can't stop eating them—so I only keep ones in the house for my family that don't turn me on. Sound selfish? It's not. They have the foods they need and they have a slim, healthy, happy mama, which is more important than a box of cookies. Another way to keep from binging is to buy things in small containers, for example, an individual pack of cookies, not a box; the miniature Häagen Dazs cups; or a snack-size, not regular-size, bag of potato chips—you get the idea.

Ideally, though, instead of going for the real thing you can find a substitute that will be equally satisfying—actually more satisfying. If I want, say, chocolate, I'll have one-half pound (about 20 pieces) of low-sugar, low-cal chocolate fudge candies. They appease my taste buds and let me know that I'm not going to feel or look like a mess the next day. I get double satisfaction. If I were to choose one-half pound of Oreo cookies instead, I might feel happy while I'm eating them, but afterward my mind and body would be going in circles, I'd be consumed with guilt and anticipating the next day's weight gain and sugar hangover. Plus, when you choose lower fat and calorie indulgences, you can eat more food and pay less for it. For Brian Wilson, who lost more than 115 pounds, his way of releasing stress was to indulge in Oreo cookies. He used to feel so guilty about it that it would stress him out even more. Now Brian has the fat-free cookies from Health Valley and can indulge himself without the added stress. For the times that he has to have the real thing, he does—and then eats lighter the next day, drinks a lot of water to flush out his system, and runs a little farther. If you do indulge in the real thing for your cravings (maybe even overindulge) then don't get crazy about it. Just wake up the next day and get back on track.

Unfortunately, when I was a dancer there weren't as many wonderful alternatives to junk foods as there are now. These days, there is a whole world of healthy substitutions. The ones I've listed here will satisfy the taste sensations we seek out most. If none of the substitutes seem appealing then, again, have the real thing, accept that you are human and clean up your act the next day. (Note: once in a while, I'll recommend junk diet foods. But, because they generally contain chemicals and because eating them all the time will keep you from getting in the habit of eating better foods, I suggest that you only have them when you're having a desperate snack attack.)

## *Chocolate*

This is probably the most commonly craved food—and eating it the most common cause of guilt. Women especially go crazy for it during PMS, those few days before their periods when they just happen to be standing in line at the supermarket and the 3 Musketeers bar that they usually ignore begins to call their names, conjuring up childhood memories and making their mouths water. That's a craving all right—*more* than just a normal desire to consume a certain food. Giving into a chocolate craving isn't so bad unless it gets out of hand, leading to a full-scale binge (the old "as long as I've blown it" syndrome). I decided after my daughter Nolina was born that I did not intend to live my life without ever having chocolate, or completely hating myself every time I did. Life is both too short and too long never to indulge in something that you truly love. I suggest keeping low-calorie chocolate foods around all the time, ones that will provide the flavor fix you need, but won't make you feel guilty and cause you to go off on a chocolate-eating rampage. And with the following products at home, you can skip the one-pound chocolate fudge bar or pint of rocky road or the bag of chocolate chips that were supposed to be for baking anyway. Look for:

- Low-cal chocolate candies—made by Taffy-Lite, they come in a variety of flavors (not only chocolate), are about 8 calories each, and look like large gumdrops. I have seen them on both coasts so they shouldn't be too hard to find.
- Low-cal, low-fat chocolate ice cream bars—Weight Watchers and Fudgesicle brands.
- Sugar-free chocolate mousse—Sans Sucre (available in the pudding section).
- Sugar-free chocolate pudding—Jell-O brand.
- Chocolate chewing gum—Bazooka.

- Diet hot chocolate—Swiss Miss and Nestlé brands.
- Diet chocolate sodas—Shasta and Famous Amos brands.
- Carob animal crackers.
- Entenmann's fat-free chocolate sponge cake.

Most of these are diet junk foods and only meant to stave off cravings—don't make eating them a regular habit.

## *Salt*

As I said earlier, salt *is not* a killer food and craving it is very natural. It's a major component in the food-satisfaction factor. That isn't to say that overdosing on it can't lead to water retention and, for some people, high blood pressure (that's why it's important to check with your doctor), so try to keep it at a minimum. Also: beware that salt is usually combined with other more harmful ingredients. When it's on potato chips, peanuts, or processed crackers, it's keeping lousy company with oils and other fats. Next time you get the munchies and are looking for something you can wash down with beer, try some of these:

- Rice crackers and puffs—see shopping guide for different varieties.
- Low-cal cheese puffs—baked, not fried.
- Sliced jicama dipped in salsa.
- Spicy salsa on anything.
- Sliced water chestnuts in lite (reduced-sodium) soy sauce.
- Pickled vegetables—mostly in the Italian foods section, under various brand names.
- Unsalted dill pickles—they'll still taste salty.
- "Baldy" pretzels—unsalted on top, they're still made with salt and taste somewhat salty.
- Caviar—not fattening, but *not* for those who have a cholesterol problem.
- Oriental rice snaps—many are made without any oils (check labels) and contain salty tamari.
- Hearts of palm or canned artichoke hearts without oil.

Instead of sprinkling salt on your food, try these seasoning substitutes:

- Lemon juice.
- Garlic—fresh, granulated, or powdered.
- Capers.
- Vinegar.

- Chilies and peppers.
- Seaweed.
- Tabasco sauce.
- Worcestershire sauce.
- Dijon or any mustard.
- Parsley Patch Garlicsaltless seasoning (has a salty flavor).

## *Fat*

This is the craving that is most misunderstood. Obviously no one craves a glass of corn oil or wants to sit down and carve up a good stick of butter. What you want is some food that has fat in it, a salt-fat or sugar-fat combo. It's the texture, and sensation, that is most appealing. Also, foods high in fat are quickly filling, and literally "stick to your ribs," giving you a feeling of immediate satisfaction. That usually translates into craving something greasy like pizza, burgers, cheesy nachos, or ice cream—you crave the food, not the fat alone. However, fat is one of the biggest factors in today's foods and most people are literally addicted to it.

Until recently, the only answer seemed to be going cold turkey and going on something like the boring Pritikin (puritan) diet. So who'd want to make the switch? This was the problem presented to me when I began working with a famous blues musician. Here was a man raised on deep-fried chicken and sweet potato pie. He had gone to Pritikin and literally locked himself in the place several times. He lost the weight, took the Pritikin products home with him, and within a week was back at the fried chicken, pizza, and pie. He was back with a weight problem too. But it does not have to be all or nothing. Unlike sugar and salt, there haven't been any real substitutes for fat that we can use in our homes. Which is why major food corporations are in the midst of turning out alternatives like Simplesse and Olestra. Are they really any better? Maybe they won't make you fat, but they're not likely to be very healthy. And they'll never get you unhooked from that fat flavor. I think if you take a real approach—that is, eat as few fats as possible—you'll be much more successful. Because the good news is that the fewer fats you eat, the harder it becomes for your body to digest them, and as time goes on the cravings really do go away or at least lighten up. But when you do have to have something that contains fat, try to define the category of fat you're craving and make the least-offensive choice. For example:

- If you crave cheese, go for one of the low-fat cheeses on the market today like New Holland or Lifetime—as I've traveled, I've found low-fat cheeses in all markets.
- If you crave a greasy burger, make it lean ground beef and grill it until it's well done (so much of the fat cooks out), leave out the mayo, and layer on mustard, pickles, tomato, and lettuce. Better yet, make it with ground turkey.
- If you crave a sandwich smothered in mayonnaise, try to use an oil-free salad dressing or mustard instead or, if you must, a reduced-calorie mayo (just don't double the portion because it's reduced). Truthfully, you are better off eliminating it from your life, including the reduced kinds.
- If you crave olive oil, just use half of what you'd normally use, and if you're trying to keep pounds off, don't use it on a regular basis.
- If you crave French fries, try new potatoes, steamed and dipped in mustard. Or look for the frozen fries in your local health food store that are baked, not fried.
- If you crave butter, go for the Butter Buds substitute but, again, don't use it on a regular basis.
- If you crave peanut butter, give up and eat it—pare down your meals the next day. There is no substitute for peanut butter.
- Ice cream. The real thing has a lot of butter fat. Face it, the good stuff is based on cream, but there are hundreds of reduced, light, low-fat, and now the Simplesse versions on the market. Pick one that has the lowest amount of butter fat (ice milk, for instance, doesn't even have enough fat to be legally called ice cream). There are also frozen non-dairy products like Rice Dream and Ice Bean, which taste like ice cream but are healthier for your body. And, of course, there are lots of nonfat kinds of frozen yogurt (but don't be fooled into thinking they are healthy like plain nonfat yogurt in a carton).

## *Sugar*

Sugar, like salt, has been picked on long enough, even though, like salt, it has been overused in the food products created this century. But sweet cravings are also as natural as salt cravings and should never be dismissed. As I said about chocolate, eating sweets is not a sin. What is a sin is to think you have to live your life without sweets or to feel terribly guilty every time you have them. Sugar by itself is not all that damaging, although I wouldn't call processed white sugar a healthy product. Yet it's important to deal with not just what's healthy, but what is a reality. And the reality is that everybody craves a little (sometimes a lot of) sugar in their lives. You just don't want to overdo or binge on it frequently so that you suffer the sugar blues or don't burn the calories off. Because sugar is mostly glucose, which the body uses for energy, sugar calories get burned quickly and are not stored as fat. Dancers and athletes often have honey or candy before they perform for a fast jolt, knowing that they'll use those calories right away. But the body will only burn what it needs, so eat too many sugar calories and it's likely to show up around your middle and on your thighs. And when you do eat sugar foods, go for ones that don't contain fat, such as:

- Low-cal, low-sugar hard candies like Lifesavers.
- Sugar-free chewing gum.
- Fruit.
- The low-cal low-sugar candies listed under "Chocolate."
- Jujubes.
- Panda red licorice.
- A small package of Jujyfruits or hard candies and hard lollipops; even mints are low cal.
- All-natural fruit drops.

When cooking, try these substitutes:

- Apple (or any fruit) concentrate.
- No-sugar jams.
- Fructose.
- Sugar substitutes—only when absolutely necessary.
- Sweet sherry or a liqueur
- Knudsen all-fruit syrups

# 7

# Real Problems, Real Solutions: $R_x$ for Day-to-Day Dilemmas

**I**F OUR DAYS were always the same, if the food available to us were always healthy and nonfattening, eating well would be a breeze. But there's inevitably something that will put a crimp in the plan: You're stuck in the middle of nowhere with only crummy diner food to eat. Aunt Betsy is foisting her famous sugary holiday cookies on you—and you *want* to eat them! You skip dinner to take the kids to a carnival, only to find that cotton candy is about the lightest thing there to eat.

There are a hundred situations that *can* trip you up, but they don't *have to* trip you up. What follows is an emergency guide for eating well under (almost) any circumstance.

# Lunch: The Meal That Most Makes You Feel Like a Victim

Aside from what I said about lunch in Chapter 6, I wanted to address it even further, because it presents a problem for so many people. If you pack your own lunch, there's no reason it shouldn't be healthy and non-fattening. If you dine out in restaurants (or order in), Chapter 9 should help put you on the right track. But all too often, there's no time to make lunch for yourself in the morning or even time to spend having a leisurely lunch out. Whatever you can grab quickly from the company cafeteria or lunch truck usually has to suffice. Lunch trucks and street vendors are especially dangerous because when you just grab something and munch it as you walk along, instead of sitting down to eat, it gives you the false sense that you're not consuming much. In fact, you may be consuming more fat and calories than you would if you were having a regular meal. It's the same idea as when you raid the refrigerator or pick at the leftover pie as you stand at the kitchen counter—it's just a quick bite, not really eating, you tell yourself. This is victimization at its worst because you are victimizing yourself.

The truth is, lunch trucks and cafeterias are out to make a living, which is why they have little to offer but low-budget, cardboard junk. There's no way they can serve anything resembling quality food and make a profit. I admit that street food has always had a special appeal in countries around the world: hot dogs with sauerkraut, giant pretzels, and hot chestnuts in New York; slices of watermelon and fresh coconut in Venice; crepes with jam in Paris; gelati in Florence; sausage in Germany; jicama with chili and lime in Mexico—these are all wonderful treats. But obviously, some of them just wouldn't do for a healthy lunch every day.

If you can, avoid lunch trucks, street vendors, and company cafeterias just like you avoid McDonald's. If you're stuck, once again, do the best you can. Most of the trucks and cafeterias have fruit and, often, a pre-prepared turkey sandwich (ask if it has mayonnaise—if so, forget it). Many have low-fat yogurts, crackers, or plain rolls, which would be fine. Try a lunch of tomato or V8 juice, a small container of cottage cheese, a roll, and fruit. Or just have a couple pieces of fruit and a roll or crackers. There may also be premade salads that, if you think ahead and bring your own oil-free dressing or sprinkle with lemon and mustard, can be a good choice.

Remember, you don't have to dine famously at every meal. If there is absolutely nothing healthy on the truck or in the cafeteria, then have some juice and crackers to tide you over and wait for your next meal to get some decent food. Or plan to treat yourself later: "Okay, so lunch was crackers and V8, I'll stop on the way home and pick up a great cut of swordfish for dinner"—or anything else that makes you feel good. (Within reason—obviously, not a pail of Kentucky Fried Chicken). This is a better way to deal with the situation than to just say, "There's no other alternative so I might as well have the enchilada and chips or roast beef sandwich and cole slaw."

The ideal lunch is one you make yourself. If you've always been too busy or just lazy about it, maybe now is a good time to change your ways. It's one of the most important things you can do in avoiding being a victim. In an office situation, there is almost as much pressure about what you eat for lunch as who you eat it with. It begins early in grade school when children start sharing lunchtime—and lunches. My daughter has begged me to let her buy a hot lunch at school because a certain friend is going to be having one and the hot lunch kids sit at a different table than the cold lunch kids. And the cold lunch kids sit, compare, and trade off most of the lunch their parents made them anyway!

Similarly, the "wrong" lunch at work can set you up for social pressure. Bring a brown bag and sit at your desk sipping a diet soda and eating carrot sticks and low-fat anything and you're instantly on trial: "Oh, are you dieting?" a co-worker will ask, and if you are trying to lose weight, the question comes across as, "Oh, are you fat?" But it's none of anyone's business whether you are trying to lose weight or if you're just observing some sort of religious holiday. What you put down your throat goes into—and on—your body and you have to live with it. Most people are slightly challenged by others who eat healthfully and a little threatened by their control. If this kind of pressure comes from someone higher on the rung than you who you want to impress, it can be debilitating. But jobs and supervisors come and go. The desire to be thin and healthy doesn't. Know your rules and stick to them and no one can take that away from you.

So now that I've convinced you to pack your lunch, what should you pack? Here are some ideas:

- Any raw vegetables (except avocado).
- Pickles or other pickled vegetables not marinated in oil (hearts of palm, artichoke hearts, even canned beets).
- Vegetables steamed the night before (you can buy them presliced at

the store or buy the frozen microwaveable packages), then tossed with an oil-free salad dressing with some baby shrimp.
- Low-fat, low-calorie crackers and rice cakes.
- Crispy bread flats instead of potato chips.
- Nonfat yogurt or a small slice of low-fat cheese.
- Individually wrapped string cheese.
- 25-calorie-per-ounce tofu and herb spread (see page 198) with crackers or raw veggies.
- Slices of chicken breast, turkey, or cold seafood.
- A turkey, turkey meat loaf, or chicken breast sandwich on whole wheat bread with mustard or fat-free dressing.
- Tuna mixed with fat-free dressing in a pita with any of the following: cucumber, tomato, lettuce, watercress, mushrooms, and hearts of palm.
- A salad with oil-free dressing.
- Soup made without oil or fats (Pritikin, or one you make yourself) or instant soups (choose Health Valley, Hain, Westbrae Natural, or any other kind made without preservatives).
- Shredded lettuce, salsa, and white meat chicken rolled up in corn tortilla.
- A can of tuna (packed in water) sprinkled with balsamic vinegar.
- A pasta salad with oil-free dressing.
- Fruit, glorious, fruit.
- Applesauce.
- 95% fat-free ham or chicken bologna (yes, they have nitrates, but if you can't get to anything else, having them once in a while won't hurt).
- Leftover goodies from the fat-free dinner of the night before—even a container of leftover pasta is really satisfying when heated up. Or make a week's worth of food (see Chapter 8) and take along any of the items you've made.

Most of the time, lunch isn't even relaxing—it's just a quick refuel. So at least try to eat foods that will benefit, not destroy you by making you heavier or unhealthy. Try to evaluate the peer pressure and what it means to you. Or whether or not the lunch you eat is a reflection of stress you're feeling at work. If it is, perhaps you should let yourself go a little during lunch and clean up the rest of your meals. Just remember, there is always a way to get the food you want and need in this world. And if your co-workers think you're a little odd because you don't join in with the burgers-for-lunch crowd, chances are they'll also envy and respect you for looking slim and healthy.

## Avoid Feeling Helpless over the Holidays

During the holidays, it's not just one meal that's troublesome, it's up to two months of meals and parties. I had someone call me for a consultation simply to help her get through the fattening months of November and December without having to face another January of guilt, repenting, and making the same old boring New Year's resolutions. Because this woman works as an editor of a West Coast magazine, she attends a lot of parties over the holidays, so it was important to give her advice that wouldn't spoil her fun. Besides, holiday time is not the time to go on a strict diet and refuse all temptation. Then again, it doesn't have to be a time when you just give up—and blow up. Basically, what I told her was to pick her sins wisely. In other words, just because there is candy over here, cookies over there, eggnog in the corner, and a tray coming round with fruit cake, don't feel you have to have everything. You know you're going to be confronted with an ungodly amount of unhealthy temptations, so figure out which of the holiday delights you love or crave most. For instance, I can pass up truffles and cheeses, but I cannot resist my mother's saffron buns on Christmas morning. But I don't let that set me off or start putting everything I see in my mouth. At one time it did, and that led to the classic binge and purge syndrome. I have no desire ever to do that to myself again. Know what indulgences you're going to go for and you probably won't feel helpless in the face of all others. Then, keep some of these other strategies in mind, too:

- *Never go to a holiday party starving.* You will usually have a drink right off and that will weaken your willpower to resist the cheeseball studded with nuts and assorted other fat-packed foods. But if you've eaten a little beforehand, the drink is less likely to go to your head and loosen your hors d'oeuvre–grabbing fingers. What should you eat before you go to a party? No, not carrot sticks. Then you'll just feel deprived. Cold chicken or turkey breast, some flavored rice cakes, bread, food that gives your stomach something to work on and makes you feel satisfied. If you're going to a party straight from the office, bring some fruit or rice cakes to work and eat them at about five o'clock. A banana might work just fine. For me I need some protein, so I have a can of water-packed tuna or some cold chicken before I go.
- *Keep a lot of your own treats around (give those sweet gooey gifts away immediately!) so that you have something special to come home to.* If you

know you have your low-sugar fudge candies at home or another treat, you might have a better chance of being able to pass on the truffles going around the office. When I have a bag of seedless red grapes at home, I forego dessert knowing that I can go home and munch on them while I soak in a hot bath. This is especially helpful when you're going home alone feeling lonely, convinced everyone else is snuggling up happily with somebody. It's great to know there's something delicious awaiting you. Again, go by your rules. Madeleine Stowe will go and buy sugarless fruit tarts or a pie from the local health food store and keep them around. This way she will pass up the double-rich chocolate cake and go home to a dessert that won't destroy her the next day. Also, for many people, one piece of that cake sets off a chain of eating every sugary treat they can get their hands on. Having something at home that you can relax with helps stop this chain. Pick a treat that you know is not going to set you back, but that you can still look forward to. It could be some fresh shrimp with a little cocktail sauce or some caviar rolled into hearts of palm or maybe just some two-calorie cheese puffs and an old movie. Be nice to yourself.

- *Just as you pick your "sins," pick your parties and meals.* For instance, I don't care much for Thanksgiving fare, so I don't eat that much. But when I attend my husband's company Christmas party, I know the food is going to be wonderful, catered exquisitely, and I intend to enjoy it — and I do. Likewise, you should choose which holiday festivities are worth throwing caution to the wind for and which are not. They very fact that food is "holiday food" doesn't mean you have to eat it — enjoy it, or not.

- *The same goes for different dishes served at parties and holiday dinners.* Which things on the menu do you care about the most? The gravy? The stuffing? The yams with marshmallows? Or the cheese-covered vegetable? You don't have to have it all. Skip the gravy and have extra cranberry sauce. It may be higher in sugar, but those carbohydrate calories are easier to burn off than the fatty gravy calories. Or skip the yams and push the cheese on the broccoli to the side. Let plain white meat turkey and dessert make up your whole meal if you like. Apply the rules that work for you. My friend Susan always flies home for the holidays. The minute she enters her mother's house, she reports, there is her brother, stirring up his yearly classic, not to mention powerful, batch of eggnog. "Between you and me," she said, "in order to deal with my mother, I *need* the eggnog. Then from there, I just go on and eat everything the entire week I'm home."

"Hold it," I said. "You feel that because the eggnog is fattening, that it is the undoing of your entire trip. Have the eggnog, especially if it relaxes you and allows you to be more comfortable with family situations. However, don't let that send you into a state of surrender so that you end up gaining six pounds. Pick the stuff you really want and need, and skip the rest. Gain two pounds, not six, and try to walk and exercise as much as possible."

- *Bring your own dish.* 'Tis the season to exercise your cooking skills. Bring a huge spinach soufflé to a dinner or scallop seviche to a cocktail party. Show off your low-calorie chocolate mousse—then be your own biggest fan. Make most of your meal the nonfattening food you brought. I attended three holiday parties in a row last year. To the first I brought a roast turkey. For the second I made an oil-free seviche. On Christmas day, I brought fat-free hors d'oeuvres and a low calorie chocolate cheesecake pie.

- *Putting in some extra workout time is the ideal way to keep the holidays from taking a toll on your hips.* However, with all the hustle and bustle this time of year, you might barely have time to squeeze in your normal workouts. If you only have a little time, try to keep the cardiovascular segment of your workout alive: you want to keep up the calorie burning, not worry about weight work and stretches. Or, if you usually do a half hour cardiovascular work and a half hour of toning exercises, you might want to devote the whole hour to cardiovascular to maximize your calorie-burning power.

## Other Sticky Situations . . . and How to Get Out of Them

Everyone expects it to be hard to eat healthfully over the holidays, but there are also countless other times when it's difficult to stick to your rules. Here are eight of the classic situations—and some not-so-classic solutions.

1.  **You're going to a baseball game or other sporting event and know that you're going to be up against snack bars full of the worst American food available.** Not to mention that everybody around you is going to be wolfing that very same food down in front of your face—it's enough to undermine anybody's willpower. Once again, take care of yourself and pack your own picnic. My friend Marcia and I always went to our local supermarket and packed a big

salad from the salad bar, tossed it with our oil-free dressing, then threw in a sack with a great loaf of sourdough bread, some nonfat cheese, and a pint of berries. Next thing we knew our husbands asked us to pack them the same picnic. Now everyone sitting around us at the ballpark is jealous. If that seems to be too much detail work, then pack your own sandwiches or bring some flavored rice cakes and fruit. Or stop at a deli and have them pack some sandwiches. You could even pick up some sushi to go. Use your imagination and enjoy the game without worrying about blowing up the next day. Marcia's husband is a baseball fanatic and a lot of times she ends up at a game on the spur of the moment—hungry. Instead of giving into the junk, she tries to eat some popcorn, maybe a few plain hot dog buns (no hot dog) and a glass of wine, until she can get home to have some protein, veggies, and fruit. Granted, it's a lot of starch but it's better than consuming all of the ballpark fats.

2. **You're attending a local PTA meeting, focus group, self-help group, or any meeting (not including Overeaters Anonymous) where the fare is most likely going to be doughnuts, cookies, and cakes.** First of all, I always carry small packets of nonfat milk powder to replace the fatty cream substitutes usually offered at these gatherings. But I also try to take charge of what's being served. Unasked, I still bring a big fruit salad or just a big bowl of fruit. Sometimes I'll bring some mini bran muffins and fat-free or oat bran cookies. Even a small bowl of diet candies is a good offering if you need something really sweet. Meetings are a time to share thoughts and feelings; share some nutritional ideas as well. If you are stuck and arrive starving, don't have something that is going to send you off on a binge. Skip the chocolate cake, and have four of the plainest cookies they have. Or have the pound cake, which is lower in fat and temporarily filling.

3. **You're going to the movies. Need I say more?** We are conditioned to start putting some kind of fun snack into our mouths the minute we hit the seat. Some people go through a large vat of popcorn even before the movie begins. Movies are a great form of relaxation so if there's anytime to pick your "sin," this is it. When you know you are going to the movies on a given night, don't have a heavy carb day; save it for the (unbuttered) popcorn. If you want to avoid popcorn, but like the crunch, pack the rice cake of your choice (remember, there are a large variety of flavors these days). I do not care for popcorn, but start to think about candy the minute I enter the theater. Sugar and movies go together in my personal thesaurus.

Sometimes I can be satisfied with some grapes or blueberries, especially if my weight is up, but most of the time I bring a small bag of low-sugar/low-cal chocolate candies. And no one gets one bite—they are for me, they're my treat! If I get stuck without the candies, I will sometimes indulge in a box of Jujyfruits, which is a much better choice than Milk Duds, chocolate raisins, or any of the other chocolate (and thus fat-packed) treats.

4. **You're going to a company picnic or a barbecue where there will be nothing but greasy ribs, burgers, and hot dogs roasting on the grill. All side dishes will be mayonnaise based, topped off with chips and supersticky desserts.** This is the time to most definitely BRING YOUR OWN! It is not a crime nor should it be an embarrassment, especially because nonred-meat eaters are pretty commonplace these days. Put a few pieces of chicken in a Baggie and politely ask them to grill it for you. If they are by chance already grilling chicken—but in a gooey sauce—just peel off the skin before you eat it. Bring a Tupperware container full of salad for yourself or offer to bring salad for all (the low-fat pasta salad on page 207 is a good choice). If you're not bringing your own green salad, bring your own dressing for the one that will surely be served. Enjoy the bread dipped in the salad dressing you brought, and indulge in the fruit salad.

5. **You're going to a Disneyland, Great Adventure, or Sea World kind of amusement park (or just the local fair) where the fare is a fantasy of gooey childhood delights.** This is a time when we revert back to our kid days, only to find our adult bodies paying the dues for those fattening, unhealthy kiddie foods. The thing *not* to do is to say to yourself, "Oh, there's no way I can possibly eat healthfully; therefore, I will just eat everything." No no no no no no no! If you look hard enough, you'll find that besides the ubiquitous snack bars, most of these places do have restaurants that serve sandwiches and even salads. And you can at least usually find unbuttered popcorn and fresh fruit. If you're not going to stop at one of the restaurants (because your kids insist you hit every ride), then either pack your lunch or opt for a grilled well-done hamburger on a (you can hope) whole wheat bun with mustard, tomato, and lettuce. Have the frozen yogurt over the deathly cotton candy and ask the candy apple people if they have a spare fresh apple. Choose one treat that really was your favorite as a child and go for it. Just don't eat everything in the whole park. Another solution: go on the most obnoxious

frightening topsy-turvy roller coaster ride there and you will be too sick to eat all day!

6. **You're traveling and must endure at least one meal during your flight.** I think we are all aware that you can now order special meals on any airline. However the diet menu is usually as bad if not worse than the regular menu. Once again, bring your own. If you can't manage to get the meal thing together before your flight, opt for the fish or poultry entrées and have the salad without the envelope of creamy goo. Ask the stewardess for any extra bread or fruit (many times they have more meals than they need) on board. Munch on crackers with your cocktail, not peanuts. Drink a lot of water, read, sleep, stretch, and try to hold your appetite until you get to your destination. If you have time to preorder a special meal don't opt for low-cal or vegetarian; they are usually still loaded with fat. Ask for a fruit or raw vegetable plate or the seafood platter. I ended up with a gorgeous shrimp salad once when I did this. As I will mention later on, if the flight is over twelve hours . . . give up, eat the stuff, then clean up your act once you land. There have been many diets suggested for avoiding jet lag and surviving a flight healthfully. They are all generally common sense: eat lightly, drink water, and avoid salty foods—basic good diet rules to follow.

7. **You arrive at your destination only to find it completely surrounded by every fast-food joint ever invented.** Just remember: in every town there is a market. In every market there is fresh produce—or at least canned or frozen vegetables. We spend many weekends and holidays in the mountains outside of LA. I bring most of our food with us, but when we decide to just up and leave, I have to do my shopping at the little market near our cabin. They always have frozen poultry as well as canned and frozen vegetables, which I buy and mix with pasta or rice and lots of seasonings. There are always apples available so I bake them instead of buying boxes of cookies, although that would seem much simpler. You just have to use your imagination and not succumb to the easiest way out. If you are staying in a hotel or motel and are stuck without a kitchen, you can still rely on the local market. Fill your room with healthy crackers, artichoke hearts, canned tuna, some diet dressing or vinegar, canned fruits without the sugar, or anything from the basic survival kit you would keep in your office (see Chapter 3). As far as eating out goes, let the chapter on restaurants (Chapter 9) be your guide. If you are depending on room service, then let them know about your

"food allergies" when you check in so that you don't have to repeat it every time you call for a meal. Have them stock your room with fruit and crackers. I'm sure they will accommodate you.

8. **A serious crisis occurs and you find you just can't face it without all those old "comfort" foods. Before you know it, you find yourself gaining weight.** Let me tell you a story about one of my clients whose mother recently died. When Dennis came to me he wasn't extremely overweight, but nonetheless had a troublesome ten extra pounds around his middle. He is a highly energetic, sweet, and giving person. First, Dennis told me that he had been a runner and so had never really had to worry about his weight, but he had stopped running six months before. He said that he knew he ate badly, but just couldn't seem to get control over it. The last time he was thin was when he went on a juice fast, but he had obviously gained the weight back. It was as if it was out of his hands. I listened to him talk, and all of a sudden his eyes welled up with tears. He then told me that his mother had died, he had made a major change in jobs, moved from one house to another, and had two friends die from AIDS. All in the past year! That's a lot of real crisis to handle, and the last thing anyone would want to think about was his weight. Dennis did not need any more deprivation. My suggestions to him was that he take baby steps. First, I told him, confront and deal with the pain of your recent losses. He mentioned that he had been thinking about seeing a therapist. "Go!" I said. The second step was to start running again. Not marathons or with any distance goal in mind, just a little here and there to remind his body of what it feels like to be in action. Third, I recommended that he ask himself two questions before he ate anything: "Why am I eating this, and do I really want it?" These are all small steps that will help get you through the pain, and back in a emotional state where you can begin to eat less, or restructure your food intake on a healthy basis. Dennis is still a good (and a slim) friend of mine, and he managed to lose ten pounds during last year's Christmas holidays.

At times like these, you are usually not emotionally capable of controlling what you eat. It's the "I just don't care" attitude that we all get when we feel depressed. However, you don't want to let this get so out of hand that you are using food as something self-destructive. Just like my client who created anorexia to avoid her real problems, don't let your real pain or problems create an unhealthy, unhappy body. Start with those baby steps, like recording what you're eating and why. Figure out how important it is to you to eat the foods you are eating. Most of the time people eat whatever is put in front of them. Start to look at what is going into your mouth, and eliminate things that you aren't really interested in. Step-by-step you will start to take more control over what you are eating.

## When to Give It Up

There will always be situations that arise when you simply don't have a choice but to eat what's accessible or has been put in front of you. Times when it's just not worth fighting. This is life. And, oddly enough, the more you accept that fact, the easier it will be for you to get through these times without letting them knock you off course. Go ahead, eat, don't feel anxious about it, and *cut back* the next day. Here's my give-it-up list:

Give it up when . . .

- Your new boyfriend/girlfriend makes you dinner—not only should you eat it, you must compliment them!
- Your new boyfriend's/girlfriend's mother makes you dinner—not only should you eat it, rave about it.
- You go to an elaborately catered wedding—just try to dance more than you eat.
- You're on a miserable plane ride for anywhere between 8 and 14 hours—just try to sleep more than you eat.
- You've had the worst week of your life—be kind to yourself and allow food to be a friend.
- You're in the hospital—the food's miserable, you're miserable, try to get well and get out.
- Your boss takes you to a great lunch—order as best you can and try for a great raise.
- You're at an elegant dinner and the meal has already been preordered and prepaid—do a predinner workout and enjoy the cuisine.
- You're at a bris—if you can eat, go for it.
- You're at any street fair that offers a city's cuisine—Taste of LA, NYC's Ninth Avenue Street Fair, the classic Little Italy feast, Garlic Festival, and so on—you're there for a reason, admit it, accept it, and clean out the next day.
- You just finished a 26.2-mile marathon—please, eat.
- The last three weeks of any pregnancy—your stomach is already hang-

ing out, you're uncomfortable, eat and worry about it after you have your baby.

- You're in Tahiti—go there and you will understand what I mean.
- You're in France, Italy, Greece, the Bahamas, the Caribbean, any great vacation spot—enjoy yourself, but come back to reality when you get home.

Certain occasions are about food. Let that be and understand that every day is not a holiday, that not every day will be fraught with crises. That is probably the hardest thing to learn about food. When to let it go, when to pull it back. And most of all, how to really enjoy it.

# 8

# Head for the Kitchen: How to Cook the Perfect Food

**I** LIKE TO REFER to my style of cooking as "Food for the 21st Century" or "The Perfect Food." Obviously, I say this without humility, but consider that the recipes ahead are all of the following:

- Healthy for you and your family.
- Nonfattening.
- Quick, easy, and convenient.
- Undeniably satisfying and delicious.

Obviously, the word *perfect* is a personal opinion, but I think that food that allows you to eat well without any worries or physical ailments to deal with is, well, *perfect*.

The reason why my food is all of the above *and* nonfattening is, quite simply, because I rarely cook with oil, never butter. Many of my clients are extremely upset when I tell them to stop cooking with olive oil.

These days they understand that butter is taboo, but not why olive oil is also taboo for a great many people. My mother cooked everything in garlic, olive oil, *and* butter, and it was wonderful. It smelled good, it tasted good, we looked terrible. Olive oil is a very healthy food, it's not evil. IT'S JUST FATTENING! Bottom line, the stuff turns to fat on your thighs, rear end, or whatever body part of yours that is susceptible to fat. It does not go into your system and supply your body with lots of vitamins and minerals, it goes into your mouth and makes a beeline for your fat cells. I think I've made my opinion on that topic clear.

The flavor of olive oil, like that of salt, sugar, butter, or any particular food, is something you become accustomed to. When you prepare food you expect it to taste a certain way on your plate. When you are expecting an olive oil taste, you feel disappointed if you don't get it. But I know that when you start to use spices and spice mixes, wines, soup broths, and other alternatives to flavoring food with olive oil and butter, you will get a pleasant surprise: great flavors, juicy foods full of gusto, and enormous satisfaction.

I would also like to clear up the matter of cooking with wine or other liquors to enhance your foods. Trust me, the alcohol burns off in the cooking process, as do the calories. Some people seem to feel guilty about cooking with any alcoholic beverage, but I really encourage you to buy some inexpensive wines and pour them on. It adds a great deal of flavor and replaces the moisture you need when you are cooking without fats.

Of all things, I encourage you to have an open mind. As I mentioned before, when I was young my mother would place strange and exotic foods in front of us and, frankly, I thought they were disgusting at the time. Now, I appreciate this education more than ever. Food has many different languages and it is important to know that no recipe is written in stone: you can experiment and change the way food is made to make it suit your life. I will not eat oils or fats. This doesn't mean I have to stop eating. Don't be afraid to cook in a way that is unfamiliar. Take a risk and you will discover a whole new world of food and have a healthier, leaner body because of it.

I believe that in the next ten years everyone will begin to cook the low/no-fat way. There's no reason to add lots of fats, salt, and sugar to food when you can cook in a manner that is healthy, gourmet, and—honestly—quick and easy. I know, you feel you've heard this before, only to find that following the recipe is like reading a legal document. I promise you that once you have all the basic ingredients in your pantry, you will find the following recipes so simple, you'll wonder how I got away with it.

I have many fancy, complex recipes (full of long procedures) in my files, but you won't find any of them here. Instead, what I've done is gather those that are extremely easy and doable, even if that sometimes means using dried herbs or premade mixes. I've found that the easier it is to cook something healthy, the more likely someone will be to cook in this fashion. That's what this book is all about—doing it. I don't want you hemming and hawing about how you couldn't make this or that dish because the ingredients were too difficult to find or the instructions were too complicated. I want to teach you how 1-2-3 convenient it can really be to make healthy, nonfattening food. Then you have no excuse but to try it or, to quote Nike, "Just Do It."

## Stocking the Larder

Just as you can look at the food in people's grocery carts and relate it to the way they look, you can also tell a body by its cupboards. As you "make over" your kitchen you will be making over your eating lifestyle, and ultimately, the way you look and feel. The following is a basic pantry list, foods to keep on hand so that you have all the things necessary for cooking healthfully at your fingertips. Cross-reference this with the shopping guide in Chapter 5 and you're all set.

### Seasonings

- McCormick Parsley Patch brand—Garlicsaltless, It's a Dilly, Salt Free Lemon Pepper, Popcorn Blend, Oriental Blend.
- Nile Spice brand—Ginger Curry, All Purpose, Cleopatra's Secret.
- Capello's chicken and vegetable seasonings.
- Paula's poultry seasoning.
- Sharwood's Tandoori.
- Chef Paul Prudhomme's blackened redfish cajun style.
- Any brand: oregano, basil, thyme, bay leaves, cumin, tarragon, granulated garlic, garlic powder, sage, rosemary, chili powder, celery flakes, parsley flakes, onion powder, minced onion flakes, ground ginger, dry mustard, cinnamon, nutmeg, regular- and coarse-ground pepper.

**Note:** Obviously you can add other spices and spice blends to this list. Just be sure to read the labels so that you don't end up with anything full of MSG, salt, sugar, and other additives.

### Cooking Liquids

- Dry white wine (preferably Italian or Spanish for a saltier taste).
- Dry red wine.
- Sweet sherry.
- Light soy sauce.
- Pritikin chicken broth (or any defatted brand).
- Bottled lemon juice.
- Bottled lime juice.
- Frozen apple and orange juice concentrates.
- Red wine vinegar.
- Apple cider vinegar.
- Balsamic vinegar.
- Tomato sauce.
- Cook's Garlic Gusto, Dijon, French Tarragon oil-free salad dressings.
- Olive oil.
- Canola oil (remember, these oils are for the person with no weight problem and high cholesterol; do not use them if you are trying to lose weight).
- Any oil-free or fat-free salad dressing.

### Miscellaneous

- Pam no-stick cooking spray.
- One of the olive oil or garlic sprays.
- Canned diced red bell peppers.
- Canned tomatoes.
- Mustards—Dijon, salt-free, and herb.
- Roasted sesame seeds.
- Sugar-free jams.
- Hain oil-free dry salad dressing mixes.
- Canned water chestnuts.
- Canned tuna.
- Tofu.
- Fresh or bottled salsa.
- Fresh garlic, red and yellow onions, shallots.
- Oat bran.
- Wheat germ.

- Variety of dry pastas—plain, spinach, herb, whole wheat, spaghetti.
- Variety of rice crackers, rice snaps, and rice puff products.
- Canned hearts of palm.
- Variety of rice—brown, basmati, wild rice.

## The Perfect Food

You will find that most of the following recipes are amazingly simple, aimed at teaching you some of the basic ideas of how to cook without oil and still have juicy, flavorful food. Once you make the transition to oil-free cooking you can take any recipe, gourmet or basic, and translate it with ease. I use the grill a lot as I live in southern California where it's always barbecuing weather, but don't give up on the grill recipes if you are caught somewhere in the dead of winter. Simply use the same ingredients and bake the food (chicken, turkey, whatever) first, then slip it under the broiler for about one to two minutes to add crispness. If you *are* grilling, make sure that when you remove the food from the grill that you place it right back in the marinade or liquid you used before. Don't forget to heat the marinade over a low flame or on the grill until it comes to a low boil (in order to kill any bacteria). The hot food will soak up the liquid and be very juicy when you serve it.

And don't be frugal with marinades, wines, or cooking liquids. You want to make sure you *replace* the moisture the food loses through cooking and that would ordinarily be replaced with oil. Plus, it's nice to have enough of the liquid remaining to flavor vegetables, rice, potatoes, or other side dishes. So pour on the juice.

As a final note, always adjust the seasonings in any recipe that you follow. Make sure you get plenty of flavor from your spices and spice mixes. I find that people tend to be too safe and, consequently, the food tastes too bland. We all know that fresh herbs are better than dried, but they are often a lot more expensive and not always easy to get. So the herbs listed in the following recipes are dried unless otherwise indicated. Also do not use ground seasonings, unless indicated, as they impart a different flavor.

Enjoy!

# Sinless Starters

## Simple Seviche

*Served with light crackers, this is a wonderful appetizer or lunch dish. Also, this is the type of dish I like to munch on to curb my appetite before I go out to eat. If available, add a diced mango to the mixture, too.*

**Makes 2 to 4 appetizer servings.**

¼ pound fresh scallops (bay or sea)

Juice of 3 limes

2 tablespoons chopped red onion

1 tablespoon minced fresh cilantro

2 teaspoons fresh basil

Pinch of pepper

2 green onions, chopped

½ each: red, green, and yellow bell peppers, diced (if you can't find yellow, then dice a whole red and a whole green)

1 can (8 ounces) stewed tomatoes

In a large bowl, marinate scallops in lime juice overnight in the refrigerator or for at least 2 hours. Drain lime juice and add remaining ingredients. Mix well and marinate for 2½ hours or more.

## Scallop Mango Seviche

*Here's a sweeter, fruitier take on the preceding recipe.*

**Makes 8 to 12 appetizer servings.**

1 pound large sea scallops, cut into quarters

Juice of 5 limes

½ cup raspberry vinegar

¼ cup bottled lime juice*

*Limes are often rather dry and lacking in juice, so I use part bottled juice. If you can find juicy limes, then use all fresh juice.

1 teaspoon salt

1 teaspoon pepper

2 each: red, green, and yellow bell peppers, diced

1 ½ red onions, diced

2 large (or 3 small) mangos, diced

6 plum tomatoes, seeded and diced

5 tablespoons chopped fresh cilantro

In a medium bowl, mix together the scallops, fresh lime juice, vinegar, bottled lime juice, salt, and pepper, and let sit in the refrigerator overnight. The next day, add the bell peppers, onions, mangos, tomatoes, and cilantro to the scallops. Taste and adjust seasonings, adding more lime juice, vinegar, salt, or pepper, if necessary. Serve alone or with blue corn chips.

## Jicama Chips with Salsa Cruda

*This fat-free alternative to chips and dip is great for munching on while watching television or if you're hungry before dinner. If jicama is hard to find in your area, use celery sticks to dip.*

**Makes 2 servings.**

1 cup chopped fresh plum tomatoes

½ cup V8 juice

¼ cup lemon juice

2 tablespoons chopped fresh cilantro

1 teaspoon Tabasco sauce

2 scallions, chopped

1 pound jicama, peeled and sliced into round disks or sticks for dipping.

Mix all ingredients, except the jicama, together in a bowl. Serve with jicama on the side. If not serving immediately, sprinkle some lemon juice over the jicama to keep it fresh looking.

# Non-Deviled Eggs

*Unlike regular deviled eggs, these contain no mayonnaise and, consequently, a lot less fat.*

**Makes 8 halves.**

4 hard-boiled eggs, halved
¾ cup soft tofu
½ cup nonfat yogurt
1 tablespoon Dijon mustard
2 teaspoons Worcestershire sauce
1 teaspoon garlic powder
1 teaspoon light soy sauce
1 teaspoon minced onion flakes
Pinch of pepper
Capers, for garnish

Separate the egg yolks from the egg whites. Place the yolks in blender container with the remaining ingredients, except the capers. Cover and blend on low until thoroughly mixed and creamy. Stuff the egg whites with the yolk mixture and place capers on top for garnish.

# Garlic-Vinaigrette Fennel Salad

*Fennel (also known as anise root) is a flavorful, licorice-tasting vegetable that has a satisfying crunch. This starter salad is made with garlic dressing, but can also be made with any other kind of oil-free vinaigrette.*

**Makes 4 servings.**

1 to 1½ cups Cook's Garlic Gusto salad dressing or other oil-free
    vinaigrette
Juice of 1 lemon
½ teaspoon minced garlic
½ pound fennel bulbs, sliced into ¼-inch rounds

In a large bowl, combine the salad dressing, lemon, and garlic. Mix in fennel and marinate overnight. Serve chilled.

# Manhattan Clam Chowder

*Of the two chowders—Manhattan and New England—always remember that Manhattan is the healthy one! New England is cream based. This version is a great recipe to cook on a Sunday so you have it around the whole week.*

**Makes 2 to 4 servings.**

I green bell pepper, diced
I yellow onion, diced
½ cup white wine
2 peppercorns
I ½ teaspoon thyme
I teaspoon basil
I bay leaf
Pinch of salt
5 new potatoes, cubed
4 fresh plum tomatoes, blanched and diced
3 carrots, diced
3 celery stalks, diced
3 cans (7 ounces each) clams
I can (28 ounces) diced tomatoes

In a large soup pot, sauté the bell pepper and onion in the wine. Once the wine has cooked off and the vegetables are transparent, add the rest of the ingredients. Bring to a low boil and let simmer for 30 to 40 minutes or until the potatoes are soft and the flavors have blended.

# Grilled Eggplant with Mozzarella
· . · . · . · . · . ·

*This is the kind of hors d'oeuvre your guests will never guess is nonfat. Use a soy-based mozzarella if cooking for high cholesterol.*

**Makes 8 servings.**

> 2 cups bottled or fresh oil-free vinaigrette*
> ½ cup lemon juice
> 2 tablespoons Dijon mustard
> ½ teaspoon cracked pepper
> I medium eggplant, sliced into ¼-inch rounds
> 6 to 8 ounces Lifetime or other nonfat mozzarella cheese, sliced
>     into ¼-inch-long sticks
> Toothpicks

In a large bowl, combine the vinaigrette, lemon juice, mustard, and pepper. Marinate the eggplant in the sauce for at least 1 hour. Grill or broil the eggplant slices until cooked through, about 5 minutes on one side, then turn and cook for about 1 minute more. When cool, wrap each eggplant round around a stick of mozzarella. Secure with toothpicks and serve.

*If you don't want to use a bottled dressing—and aren't fighting weight—then use olive oil and fresh minced garlic.

# Onion-Garlic Crackers with Herb Dip
· . · . · . · . · . ·

*Whenever I get an attack of the munchies, these crackers alone save me from dipping into the corn chips. With the dip, they're a perfect family snack.*

**Makes 6 servings.**

> 2 cups nonfat yogurt
> I package (I I ounces) Hain dry salad dressing mix, any flavor*
> Pepper
> Garlic powder
> I package (3.5 ounces) Edward & Sons Onion-Garlic Rice Snaps†

*If you can't find Hain mixes, use any other no-oil salad dry dressing mix.
†Again, if you can't find the same brand, look for any kind of low-fat rice snap. There are a variety in the Oriental section of your supermarket.

Combine the yogurt and salad dressing mix in a medium bowl. If desired, add pepper and garlic powder to taste. Serve with crackers.

## Munch-Crunchy Oriental Water Chestnuts
. . . . . . . . . .

*These will satisfy a salt craving, but without all the fat (although just as much crunch) that comes with chips. I have served these with beer at our Super Bowl–and boxing match–watching parties instead of peanuts, and they are a great hit. Men are more worried about their cholesterol than women are, and they are thrilled they can munch out and not sacrifice their hearts. This recipe gives you a choice of two different marinades—one that's really spicy, one that's sweeter tasting. If you want to save yourself the trouble of mixing the spices, try adding 1 teaspoon Nile Spice Ginger Curry seasoning to ¾ cup light soy sauce and toss with the water chestnuts.*

**Makes 6 servings.**

SPICY

  **¾ cup light soy sauce**
  **½ teaspoon turmeric**
  **½ teaspoon coriander**
  **½ teaspoon cumin**
  **½ teaspoon pepper**
  **¼ teaspoon garlic powder**
  **⅛ teaspoon cardamom**
  **⅛ teaspoon nutmeg**
  **⅛ teaspoon cinnamon**
  **Pinch of red chili flakes**
  **Pinch of ground cloves**
  **2 cans (5 ounces each) sliced (or whole) water chestnuts**

**OR**

SWEET

  **½ cup light soy sauce**
  **¼ cup apple juice concentrate**
  **I teaspoon ground ginger**
  **I teaspoon curry powder**

**Pinch of cinnamon**

**2 cans (5 ounces each) sliced (or whole) water chestnuts**

In a medium bowl, combine all ingredients except the water chestnuts and mix. Add water chestnuts and allow to sit for 30 minutes in the refrigerator before serving.

# Slivered Balsamic Carrots

*There are barely any calories in this recipe, but lots of gourmet flavor.*

**Makes 8 servings.**

**5 to 8 large carrots, peeled and cut on the diagonal into ovals**
**¾ cup balsamic vinegar**
**2 packets Equal\***

Lightly steam carrots until al dente. In a medium bowl, toss carrots with vinegar and Equal, then let marinate in the refrigerator for at least 1 hour.

*If you don't want to use Equal, use 2 teaspoons of honey.

# Pared-Down Poultry Dishes

## Chicken Tarragona
· · · · · · · · · · ·

*This recipe is simple and delicious, plus the gravy goes great over veggies or potatoes, not to mention soaked up on a good piece of sourdough bread. Or serve it over a bed of brown rice with a side of steamed broccoli.*

**Makes 4 to 8 servings.**

    8 skinless, boneless chicken thighs
    3 tablespoons Dijon mustard, regular or preferably with tarragon
    ½ pound mushrooms, thinly sliced
    I lemon, thinly sliced into rounds
    I ½ cups red wine
    I ½ tablespoons tarragon

Preheat oven to 500°. Line a 7 × 11 inch shallow baking pan with aluminum foil. Slather the chicken thighs with mustard and place "meaty" side down in the pan. Surround the chicken with mushrooms, lemon slices, and red wine. Sprinkle with tarragon. Bake until cooked through and the sauce is bubbling, about 20 minutes. Slide the pan under the broiler for about 2 minutes to crisp. Remove thighs from pan and serve with mushrooms spooned on top.

## Orange Teriyaki Chicken
· · · · · · · · · · ·

*This is as good cold as it is hot and the marinade is also great for fish and turkey. Serve with brown rice and steamed snow peas. You might want to make a double batch of the marinade and let half sit in the refrigerator for a week so that the sesame seed flavor expands, then make the dish again. I have friends who also use it as a salad dressing or pour it over their baked potatoes.*

**Makes 2 to 4 servings.**

> Pam no-stick cooking spray
> ¼ cup sesame seeds
> ½ cup frozen apple juice concentrate
> 6 ounces light soy sauce
> 4 tablespoons ground ginger
> 3 tablespoons dry mustard
> I can (12 ounces) frozen orange juice concentrate
> I teaspoon cornstarch mixed with ¼ cup water
> 4 skinless, boneless chicken breast halves (4 to 6 ounces each)

Preheat oven to 400°. On a baking sheet sprayed with Pam, roast the sesame seeds until a dark golden brown. (Keep turning over until evenly browned.) Place all of the remaining ingredients, except for cornstarch mixture and chicken, in a large saucepan. Simmer over low heat until all the flavors have blended, about 20 to 30 minutes. Add the cornstarch mixture and bring to a boil. Remove from heat and cool.

Place chicken breasts in a baking pan or bowl and pour the cooled marinade on top. Marinate for at least 1 hour in the refrigerator, then grill the breasts over a medium flame for 15 to 20 minutes on one side, 5 minutes on the other. In the meantime, place marinade in a saucepan and bring to a boil. Remove from heat. When chicken breasts are cooked through, place them back in the marinade to cool. Serve with slices of quickly grilled oranges.

# Grilled Lime Chicken with Two Salsas

*You can serve this dish with bottled salsas—a time-saver—or make your own salsa cruda (see Jicama Chips with Salsa Cruda on page 185). Serve with steamed new potatoes and steamed yellow squash.*

**Makes 2 to 4 servings.**

> 4 skinless, boneless chicken breasts (4 to 6 ounces each)
> 4 limes
> I cup bottled lime juice*

*If can find juicy limes, use all fresh lime juice.

½ cup frozen apple juice concentrate

2 cups red salsa

2 cups tomatillo salsa†

Preheat your grill, or make sure that your coals are red-hot to barely white around the edges. Place the chicken breasts in a baking dish. Squeeze the limes over them, then pour the bottled lime juice and apple concentrate over. Mix well and marinate in refrigerator for at least 1 hour. Grill breasts on medium heat 20 minutes on one side, then 5 minutes on the other. Place marinade in saucepan, bring to a boil, then remove from heat. Then place breasts back in the marinade after they come off the grill. Serve with bowls of salsa on the side.

†Preferably Scotty's salsas. If you can't find a tomatillo salsa, then use the recipe for Salsa Cruda (page 185) and the recipe for Papaya Salsa (page 197).

# Grilled Cajun Chicken

*This dish can be very spicy or mild, depending on the amount of seasoning you use. You can also use the cajun seasoning on red snapper, tilapia, or sole. Serve with wild rice and steamed broccoli or okra, for a Southern flair.*

**Makes 2 to 4 servings.**

4 skinless, boneless chicken breast halves (4 to 6 ounces each)

3 teaspoons cajun seasoning*

I cup lemon juice

Place the chicken in a baking dish and sprinkle with cajun seasoning. Pour in the lemon juice and marinate chicken for about 15 minutes. Preheat grill on high for 3 to 5 minutes. Reduce to medium heat and grill the breasts evenly on both sides, turning only once (about 7 minutes one side, about 5 on the other). If you can't grill, then heat a sauté pan until sizzling, pour in some chicken broth and sauté the breasts on both sides. Serve hot or cold.

*Cajun seasoning can be found under different brand names in many markets. If you are concerned about the salt, look for a salt-free version in the health food store.

# Cha Cha Cha Chicken

*This is a Caribbean dish that has a delightful blend of flavors, primarily an orange and cumin mix. Serve over a bed of brown rice with a light salad on the side.*

**Makes 2 to 4 servings.**

- 4 skinless, boneless chicken breast halves (4 to 6 ounces each)
- 3 teaspoons cumin
- ½ teaspoons pepper
- 2 to 3 cups Pritikin or other defatted chicken broth
- 1 to 2 cups white wine
- 3 garlic cloves, slivered
- 1 each: red, green, and yellow bell peppers, cut into ¼-inch julienne strips
- 1 orange, peeled, cut into ½-inch chunks (be sure to remove all white)
- ½ cup frozen apple juice concentrate

Season the chicken with 1½ teaspoons cumin and ¼ teaspoon pepper (rub the seasonings into the breasts with your fingers); set aside. In a large sauté pan, heat 2 cups broth, 1 cup wine, the garlic, and the remaining cumin and pepper. Bring to a low boil, then add the chicken. Sauté on both sides until done. Remove the chicken, drain, and set aside. Add the remaining wine and broth, and the sliced bell peppers. Continue to sauté over a medium heat. Sauté until bell peppers are tender-crisp, remove from pan and place on top of chicken. Add orange chunks and apple juice concentrate to pan and sauté for 1 minute, turning frequently. Remove and scatter the orange chunks over the chicken and peppers. As you cook this dish, you can add more cumin and pepper to the broth and wine according to your taste. By simmering, reduce the remaining liquid in the pan until slightly thick and pour over chicken dish.

# Southern Baked Chicken

·.·.·.·.·.·.·.·

*This dish—a healthy knockoff of fried chicken—is proof positive that food doesn't have to be greasy to taste good: It's so spicy and crunchy, you'll never miss the fat. Serve with a dipping sauce made of no-sugar marmalade combined with a touch of Dijon mustard and cold potato salad made from steamed new potatoes tossed in my version of mayonnaise (page 198). Or try it with classic baked potatoes and a green salad. The chicken is also ideal cold, packed for lunch.*

**Makes 4 to 8 servings.**

**3 egg whites**

**I teaspoon Worcestershire sauce**

**White pepper**

**I cup whole wheat flour**

**½ cup oat bran**

**¼ cup wheat germ**

**I tablespoon garlic powder**

**I tablespoon onion powder**

**½ teaspoon cinnamon**

**¼ teaspoon paprika**

**½ teaspoon red chili flakes**

**¼ teaspoon ground cloves**

**2 each: skinless chicken breasts, thighs, and drumsticks**

**I small can (13¾ ounces) Pritikin or other defatted chicken broth**

Preheat oven to 400°. In a large bowl, whisk together egg whites, Worcestershire sauce, and a pinch of white pepper; set aside. In another large bowl, combine remaining ingredients, except chicken and chicken broth. Add a pinch of white pepper. Roll the chicken in the egg mixture, then roll in the flour mixture until completely coated. Pour enough chicken broth in a large baking pan to coat bottom. Place the chicken in 9 × 12 inch shallow baking pan and cover with wax paper. Bake for 10 minutes, remove the wax paper, and cook until golden brown, about 10 to 15 minutes more.

# Roasted Whole Chicken

*If you are trying to lose weight—or just put on a pound looking at fat—make sure you remove the skin before eating the chicken. This is a classic and is best served with mashed potatoes (made with nonfat yogurt), roasted onions, carrots, and steamed green beans, or a nice green salad. Always keep the wishbone. Let it dry, then make a wish!*

**Makes 6 servings.**

- 1 three-pound whole fryer or roasting hen
- 1 apple, quartered and seeds removed
- 1 medium onion, quartered
- 4 cloves garlic, diced
- 3 tablespoons herb mustard
- 2 tablespoons rosemary
- 2 cups Pritikin or other defatted chicken broth
- 2 cups dry red wine

Preheat oven to 450°. Remove the giblets from the cavity of the chicken and place them in the bottom of a roasting pan. Rinse the chicken with cold water, inside and out. Stuff the cavity of the chicken with the apple and onion. Slip pieces of garlic under the skin of the chicken. Next, cover the chicken with the mustard and rosemary. Place the chicken on a rack in the roasting pan, then pour the broth and wine over chicken. Let the liquid stay in the bottom of the pan. Bake the chicken uncovered for 1 hour, or 20 minutes per pound, basting every 15 minutes with the liquid in the pan. To test for doneness, pierce the breast with a toothpick or fork—if the juice runs clear, it's done, if the juice runs slightly red, continue cooking for a few minutes more.

# Tandoori Chicken with Papaya Salsa

*This is a classic East Indian dish excellent cold or hot and best served with freshly chopped papaya or mango. I would almost insist that you serve this with the Papaya Salsa as it is a wonderfully sweet complement to the spicy tandoori flavor. If you don't have time to make the fresh salsa, then pick up Knudsen's Chunky Apple Pourable Fruit and mix it with a little ground ginger, cinnamon, and nutmeg. To round out the meal, serve brown rice and marinated cucumber slices on the side.*

**Makes 2 servings.**

**Papaya Salsa (below)**
**Sharwood tandoori seasoning***
**4 medium chicken breasts, skinned**
**6 limes**
**½ cup apple juice concentrate**

Make the Papaya Salsa. Sprinkle the tandoori seasoning over the chicken breasts; they should look bright orange. Place the breasts in a deep 11 × 7½ inch pan and squeeze the juice of the limes over them; add the apple juice concentrate. Marinate for at least 1 hour in refrigerator. Pre-heat the grill to high or until coals are red-hot. Grill for 20 minutes, and check for doneness by pricking to see if juices run clear. While chicken is cooking, place marinade in a saucepan and bring to a boil, remove from heat. Place the chicken back in the marinade before serving. Serve with the Papaya Sauce.

*If you can't find Sharwood seasoning, then look in your local ethnic food market for a tandoori seasoning.

## Papaya Salsa

I cup diced papaya (usually I whole fruit)
¼ cup diced red onion
¼ cup chopped fresh cilantro
2 tablespoons fresh lime juice
¼ to ½ jalapeño pepper, diced (depending on how spicy you want your salsa)
2 tablespoons fresh orange juice

Combine all ingredients in a medium bowl and let marinate in the refrigerator for at least 2 hours. Makes 4 3-ounce servings.

# Garlic Herb Chicken Salad
. . . . . . . . . .

*Well, here it is, the recipe that I have talked about all through the book. The answer to those gloppy mayonnaisey salads served at every restaurant across the country. You can use the tofu mixture in this recipe as an oil-free substitute for mayonnaise anytime—for sandwiches, tuna salad, baked potatoes, anything that calls for a great spread. I make tons of the stuff and keep it bottled in the fridge—it lasts about 8 weeks. The base for the spread is tofu and nonfat yogurt, but use your imagination and vary it with your own choice of spices. This recipe also calls for wheat berries, which I use in place of nuts in many recipes. They have a nutty flavor, but no fat.*

**Makes 2 servings.**

1 package (14 ounces) soft tofu

1½ cups nonfat plain yogurt

1 package (11½ ounces) Hain Caesar Salad Dressing dry mix (no-oil)

1 teaspoon dill weed

1 teaspoon lemon juice

1 teaspoon Grey Poupon Dijon mustard

2 grilled or other leftover cooked chicken breast halves, seasoned with garlic powder and cubed

2 green onions, chopped

½ cup cooked red wheat berries (optional)

Place the tofu, yogurt, dry mix dressing, dill weed, lemon juice, and mustard in a food processor or blender. Cover and blend well. (This mixture makes your basic "mayonnaise.") In a large bowl toss the tofu mixture with the chicken, green onions, and wheat berries.

# The Famous Turkey Meat Loaf
. . . . . . . . . .

*This recipe is a good example of how to take an old favorite and make it healthy and lean. Instead of using flour or bread crumbs to bind the meat loaf together, I use vegetables and wheat germ, a combination that also adds moisture (turkey is drier than ground beef), color, and texture. Serve*

*with the classic mashed potatoes (mixed with nonfat yogurt instead of milk) and peas or corn. The meat loaf leftovers make great sandwiches or can be kept frozen.*

**Makes 6 servings.**

¼ cup defatted chicken broth
½ cup white wine
½ large yellow onion chopped
I green bell pepper, chopped
2 cloves garlic, chopped
I zucchini, finely grated
I large carrot, finely grated
I pound ground turkey (breast is best)
¾ cup wheat germ
I egg
I tablespoon oregano
I tablespoon basil
I tablespoon pepper
2 cups tomato sauce

Preheat oven to 350°. In a large skillet, heat chicken broth and white wine over medium heat. Add onion, bell pepper, and garlic. Sauté until al dente. In a large bowl, mix the sautéed vegetables, zucchini, carrot, turkey, wheat germ, egg, and herbs. Mix well by hand. Form the turkey mixture into a loaf in a shallow (2-inch high) loaf pan. Cover with tomato sauce. Bake until cooked through, about 20 to 30 minutes.

# Roast Turkey Breast with Mustard Sauce

*After you read this recipe, you'll see just how easy preparing a nonfattening meal can be. I also like to just keep the turkey in the refrigerator for quick, nonfattening snacks. It is very versatile and can be served with any vegetable and potato or rice, plus it makes great sandwiches. Try spooning the leftover mustard sauce over a baked potato. If you can't find an herb mustard, then use a good Dijon and let the tarragon sit in it a while before preparing the turkey. Look for the boneless turkey breasts by Louis Rich that have a built-in thermometer.*

Makes 8 servings.

> 3 to 4 tablespoons mustard with Herbes de Provence (or any herb
> mustard)
> ½ turkey breast with the skin (2 to 3 pounds)
> 1½ teaspoon tarragon
> 1 teaspoon minced onion flakes
> 1 teaspoon dillweed
> ½ teaspoon white pepper
> 1½ cups white wine

Preheat oven to 350°. Slather the mustard on both sides of the turkey; don't be frugal. Sprinkle half the tarragon on the skin side of turkey; place skin side down in a shallow baking pan. Sprinkle remaining tarragon on top of turkey. Add the remaining spices to the white wine and pour over the turkey. Tent aluminum foil over the top of the baking pan. Place the turkey in the oven and bake for 15 to 20 minutes. Remove the foil and turn the breast over. Cook until done, about 7 minutes. To test for doneness, pierce the breast with a toothpick or fork—if the juice runs clear, it's done, if the juice runs slightly red, continue cooking for a few minutes more. Don't overcook—the turkey will keep cooking in its own heat after it's removed from the oven.

# Turkey Scallopini

*Another great version of an old favorite that is usually fattening and un-healthy. Serve this dish with some herb noodles or regular pasta and steamed asparagus. If you are cooking for people with no weight problem then feel free to use about a tablespoon of olive oil during the sautéing.*

Makes 6 servings.

> 1 pound turkey breast slices
> ¼ cup lemon juice
> ¼ cup dry white wine
> 2 cloves garlic, diced
> 1 teaspoon granulated garlic
> 1 teaspoon dry mustard

Pinch of white pepper

2 teaspoons capers

Rinse the turkey slices under cold water, then pound between sheets of wax paper very lightly to soften (use the bottom of a glass if you don't have a pounder). Place the lemon juice, wine, garlic, and seasonings, in a large skillet. Sauté the garlic until the liquid boils and the garlic has released its flavor. Add the turkey slices to the pan with the capers and cook very quickly (3 minutes one side, 1 minute the other) over high heat, turning only once. Cook until slightly pink in the middle (they'll finish cooking once removed from the pan). Pour the remaining sauce over turkey slices and serve.

# Stuffed Red Bell Peppers

*This dish is one of my best sellers in my home delivery service. Cher used to order these on a regular basis.*

2 medium red bell peppers

I pound ground turkey

I ½ cups brown rice*

5 medium plum (roma) tomatoes

I tablespoon Paula's Poultry seasoning

I tablespoon worcestershire sauce

I teaspoon parsley flakes

I ½ teaspoons dried minced onion flakes

I tablespoon Granulated Garlic

½ cup dry white wine

2 cups Pritikin Spaghetti Sauce (or any no-oil pasta sauce)

Preheat the oven to 400°. Prepare the brown rice according to package directions, then toss with the poultry seasoning, worcestershire sauce, parsley flakes, and onion flakes. Set aside. Slice the bell peppers lengthwise and remove seeds and cores, set aside. Saute the ground turkey in

*If you can find Hain's Chicken and Vegetable Side Dish, it is a great substitute for the brown rice and seasonings listed above. Make sure that you prepare it without oil.

the white wine and the granulated garlic, set aside to cool slightly. Mix the rice and ground turkey together in a bowl. Chop the plum tomatoes and mix in with the turkey and rice. Spray a 2-inch shallow baking pan with a non-stick cooking spray and place the bell peppers skin side down in the pan, close together. Stuff the bells with the turkey, rice, and tomato mixture and pour the pasta sauce over the top of each bell pepper until completely covered. Place aluminum foil over the top in the shape of a tent. Bake at 400° for 15 minutes, then remove foil and bake for another 7–10 minutes, until the peppers are soft. Serve with a salad.

# Barbecue Turkey Tenderloins

*If you like flank steak, you'll like this dish, particularly because it contains a lot less fat. A poultry tenderloin is the piece of meat that is underneath the turkey or chicken breast. It is easy to separate from the breast and very juicy and tender. Serve with a rice pilaf and steamed zucchini, or a green salad and baked potato.*

**Makes 6 servings.**

**I pound turkey tenderloins**
**I ½ cups Yolanda's BBQ Sauce (page 221) or other oil-free barbe-**
**cue sauce**

Slice the tenderloins on the diagonal into ½-inch slices. Place one cup of the BBQ Sauce in a baking pan and add the turkey. Marinate for ½ hour. Preheat the grill on medium, as these cook very fast. Brush with more sauce as the tenderloins cook. Grill the turkey until cooked through, about 5 to 7 minutes. Spoon the remaining BBQ Sauce over the turkey and serve.

# No-Fat Fish Dishes

## Orange Roughy with Ginger Sesame Sauce

*Sesame is a very popular flavoring in restaurants these days—however, sesame flavor on the menu usually means tons of sesame oil on the plate. This dish has good Oriental taste without all the fat and the marinade is another versatile sauce I make in bulk and keep in jars in the fridge. Then I can just pour it over sole, snapper, orange roughy, or even chicken and bake or broil. Serve this particular dish with steamed rice and Oriental vegetables (usually you can find mixed Oriental vegetables in the frozen food section, just make sure that they're plain and not filled with additives).*

**Makes 2 servings.**

2 orange roughy fillets (6 to 8 ounces each)

I lemon

1 ½ cups sherry

I cup water

2 cloves garlic, chopped

I tablespoon grated gingerroot

I bunch scallions, finely chopped

½ cup light soy sauce

½ cup apple juice concentrate

½ cup roasted sesame seeds (see page 192 for roasting method)

Place the fish fillets in a shallow baking pan and squeeze the juice from the lemon over them; set aside. Place the sherry, water, garlic, and gingerroot in a medium saucepan and bring to a boil. Reduce the heat and cook until the sherry mixture is reduced by half, about 10 minutes. Add the scallion, soy sauce, apple juice concentrate, and sesame seeds and let simmer for 15 minutes. In the meantime preheat the oven to 400°. Pour the sauce over the fish and cover the baking pan with waxed paper. Place in the oven and cook for 10 minutes. Remove the waxed paper and cook another 3 to 5 minutes or until fish flakes when touched with a fork.

# Capered Swordfish

*This is a recipe inspired by a dish I had at one of my favorite restaurants in LA. I love swordfish served with steamed asparagus and new potatoes.*

**Makes 2 servings.**

I lemon
2 6-ounce swordfish steaks
I cup white wine
½ cup Grey Poupon Dijon mustard
I tablespoon capers
I tablespoon granulated garlic
I teaspoon paprika
Pinch of pepper

Squeeze the juice from the lemon over the fish and set platter aside. Mix the remaining ingredients in a small bowl, wisking with a fork (or mix in the blender). Crush the capers as you go. Pour the wine mixture over the fish and let the steaks marinate for at least 1 hour in refrigerator. Preheat the grill to high or until coals are red-hot. Reduce to medium heat. Place the steaks on the grill* for about 5 minutes on one side, turn and cook 1 to 2 minutes on the other side. Return to the marinade and serve.

# Halibut with Red Pepper-Caper Sauce

*When you make this accompanying sauce, it's a good idea to make a lot and keep it in the refrigerator—it's great over trout, catfish, or snapper as well. Serve the halibut with steamed banana or butternut squash and steamed spinach.*

**Makes 4 servings.**

I 8- to 10-ounce halibut fillet
I lemon

*If you can't grill, bake the fish for about 15 minutes at 450° then broil for 1 minute.

3 roasted red bell peppers*

I teaspoon capers

I tablespoon Grey Poupon Dijon mustard

½ cup white wine

I tablespoon rosemary

½ teaspoon white pepper

I teaspoon Paula's poultry seasoning (optional)

½ cup Pritikin defatted broth

Preheat oven to 450°. Line a baking pan (11 × 7½ inches) with aluminum foil. Place halibut in pan and squeeze the juice from the lemon top. Place bell peppers, capers, mustard, wine, and spices in a food processor or blender and quickly blend until smooth. Pour the red pepper-caper sauce over the halibut. Pour broth into the bottom of the pan. Bake about 10 to 15 minutes or until cooked through and fish flakes when touched with a fork.

# Cumin-Spice Shark Steak

*The shark in your market is not the same fish that starred in* Jaws. *It's a hearty, but mild-tasting fish that's great grilled or baked. It is a steaklike fish without bones, and has been known as "poor man's swordfish," because it is affordable. I like to serve this with grilled vegetables (eggplant or a mixture of your choice) and baked acorn squash.*

Makes 2 servings.

I pound thresher shark steaks

I tablespoon cumin

Juice from 1½ lemons

½ cup white wine

¼ teaspoon white pepper

Preheat the grill or oven to 500°. Cover the fish with cumin (you can just rub it on with your fingertips) and place in an aluminum foil "boat." Pour the lemon juice and wine over the fish and sprinkle with the white pepper. Place the "boat" on a hot grill or in the oven. When the juice and

*If you can't get fresh red bell peppers, then use canned diced red peppers that are not packed in oil. To roast, place the peppers on a grill over low to medium heat. Turn until all sides are grilled and the peppers are soft (you can get the same effect on your stove top).

wine are boiling at the bottom of the foil, turn the fish. If you are cooking it in the oven, place it under the broiler for 2 minutes. If cooking the fish on a grill, just turn it and let it cook until done, about 3 more minutes.

# Sole Veracruz

*You can use almost any fish fillet or white fish such as orange roughy, halibut, or dover sole for this recipe. You can even use frozen fish, because the sauce makes anything taste good. I think this recipe is a perfect example of how much moisture and flavor cooking with sliced vegetables can add.*

**Makes 6 servings.**

>   8 petrale sole fillets (6 to 8 ounces each)
>   Pam no-stick cooking spray
>   Juice of 1 lemon
>   1 teaspoon low-sodium vegetable seasoning (like Capello's chicken vegetable)
>   ¼ cup dry vermouth or white wine
>   1 large onion, chopped
>   2 shallots, chopped
>   4 large ripe tomatoes, peeled, seeded, and chopped or 6 canned Italian plum tomatoes, drained
>   1 cup fresh orange juice
>   2 tablespoons frozen orange juice concentrate
>   2 tablespoons frozen apple juice concentrate
>   Pinch of crushed red pepper
>   ½ teaspoon fennel seeds
>   Pinch of black pepper

Place the fish fillets in a shallow baking dish (8 × 8 inch) sprayed with Pam. Pour the lemon juice over them and sprinkle with vegetable seasoning; set aside. Place the vermouth in a small saucepan and bring to a boil. Reduce the heat, add the onion and shallots, and sauté until transparent. Add the tomatoes and simmer for 10 minutes. Add the fresh juice and juice concentrates, red and black pepper, and fennel. Simmer for 5 minutes more. In the meantime, preheat oven to 350°. Pour the sauce over the fish fillets and bake for 25 to 30 minutes or until fish flakes when touched with a fork.

# Pasta Without the Pounds

## Pasta Bolognese

*Check out a traditional recipe for this dish and you'll find that it contains cream, butter, and fatty meats. Needless to say, this version calls for none of the above. This is a hearty meal in itself and only needs a good salad on the side. If you'd like to make a quick sauce to keep on hand, try this one— it freezes well.*

**Makes 6 servings.**

I cup water
½ cup apple cider vinegar
½ cup red wine
1 ½ tablespoons basil
I tablespoon oregano
½ teaspoon pepper
5 cloves garlic, diced
2 large stalks celery, diced
I carrot, minced
I large onion, diced
2 cans (12 ounces each) diced tomatoes
I can (8 ounces) tomato paste
Pam no-stick cooking spray
½ pound ground chicken
I teaspoon granulated garlic
3 cups rotelle pasta

Place all the ingredients, except the Pam, chicken, granulated garlic, and rotelle in a large pot. Heat to a boil, then reduce the heat and let simmer for 20 to 30 minutes. Allow to cool. Spray a large skillet with Pam and sauté the chicken and granulated garlic over medium heat. When the chicken is cooked through, add to the sauce. Pour in ¼ cup more red wine, then adjust the seasonings. Cook the pasta according to package directions, eliminating the salt. Pour Bolognese sauce over cooked pasta and serve.

# Manicotti

*This recipe proves that tofu is not just for Oriental or alfalfa sprout menus. Believe me, when you serve this dish everyone will think it's made with ricotta cheese. Go ahead and sprinkle on the Parmesan, as this dish is low in fat. Serve with zucchini sautéed in white wine, garlic, and oregano.*

**Makes 4 servings.**

**12 manicotti noodles (preferably whole wheat)**
**3 cans (8 ounces each) tomato sauce**
**2 packages (12 ounces each) tofu**
**2 tablespoons oregano**
**2½ tablespoons basil**
**3 tablespoons garlic powder**
**1 teaspoon pepper**

Prepare the manicotti noodles according to package directions—except eliminate the salt and cook about 1 minute less than directed. When done, place noodles in a colander and run under cold water. Preheat oven to 400°. In a large bowl, toss the noodles lightly with about one-quarter of the tomato sauce; set aside. In a separate bowl, blend tofu, oregano, basil, garlic, and pepper. Stuff each manicotti noodle with the tofu mixture. Line the stuffed noodles up in a baking pan and pour the rest of the tomato sauce on top. Make a tent of aluminum foil over the baking pan and cook the manicotti for 10 minutes. Remove the foil and cook another 15 to 20 minutes.

# Angel Hair with Quicky Tomato Sauce

*My mother used to make this sauce with tons of olive oil and butter, and it was wonderful. But it took 3 days to digest and weeks to burn off. You can doctor this sauce with your own seasonings, then keep some extra in the fridge to pour over your favorite pasta. If you can, use fresh basil to make this dish. Serve with salad and you've got a well-rounded meal.*

**Makes 4 servings.**

- 1 small onion, diced
- 1 garlic clove, minced
- 1 small green bell pepper, diced
- 1 pinch black pepper
- 2 tablespoons dry white wine
- 8 large ripe tomatoes, seeded and chopped
- 3 tablespoons chopped fresh basil, or 3 teaspoons dried basil if absolutely necessary
- 1 tablespoon chopped fresh Italian parsley
- 1 can (8 ounces) tomato sauce
- 1 pound cooked fresh angel hair pasta (cook without salt)

In a medium saucepan, sauté onion, garlic, bell pepper, and pepper in the white wine until softened. Add the tomatoes and bring to a boil. Reduce heat and simmer 10 to 15 minutes or until most of the liquid has evaporated. Add basil, parsley, pepper, and tomato sauce. Toss with the angel hair pasta.

# No-Junk Junk Food

## Halibits

When my daughter begged for McDonald's Chicken McNuggets, this is what she got instead—healthy, nonfried fish nuggets that she thought were as much fun as the fast-food kind. And because kids love the dipping process, I always include Nolina in the making of her own "McNuggets." The recipe calls for halibut, but any firm fish (swordfish, shark, or even chicken) can be substituted. To serve alongside, making dipping sauces of sugar-free ketchup and a mixture of Dijon and sugar-free marmalade; summer squash and rice make nice sides. Or just serve your child's favorite vegetable of the moment.

Makes 2 servings.

    1 4- to 5-ounce halibut fillet, cut into 1-inch cubes
    2 eggs, beaten
    1 cup wheat germ
    Paula's poultry seasoning (optional)
    Pam no-stick cooking spray or canola oil

Drench the halibut pieces in the eggs, then roll the fish in the wheat germ and, if desired, poultry seasoning. Spray a large skillet with Pam, or add a little canola oil, and sauté fish cubes over a medium heat until toasty brown.

## Shrimp Egg Rolls

If it weren't for all the frying and oil used to make this Chinese dish, it wouldn't be too unhealthy or fattening, so I took out all the frying and oil and came up with this version. This recipe is a good lesson in how to "fry" food without the grease. Make a large batch of the filling and freeze in individual-size freezer bags. Then you can thaw them and make egg rolls quickly anytime. Serve with Dijon mustard mixed with some sugar-free *marmalade, or just dip them into some light soy sauce and wasasbe (hot green) mustard.*

**Makes 5 servings.**

> **4 egg whites**
> **10 egg roll skins**
> **½ cup defatted chicken broth**
> **1 cup light soy sauce**
> **1 tablespoon minced gingerroot**
> **1 tablespoon minced garlic**
> **3 cups assorted mixed vegetables (like celery, carrots, mushrooms, and bean sprouts) finely chopped (frozen vegetables can be used)**
> **1 pound baby shrimp (frozen is fine)**
> **Pam no-stick cooking spray**

Preheat oven to 400°. In a small bowl, lightly beat the egg whites; set aside. Separate the egg roll skins from one another and lay out flat on a platter or cutting board. In a wok or large skillet, bring chicken broth, soy sauce, ginger, and garlic to a boil. Add the vegetables, then the shrimp. Stir constantly until vegetables are tender-crisp. Using a slotted spoon, place about 2 tablespoons of vegetable-shrimp mixture in the middle of each egg roll skin. Fold the skins as you would a handkerchief. Brush outside of the skins with egg white. Place on a Teflon-coated baking sheet sprayed with Pam, and bake for 7 to 10 minutes or until golden brown.

# Crustless Pizza

*This is a dream dish for anyone trying to lose weight—pizza without all the fat and calories. It is also a complete meal in itself or serve it with a salad. You can, of course, add your favorite pizza variations—no, not pepperoni! Make an extra pizza base, freeze it, then thaw when you want to make a quick meal.*

**Makes 8 servings.**

BASE

**Pam no-stick cooking spray**
**I pound ground turkey**
**½ cup wheat germ**
**½ cup oatmeal**
**2 egg whites, beaten**
**I tablespoon granulated garlic**
**I teaspoon basil**
**I teaspoon oregano**
**½ teaspoon black pepper**
**½ teaspoon crushed red chili peppers**

TOPPING

**½ cup white wine**
**I green bell pepper, diced**
**I onion, diced**
**I cup mushrooms, sliced**
**I can (8 ounces) artichoke hearts, quartered**
**¾ cup grated low-fat jack cheese**
**I ½ cups tomato sauce**

Preheat oven to 400°. Spray a large rectangular pan (11 × 7½ inches) with Pam. In a large bowl, combine all the remaining ingredients for the base. Press the turkey mixture into the pan, until it looks like a regular pizza crust.

To make the topping, heat the wine in a large skillet over medium heat. Add bell peppers, onion, and mushrooms and sauté lightly until tender-crisp. Drain and set aside. Prebake the pizza base for 5 minutes. Remove from the oven and top with the sautéed vegetables and artichoke hearts. Then sprinkle on the cheese. Top with the tomato sauce. Return the pizza to the oven and bake for 15 minutes. Cut into wedges and serve immediately.

# Turkey Burgers

*This is one of my most famous recipes and it couldn't be any simpler. It only has three ingredients, but—wow!—those three ingredients really hit it off. Serve the burgers on whole wheat buns with your favorite hamburger relishes. Or just serve them plain with sliced tomatoes, lettuce, and pickles. If you are trying to lose weight, have jicama sticks and new potatoes on the side. Many of my clients keep three to four of these burgers in the fridge and use them as "diet pills"—that is, something to grab and munch on before they go out or simply when they're ravenous and want a healthy snack. They are so tasty and really stave off hunger.*

**Makes 6 to 8 servings.**

  1 pound ground turkey
  1 medium yellow onion, diced
  ¾ cup Grey Poupon Dijon mustard
  Pam no-stick cooking spray

Preheat oven to 400° and preheat the grill to high. Combine all the ingredients, except the Pam, in a large bowl. Shape the turkey mixture into 6 to 8 patties. Spray a baking sheet with Pam and prebake the patties in the oven for about 10 minutes. Turkey does not have the fat of ground meat and tends to fall apart on the grill if you don't prebake it first. Remove the burgers from the oven and grill them until they are cooked through. Turn only once.

# Cajun Quesadillas

*This recipe is similar to burrito and enchilada recipes. A quesadilla, burrito, or Mexican anything wouldn't be even close to the real thing without cheese, but it's a healthier dish when the cheese is nonfat like in this recipe. In this take on the Mexican classic I've also added ground turkey (to make it a more substantial meal) and cajun spices just for some extra flavor. You can make your own variations on this theme; all are great cold, packed for lunch.*

**Makes 5 servings.**

½ pound ground turkey

I tablespoon cajun seasoning

4 to 5 large chapati bread (look for a fat-free chapati or Bible
   bread), or corn tortillas

½ cup each: grated nonfat Cheddar and jack cheeses

I cup chopped red bell pepper

I cup tomatillo salsa*

6 egg whites, lightly beaten

Pam no-stick cooking spray

In a Teflon skillet, sauté ground turkey over medium heat. Add the cajun
seasonings and continue sautéing until turkey is cooked through. Remove from heat. Lay chapatis out on a flat surface. Place turkey in the
middle, then top with cheese, bell pepper, and salsa. Roll up the quesadillas and fold the ends under. Lightly coat with beaten egg white, Reheat the skillet and spray with Pam. Place the quesadillas in the skillet
and brown on all sides over medium heat. Remove from the pan and
serve.

# Turkey Tacos

*Kids love these. Even though the ingredients are ten times better for them
than the ones at Taco Bell, your kids will never know the difference. This
recipe is a good example how you can start to redefine the "bad" foods as
healthy and lean. Also see page 228 for the family Taco Bar Dinner. It's
one of my family's favorites.*

**Makes 4 tacos.**

Pam no-stick cooking spray

¼ pound ground turkey (or chicken)

4 ounces canned kidney beans

¾ cup Pritikin Mexican Sauce*

4 corn tortillas

*Tomatillo sauce is available in the Mexican food section of most supermarkets. If you can't find
tomatillo, use a bottled picante sauce.

*If you can't find the Pritikin, use 1 can (8 ounces) tomato sauce with 1 tablespoon Parsley
Patch Mexican Blend.

2 ounces grated Lifetime or other nonfat Cheddar cheese
½ cup shredded lettuce
½ cup bottled or fresh red salsa

Spray a large skillet with Pam and sauté the ground turkey until almost done. Add the beans and Mexican sauce and cook until the turkey is done. Set aside. Turn a stove burner on low and place the tortillas on top of it for a few seconds to crisp both sides. Make a "boat" out of the tortillas and fill them with the turkey mixture. Top with grated cheese, salsa, and lettuce.

## Cinnamon-Vanilla French Toast

*The details that make a fat difference in this breakfast recipe are the absence of egg yolk and the use of nonfat instead of whole milk. Of course, it's cooked without butter, too, but any flavor loss is made up for with the addition of cinnamon and vanilla. Top with any of R. W. Knudsen Family sugar-free fruit syrups.*

**Makes 4 servings.**

6 egg whites
½ cup nonfat milk
1 teaspoon cinnamon
½ teaspoon vanilla
¼ teaspoon orange extract (optional)
4 slices whole wheat or oat bran bread
Pam no-stick cooking spray

Combine the egg whites, milk, cinnamon, vanilla, and, if desired, orange extract in a shallow bowl. Place the bread in the mixture until soaked through. Heat a large skillet over medium heat. Spray with Pam and place the soaked bread in the skillet. Cook about 5 minutes on one side, then flip and cook about 1 minute more.

# Just Desserts

## Apple Tart

*You can vary this recipe with other fresh or frozen fruits.*

**Makes 2 servings.**

- 2 cups apple juice
- 1 teaspoon cinnamon
- 1 tablespoon cornstarch
- 1 cup Post grape-nuts cereal
- 2 small, tart pippin or golden delicious apples, quartered, seeded, and sliced

In a small saucepan, mix the apple juice, cinnamon, and cornstarch. Bring to a boil and cook until slightly thick. Combine just enough of the liquid mixture with the grape-nuts to form a crumb crust to line the bottom of a small tart shell or 6-inch pie pan. Place the apples in the saucepan with the remaining liquid and cook 2 to 3 minutes or until slightly soft. Distribute the apples evenly over the crust; pour remaining liquid on top. Can be served warm or cold.

## Baked Apples

*These are delicious, and have saved me many times when I knew that I could come home to them and resist the chocolate dessert of the evening. They are also great for a snack—or even for breakfast.*

**Makes 4 servings.**

- 4 pippin or Rome apples, cored
- 4 teaspoons sugar-free jam, any flavor
- Cinnamon
- 1½ cups orange juice

Preheat oven to 400°. Place the apples in a shallow baking pan lined with aluminum foil. Place a teaspoon, more or less, of the jam in the hole of each apple. Sprinkle a little cinnamon on top of each, then pour the orange juice into the bottom of the pan. Bake apples for 15 minutes.

## Poached Sherry Peaches

*You can change the flavor accent of these peaches by using different liquors, or try substituting pears for the peaches.*

**Makes 6 servings.**

**2 cups water**
**I cup cream sherry**
**I can (6 ounces) frozen apple juice concentrate**
**Zest of 2 lemons**
**½ teaspoon cinnamon**
**I vanilla bean, split lengthwise**
**4 large ripe peaches**
**I cup nonfat plain yogurt**
**I cup strawberries, crushed or puréed**

In a large saucepan, combine water, sherry, apple juice concentrate, lemon zest, cinnamon, and vanilla bean. Bring to a boil, then reduce heat and simmer for 20 minutes. Add peaches to liquid and simmer about 10 minutes more or until just tender. Remove from the heat and let the peaches cool in the liquid, then remove and slip off their skins. Halve the peaches, remove the pit, then slice them. Before serving, blend the peaches with the yogurt and strawberries. (Reserve the leftover syrup and refrigerate to use another time.)

# Feijoas in Orange Syrup

*Feijoas are a trendy new tropical fruit—also known as pineapple guava—that's been showing up in Los Angeles these days. If you can't find them, kiwi will do just as well. Much of the flavor of this dessert comes from the oranges—you'll need about four in all.*

**Makes 4 to 5 servings.**

> 1 cup fresh orange juice
> Peel from 1 orange, cut into thin slices
> ½ cup sugar
> ¼ cup water
> Dash almond liqueur (optional)
> 5 feijoas (or kiwi), peeled and cut widthwise into ¼-inch slices
> 1 cup orange segments

In a medium saucepan combine the orange juice, orange peel, sugar, water, and, if desired, liqueur. Bring the mixture to a boil over high heat; continue to boil rapidly, uncovered, until the syrup is reduced to 1 cup. Remove from heat. Drop the sliced feijoas into the hot syrup, add the orange segments and stir gently. Refrigerate overnight so the flavors meld.

# Minted Poached Pears with Chantilly Custard Sauce

*One bite of these sugarless poached pears and you'll swear off those syrupy canned versions for ever. The pineapple concentrate adds all the sweetness anyone can desire and, for those who want to be a bit decadent, the chantilly cream is a sensuous pleasure.*

**Makes 4 servings.**

> 2 cans (12 ounces each) frozen pineapple juice concentrate
> 4 small seckel pears, cored and peeled with a circle of skin left at the stem
> 2 tablespoons crème de menthe or ¼ teaspoon mint extract
> Fresh mint sprigs for garnish
> Chantilly Custard Sauce (on page 219) (optional)

Pour the pineapple juice into a large saucepan and heat over medium heat. Place the pears in the juice; bring to a boil, reduce the heat, and simmer for 15 to 20 minutes. Lift the pears out of the juice with a slotted spoon and place in a serving dish. Reduce the juice to about 1 to 1⅓ cups. Add the crème de menthe. Pour the syrup over the pears and garnish with the fresh mint and, if desired, a dollop of Chantilly Custard Sauce.

## Chantilly Custard Sauce

*This, admittedly, is one of my more decadent recipes because it contains sugar (although not too much), egg yolks, and crème fraîche. But, hey, we've all got to indulge sometime and serving this custard alongside these pears (or any fruit) is as good a way, if not better, than any. And, besides, it's so rich a little dab will more than do you.*

**Makes 4 2-ounce servings.**

½ cup low-fat milk

I piece vanilla bean, split lengthwise

I ½ tablespoons raw sugar

3 egg yolks

I tablespoon almond liqueur

½ cup crème fraîche

Place the milk and vanilla bean in a medium saucepan. Heat until the milk is scalded. In a large bowl, beat the sugar and egg yolks with a whisk. Beat in about one-third of the hot milk, then pour the mixture back into the pan. Reduce the heat to low and cook until the custard is velvety and coats the back of a metal spoon. Remove from the heat and stir until cooled. Stir in the liqueur, remove the vanilla bean, and chill. When thoroughly chilled, whisk in the crème fraîche until stiff peaks form. Place in ramekins or bowls and serve.

FOOD COP

# No-Cholesterol Oatmeal Cookies

*Oatmeal cookies can so often be greasy, but there's no reason they should be: the true taste of oats combined with spices is wonderful on its own. These cookies are not only not greasy, they are made with egg whites only so they contain no cholesterol.*

**Makes about 12 to 18 cookies.**

**2 cups whole wheat flour**

**1 cup oatmeal**

**½ cup Post grape-nuts**

**6 egg whites, beaten**

**1 cup apple juice**

**1 tablespoon vanilla**

**1 teaspoon baking soda**

**1 teaspoon cinnamon**

**½ teaspoon cardamom**

**⅛ teaspoon nutmeg**

**Pam no-stick cooking spray**

Preheat the oven to 350°. Place all the ingredients except the Pam in a large bowl of an electric mixer and mix on low for about 3 minutes. (Or use electric hand beaters.) Place teaspoon-size drops of dough onto a baking sheet that has been sprayed with Pam. Bake for about 10 minutes, or until golden brown.

# Slimming Sauces and Dressings

## Yolanda's BBQ Sauce

. . . . . . . . . . .

*Make a lot of this sauce and store it; it keeps for about 6 months.*

**Makes about 2 cups sauce.**

- I can (16 ounces) tomato sauce
- ½ green bell pepper, diced
- 2 tablespoons lemon juice
- 2 tablespoons frozen apple juice concentrate
- I tablespoon Worcestershire sauce
- I tablespoon dehydrated onion flakes
- I tablespoon celery flakes
- I teaspoon dry mustard
- I teaspoon Capello's seasoning (or any poultry seasoning)
- I teaspoon natural hickory flavoring
- ¼ teaspoon garlic powder

Combine all the ingredients in a large saucepan and bring to a boil. Reduce heat and let simmer for about 20 minutes. Use as a marinade for fish, poultry, or lean meat.

## Oil-Free Vinaigrettes

. . . . . . . . . . .

*Bottled oil-free dressings are filling the grocery store shelves these days. If you find them bland, try adding a little high-quality flavored or balsamic vinegar and some granulated garlic. It's difficult to make a vinaigrette stick to lettuce without using oils or natural stabilizers like xanthum gum or carageenan, but the following three have pretty good stick-ability. And to me, they're just as tasty as any oil-based vinaigrette.*

## Mustard Vinaigrette

*You can make this yourself at any restaurant, too.*

**Makes about 1 cup dressing.**

1 cup red wine vinegar
½ packets Equal
1 tablespoon Dijon or herb mustard
½ teaspoon black pepper
1 teaspoon Parmesan cheese

Vary it with a choice of, or combination of, the following:

Crushed garlic cloves
Tarragon
Dillweed
Basil and oregano
Parsley Patch Garlicsaltless seasoning

Blend all ingredients well.

## Balsamic Vinaigrette

**Makes about 1 cup dressing.**

1 cup balsamic vinegar
1 tablespoon Grey Poupon Dijon mustard
1 teaspoon capers

Blend all ingredients well.

## Creamy Tomato Vinaigrette

**Makes about 3 cups dressing.**

2 cups nonfat plain yogurt
1 cup red wine vinegar
½ cup no-sugar ketchup
½ cup sweet pickle relish

Blend all ingredients well.

# How to Fill Your Refrigerator with Food for One Week (in an Hour and a Half)

Take a little bit of time on a Sunday, go to the store, stock up, put on your favorite album or CD, and cook. Take this time to make your week easier, and you'll be able to come home to lean, healthy, and delicious meals the rest of the week. This is the best way to avoid feeling like a "victim"—no excuses for ordering pizza or Chinese food because you're too tired to cook. You've got everything you need right there in the fridge. Feel free to add your own variations to the following menu.

## Menu (for Two to Three People)

1. Roast Turkey Breast with Mustard Sauce
2. Grilled Cajun Chicken
3. Shrimp Pasta Salad Primavera
4. Chicken Tarragona
5. Angel Hair with Quicky Tomato Sauce
6. Steamed veggies
7. Jicama Chips with Salsa Cruda
8. Baked Apples

## Equipment Needed

4 baking pans (about 2- to 3-inches deep) plus a shallow (11 × 7 inch)
    rectangular pan
1 steamer
1 medium saucepan
1 skillet
1 colander
Aluminum foil

## Shopping List

1 four- to five-pound turkey breast
4 skinless, boneless chicken thighs
4 skinless, boneless chicken breasts
1 pound frozen shrimp (fresh is always best)
1 pound angel hair pasta
4 pippin or baking apples

1 jar herb mustard
1 bottle cheap white wine (preferably Italian)
1 bottle cheap red wine
1 can Pritikin or other defatted chicken broth
1 bottle ReaLemon juice or juice of 2 to 3 lemons
1 fresh lemon
1 bottle Cajun seasoning
1 bottle oil-free salad dressing of your choice
1 bottle salt-free herb seasoning (like Parsley Patch Garlicsaltless)
1½ cups orange juice
1 can (12 ounces) diced tomatoes
1 can (8 ounces) tomato sauce
1 large onion
Fresh garlic cloves
1 bag frozen vegetables with pasta (no sauce)
Oregano
Basil
Cinnamon
Tarragon
Assorted veggies—zucchini, peppers, crookneck squash, mushrooms, carrots, and green beans
1 medium jicama
1 container fresh salsa (available in the refrigerator section)

## *Preparation*

- Line the 4 baking pans with aluminum foil. Preheat the oven to 400°.
- Slather the turkey breast with herb mustard and place it skin side down in one of the pans. Pour 1½ cups of white wine in the pan. Place in the oven for 20 minutes; turn the breast over and cook for 10 to 15 minutes more. Pierce the turkey with a fork or toothpick; it's done if the juices run clear.
- While turkey is cooking, place the chicken thighs in another baking dish and slather with a tablespoon of the herb mustard and 1 teaspoon tarragon. Slice the lemon and place the slices around the chicken. Pour one cup of red wine over the chicken, then place the baking pan in the oven. Bake until done, about 15 to 20 minutes.
- Season the chicken breasts with 1 tablespoon Cajun seasoning and place in the third baking pan. Pour ½ cup of the lemon juice over them, then place the baking pan in the oven. Bake until done, about 15 to 20 minutes.

- Core the apples and place them in the fourth baking pan. Sprinkle ½ teaspoon of cinnamon in the core of each apple. Pour the orange juice into the bottom of the pan. Bake until the apples are soft, about 20 minutes.
- Thaw the shrimp and frozen vegetables and pasta in the colander. If necessary, run under hot water to expedite thawing. Drain, place in a bowl, sprinkle with a little lemon juice, then toss with the oil-free salad dressing.
- Cut assorted veggies into large chunks, you need 1 cup of each. Place them in a steamer. Liberally sprinkle with salt-free seasoning. Fill the bottom of the steamer with about 2 inches of water and steam the veggies until tender-crisp.
- Dice the onion and 3 cloves of garlic. In the skillet, sauté the onions and garlic with ½ cup white wine until translucent. Add the can of diced tomatoes. Add 1 tablespoon each of oregano and basil; pour in the can of tomato sauce. Let the sauce simmer for at least 20 minutes while you start a pot of water to boil for the angel hair pasta. Prepare the pasta according to package directions, without adding salt or oil. When the pasta is done, transfer to the colander and run it under cold water. Drain and toss with the pasta sauce.
- Slice the jicama into large matchsticks and squeeze lemon juice over them. Place in a bowl with the fresh salsa.
- When everything has cooled, place each entrée on a plate or in a bowl and wrap with plastic. Store in the refrigerator.

During the week, you can walk in the door and simply pop whatever you feel like having into the oven or microwave. All these dishes can be eaten cold as well.

## Meals for Mixed Needs

Life would be so simple if everyone had the same body and, of course, if none of us had any food problems at all. Dream on. That's just not the way life has worked out. But as I have said throughout this book, no person should be forced to eat like another person for the sole reason of convenience. Food has just too much of an impact on our lives to be eaten without any more thought to it than what makes things uncomplicated. Especially because it only takes a tiny bit of effort to make sure everyone in your family eats well.

"Okay," you say, "so how am I supposed to handle the fact that in my family we have one normal, healthy person, one person (me) trying to lose weight, and a skinny husband with high cholesterol? How can we realistically sit down to a meal at the same time and have all our needs met?" Maybe it's not as easy as sitting down with a bucket of fried chicken, but it's still easy, I mean really easy. And even if it does require a little extra time and effort, sometimes it's worth it. I have been known to sit down to a dinner of fish and vegetables, while my family has pasta. They don't care, as long as I'm happy.

No matter if your family's needs are mixed or homogeneous, always buy food that is healthy. That must be a given. Once you have the raw materials, during the cooking process you can apply rules for weight control, high cholesterol, whatever anyone needs. To give you an example of how to make meals multipurpose, here are meals for two different kinds of eaters: a person who shouldn't have any added fats in his or her diet and a person who can afford to eat some oil and dairy products. As you'll see, the same preparation techniques can be used to serve them both (or any amount of people who have different needs). When I'm doing the cooking, I always think "this is for me, this is for them." Same thing when I shop. That's what you should do too. I've written the following menus in a way that assumes you're the person who needs to cut fats, yet also has the job of cooking for someone who doesn't. Recipes for starred dishes can be found in this chapter.

## *Pasta Dinner*

### Menu

Angel Hair with Quicky Tomato Sauce*
Steamed green beans
Fresh green salad
Garlic and plain bread
Fresh strawberries in balsamic vinegar and Equal, and honey (or sugar)

### Preparation

Cook the pasta (without oil or salt), rinse and divide in half. Toss the half for the other person with a little olive oil, then again with the tomato pasta sauce. Divide your portion in half again. Take half the noodles, combine with green beans (so you end up eating less starch) and toss with the pasta sauce only. Place a bowl of Parmesan cheese on the table: you can have a sprinkle, he can have a few sprinkles more. Serve the salad with two dressings on the side, one that's oil-free, the other made the traditional way. He gets garlic bread, you can have plain bread if you're just trying to maintain, not lose weight. Marinate your berries in balsamic vinegar and Equal, his with honey or raw sugar.

## *Steak and Swordfish Dinner*

**Menu**

Steak
Swordfish fillet with wine, mustard, and capers
Baked potatoes
Steamed broccoli with Parsley Patch Garlicsaltless

**Preparation**

Salt and pepper his steak. Season your swordfish (make sure it's a big steak so you don't end up staring at his) with wine, mustard, and capers and cover with aluminum foil. Place both the steak and swordfish in the broiler at the same time. Sprinkle the broccoli with the garlic seasoning and divide the steamed broccoli and serve yours with some of the sauce leftover from the swordfish, his tossed with canola oil or healthy margarine and a bit of Parmesan cheese. Have light sour cream and chives on the table for his baked potato, oil-free salad dressing or nonfat yogurt for yours. If he insists on ice cream for dessert, fine—you'll have frozen yogurt or low-sugar candies, even a junky diet ice cream bar if you must. But always try to opt for fruit.

## *Stuffed Trout Provencal Dinner*

**Menu**

Trout Provencal
Steamed summer squash
Hain Chicken Rice Pilaf (or Pritikin Rice Pilaf) mix
Baked Apples*
Frozen yogurt and diet chocolate mousse

**Preparation**

Take two boneless trout and spread Dijon mustard on the white meat. Stuff both with sliced plum tomatoes and chopped green onions; add a sprinkle of Romano cheese to one. Put each fish in its own aluminum foil "boat," then place in a shallow baking pan. Pour ½ cup of white wine and squeeze some lemon over each. Drizzle a little olive oil over the fish containing the Romano cheese. Place in a preheated 450° oven for 20 minutes. Then place under the broiler for 2 minutes, to get the top skin of the trout to pop off. Serve with steamed summer squash (or zucchini)—pour the nonoil fish juices over your portion and let Mr. Skinny have his tossed with margarine. While the trout is baking, prepare the rice side dish according to directions on the box, but instead of sautéing the rice in oil to start, use a little defatted chicken broth and wine. Then follow the rest of the directions on the box. Place the trout over the rice and pour the juices from each fish over the rice and squash. Prepare the Baked Apples according to the recipe on page 216. Serve frozen yogurt on his, whip up some diet chocolate mousse to have on yours. But if you're really weight watching, then skip the mousse.

## *Taco Bar Dinner*

The nice thing about Mexican cuisine is that the ingredients are wonderfully healthful and nonfattening. It's just the American way of cooking them that spoils everything. When I set up a Mexican buffet and let my guests make their own tacos, I fill the table with options for people who are watching their fat intake and those who want to go for it, fat and all. The end results are so flavorful that even those guests who stick to the low-fat ingredients can hardly believe they're eating so well at such a low cost to their thighs. The best taco bar includes the following choices.

| Ingredients for Everyone . . . | Higher Fat Indulgences . . . | Low-Fat Adds |
|---|---|---|
| Ground turkey sautéed in Pam and seasoned with a pinch of cayenne or chili powder (Parsley Patch Mexican Blend) Slices of chicken breast Chopped red onion Shredded lettuce Chopped plum tomatoes Steamed corn tortillas Salsa (both regular and tomatillo) Hot Chili verde sauce Sliced jicama | Refried beans Sour cream Chopped olives Guacamole | Plain kidney bean Fantastic Foods instant beans Nonfat yogurt Pritikin Mexican Sauce Grated low-fat Cheddar cheese |

NOTE: If you are watching your weight, take the corn tortilla and put on a mixture of everything except the items listed in the higher fat indulgences category. If you have high cholesterol then skip the guacamole, sour cream, and refried beans and choose either the nonfat yogurt or the cheese, not both.

# 9

# Order It Your Way: Getting the Food You Want in Restaurants

**R**ESTAURANT EATING HAS become a way of life. Years ago, it was a rare treat to eat out. You knew it was going to be special so you got dressed up, you spent money. There were casual restaurants, of course, but mostly dining out was an "occasion." Why, I even remember when manners were involved. Restaurant manners.

That, though, was before women went from the postfifties idea of "We know it's okay to work" to the current philosophy of "I will own the company, raise a family, and still have a good love life!" The pressure on women to work, raise a family, and look good has gotten out of hand. And it doesn't leave much time for making dinner. Try to work nine to six, make a shopping stop at the grocery store, then come home and slave over a stove. By the time dinner is on the table, it's eight o'clock and everyone's cranky or screaming at each other. It's *easier* to eat out, or even to order in. For the executive with a high salary who can afford to stop off for sushi or have gourmet take-out delivered, the absence of home cooking might not be so unhealthy. But for most people looking for convenience, eating out or ordering in poisonous fast food is more the reality.

But aren't men more willing to lend a hand with cooking and other household drudgery now? The truth is, even if their intentions are good, many men—same as many women—don't have the energy or know-how to make a good meal. Just a trip to the supermarket can be taxing. With junky fifties food (that is, the fatty, overprocessed foods that came of age in that decade) on one side, health foods (which usually provokes rebellion when you try to serve them anyway) on the other, there's confusion in the aisles. Is it any wonder that statistics show that on a typical day, close to 50 percent of the adult population eat out or purchase food to go? And I'm willing to bet that the numbers are even higher in most big cities around the country.

That's partly because of business meals. For professionals, dining out is a major and required part of success. Business meetings have even taken over *breakfast*. There's so much competition in the American work force now that work has invaded what used to be considered strictly private time. We're motivated, but we're motivated maniacs! It's positively hip to be obsessed and stressed, to have a calendar full of business meals. And it's just one more reason why people are eating out day and night, and why it's becoming essential to gain some control over what ends up on your plate. Because let's face facts: Restauranteurs are business men and women, not families. They're in it to make money, not to worry about your waistline and cholesterol count the way your mother would or to tend to the well-being of your kids as you do. No matter how conscientious the restaurant owner, ingredient costs force them to use bulk items, many of which are poorly produced and overprocessed. It's pure economics. Unfortuntely, even at the finest restaurants, what goes on in the kitchen isn't always to your benefit.

## Asking for What You Want . . . and Getting It

When you go out to eat, you're not always going for the sole purpose of experiencing the culinary talents of a fine chef. When you *are*, I suggest you go, eat, and *enjoy*. But when you're dining out on the more mundane, everyday level, don't let the menu dictate to you—the kitchen is not as limited as it would have you believe. The waiter and chef's job is to serve you, to make you want to come back again. You are paying (and you work hard for that money) for the food in front of you. Not that you're a fool: you have no qualms, for instance, about asking for your steak prepared rare or requesting a certain salad dressing or insisting that your martini be shaken not stirred. But why does it stop there? To ask for no sauce on your fish or that the cheese be left off your pasta doesn't mean you have to have the restaurant prepare a whole new dish for you. Or that you have to appear loud, fussy, or obnoxious. You shouldn't be afraid that people will think you're a health nut, or "on a diet," or that you're calling attention to your weight. It is simply the way you eat. Period.

Not too long ago, a high-powered LA attorney, forty pounds over-weight, came to me for help. She ate out all the time, but complained that she didn't want to order foods like fish grilled without butter and steamed vegetables because "everyone will think I'm on a diet." "Well," I asked, "didn't you just pay me a lot of money to help you because you're fat?"

"Yes."

"Did it ever occur to you that the people you're eating out with might have noticed that you're fat and will respect you for trying to lose weight? People respect others when they quit smoking. They should respect you for wanting a healthier body."

She rolled her eyes, shook her head, and looked around for another excuse. "Oh—but I also eat badly because I'm stressed out."

"Did you ever think you might be creating more stress for yourself by eating badly?" I asked. "If you order Fettucine Alfredo, are you going to enjoy it or subconsciously feel guilty and anxious because you know your cholesterol level is rising with every forkful and the fat is heading straight for your hips?" She got the point.

When I was a ballerina, eating out always presented a problem for me too. I felt that once I was in a restaurant I was trapped: there was no way I could get out of the place without gaining weight. So I either avoided eating out entirely or I went and completely pigged out, knowing I would feel lousy the next morning. This was not my idea of a good time—restaurant dining was a dilemma instead of a joy. But many years later, I found the secret to making the experience enjoyable again, oddly enough, while on a bad date.

The date, a wealthy, successful, and neurotic man in his thirties, told me before we went out that he was allergic to chocolate, alcohol, and garlic (he wouldn't have been much fun in Italy—or anywhere for that matter, but that's another story). At dinner (a very chic Chinese restaurant), he asked the waiter which entrées contained garlic and whether or not the chef could leave it out. Garlic, he said, gave him migraine headaches. So I watched as he got his food prepared exactly as he'd asked for it. I was impressed. I went home and thought, if he can get food his way, I can get my food my way. I decided right then and there that I was allergic to oil and butter. He gets migraines—well, I get fat! And that gives *me* migraines.

The next time I went to a restaurant I told the waiter that I was allergic to all oils. Sure enough, it worked. I learned that I could go out, order a salad to start (make my own nonfattening dressing on the side), eat the bread, have grilled fish or chicken, veggies, and fruit for dessert—and have a great time. As long as I avoided fats I could actually even lose weight. The concept of being "allgeric" to oil and butter made it easier for me to ask restaurants to prepare my meals the way I really wanted them. And without the worry of putting on pounds every time I stepped foot in a place, it became a pleasure to dine out once again.

In the August 1988 issue of *New York* magazine, the cover story was titled "How to Eat Healthy at New York's Great Restaurants." Isn't it sad that our restaurants are so unhealthy that a magazine has to dedicate a major story to teach us how to get them to serve decent food? The article was proof, too, that the desire to eat better is not just West Coast neurosis anymore—it's a fact of life cross-country. Let me quote Gael Greene, the famous food writer who penned the *New York* article: "Passionate excess can lead to ugliness and inconvenient disrepair, to a hasty and painful exit." In other words, for all of you out there who continually say, "I don't care, I'm above that weight-consciousness nonsense, I'm more intellectual than that," snobbery is going to cut your intellectualism short!

Even Greene, the food critic who wrote, "I love to eat, I love to drink, I love to sloth," finally faced up to the facts: If you eat, drink, and sloth in overabundance as your regular lifestyle, your lifestyle will be cut short. Yet the mistake most people make is thinking that if you make the effort to change, you have to go the straight, narrow, and masochistic way Nathan Pritikin encouraged his followers to go. "Stay out of restaurants, they are enemy camp," he once said. No wonder few could stay on the Pritikin plan! Restaurants are a great joy, a necessary part of social and business interactions in our lives today—not the enemy. And any diet program that keeps you from social and business entertaining will eventually fail. It's our conditioning and acceptance of unacceptable food that is the enemy.

Every restaurant you enter has the foods and facilities to prepare dishes the way you need and want them to be prepared. They all have steamers, broilers, and/or grills. They all have fresh produce, which they can bring to you raw, if necessary. If you ask, you can have the chef work for you and accommodate your "allergies." You can enjoy eating because it's not going to make you feel guilty or give you fat thighs.

Many people thought the fitness boom was a fly-by-night trend, but now they're all out there walking, if not engaging in an even more vigorous form of exercise. And like the fitness boom, "fit eating" is here to stay. Any chef whose artistic impulses won't let you have your fish or chicken grilled with lime juice instead of the macadamia sauce is going to be out of a job in the next five years. Right now every exclusive eatery, every coffee shop, and truck-stop diner serves diet sodas and has Sweet 'N Low on hand. In the next few years, and you can quote me on this, low-calorie salad dressings are definitely going to be just as commonplace.

Let me give you just one example of how restaurants are changing. Upon the signing of the contract for this book, I had lunch with my editor, agent, and co-writer at a trendy New York trattoria. I ordered some vegetables, but asked that they be cooked without any oil. The Italian waiter looked at me as if I were from Mars; he just didn't get it (and it wasn't because of a language barrier either). I ended up ordering the fruit and cheese plate instead and pushing the cheese to the side. Needless to say, I got some strange looks from the staff for not eating the cheese. But now, a year later, that very same trendy trattoria has a note at the bottom of its menu that says "Let us know if you have any allergies and we will accommodate them." Ha! Not only is that proof that the allergy trick works, but that's proof of where restaurants are heading. There's no reason, though, that you can't get a jump on the trend: start asking for nonfattening food NOW. To quote Greene one last time: Start by asking, "What have you got that I *can* eat?"

## Men and Menus: Overcoming the Fear of "Rabbit Food"

Many men that I talk to are suffering from one too many business lunches. They're concerned about their weight—although perhaps not as consumed with it as women—yet they don't want to let on that they care, particularly at a business lunch. A lot of them will order a tuna sandwich because they think it's healthy to eat fish, but not realize that

the mayonnaise is killing them. The same with Caesar salad (fatty croutons, Parmesan cheese, and egg yolks) and chef salad (cheese, ham, and
an oily dressing). The thing to do is replace the ham and cheese in the
chef salad with extra turkey, tomatoes (eggs if you're not watching your
cholesterol) and use some Parmesan cheese. Or order a seafood salad
sans dressing; ask for vinegar and mustard on the side. A turkey sandwich with mustard instead of mayo or broiled chicken with a baked potato
would both be less fattening than the tuna sandwich, too. Many restaurants now even offer turkey burgers instead of hamburgers.

Men hate "rabbit food." I know, but you won't feel wimpy if you order
a salad bulked up with chicken or plain tuna and have some bread on the
side. For years I was chastised for bringing my own little jar of salad
dressing to restaurants in my purse. I was thought to be neurotic.
("What's that, a urine sample?" was the joke) Well, I always preferred to
be neurotic about bringing my little jar than neurotic about a large rear
end. Eventually, most of my clients have taken on the same habit and it
has become pretty commonplace in Los Angeles. However, I knew that
I was on the right track when an article in *Newsweek* magazine about how
"power dieting" has finally hit Washington, D.C., revealed that all of the
major politicians are trying to trim the fat off their bodies, not just the
budget. "House Speaker Thomas Foley didn't touch the smoked-buffalo
entrée or the poached baby pears at last month's Gridiron dinner," tat-
tled *Newsweek*. "He ate the broccoli, and he doused the salad with the
low-calorie dressing he brought with him in a jar." I always knew it was
the classy thing to do.

My father is a classic example of a man too "macho" to worry about
his diet. He is sixty and from a generation where weight loss was strictly
for women or really obese men, and certainly not to be talked about in
public. While all his life he was average weight and able to eat exactly
how he pleased, he began to notice a few extra pounds around his middle
in his later years. So he'd swim regularly and the weight would come off.
But change his eating habits? Never.

My father thought I was a complete pain at restaurants and that my
eating habits were pretty crazy. Then he got hit with his cholesterol
count! It was very high, high enough to make him say to me, "Okay,
you're right. What should I do?" So I went over the basic facts with him
and let it go at that, thinking he got the message. No more peanuts
(which contain some saturated fat) at four o'clock every day, no more
snacking on cheese, and so on. Then one night we met for dinner and he
ordered the marinated tuna, pasta salad, and cole slaw. "Aren't you
proud of the way I ordered," he asked. I laughed out loud. "The only

reason I didn't jump on you was because you had a bad day," I replied. I asked the waiter to bring us the marinade in a bowl so that my father could see all the oil it contained. I explained that the dressing on the pasta salad was based on mayonnaise and that the cole slaw is almost all sour cream. "You might as well go check into a heart attack clinic right now." We went over basic restaurant strategy again and this time he resentfully agreed to try.

About a year later, we were visiting New York. Before going to the theater we had dinner in a very elegant Italian restaurant. "What are you going to order, Dad?" I asked. He looked directly at me and said "Yo, I'm not going to pull that here. This is New York, not LA, and I'm not going to insult the chef." I then said that it would insult me to see him drop dead. That didn't seem to faze him so I said it would insult me to have to push his drooling body around in a wheelchair after he had a stroke. That did it. The waiter came to our table and my father struggled to get out his order for fish prepared with olive oil instead of butter. "But, of course, it is no problem," said the waiter, thereby closing a generation gap. In other words, the times they are a changin'!

## The "I Spend Half My Life in a Restaurant Syndrome"

"I have absolutely NO FOOD in my house/apartment," is a cry I hear frequently from people who virtually eat every single meal out or ordered in from a restaurant. "Well, it is very obvious to me that you should not allow that to dictate your health and body shape. That is the ultimate in victimizing yourself. Stop pointing that (fat) finger at everything else in your life and take some responsibility for yourself," I tell them. "Learn how to order!"

This is a problem almost always associated with the young, upwardly mobile people (a.k.a. yuppies). I point out to clients like these that they are educated, climbing the ladder (or already there), and have an incredible ability to take control of everything else in their lives. Why not take control of their eating lives? If you know that you're going to have lunch at a certain *fabulous* restaurant and dinner at your favorite bistro, then order a lean breakfast at the coffee shop, have a *fabulous* lunch, and perhaps just a salad for dinner. If you go to certain places on a regular basis—believe me—they want to keep you there. The restaurant business is unbelievably competitive. Ask them to keep some oil-free salad dressing for you. Ask the coffee shop you stop by every morning (who knows just how you like your coffee, by the way) to stock some bran muffins along with all the other Danish. Perhaps you always have lunch at the corner drugstore—ask them to carry some balsamic vinegar for your salads, or make a certain salad with more chicken and veggies than avocado and cheese. You get the idea. You're spending a lot of that paycheck supporting these people's businesses, not to mention tipping all of those waiters. All that to feel fat and unhealthy! Think about it.

My husband and I frequent a local restaurant every Friday night, because they always have carrot sticks for me to munch at the bar, we like the house wine, and they will prepare anything for me without oil. The bread is great and they have a big TV so my husband can watch sports. We are both comfortable there, and sometimes comfort is just what it's all about.

## What to Eat Where: A Guide to Every Kind of Restaurant

I have two different approaches to dining out: One is for those special nights when I'm going to go all out and indulge in a gourmet meal (or am just in the mood to indulge, period); the other is for regular nights when I'm going out socially, but the meal is no big deal.

When dinner is a special occasion—and a calorie extravanganza—I save up by eating a minimum of lean foods during the day. That way I'm prepped for a guilt-free pig-out at night. The next day I cut back and try to exercise a little more, too, so that in the end it all balances out.

On the average night out, when I'm having a business meal or just a casual dinner with friends, I actually eat before I go. At home, I usually munch on fresh veggies while I cook dinner, which cuts my voracious appetite. So, when I'm going out, I try to do the munching while I'm getting ready to go. For instance, the other night I was invited to eat at a very elegant gourmet Chinese restaurant before a concert at the Hollywood Bowl. I called the restaurant ahead of time to see if they could prepare some of the dishes without oil. They practically hung up on me and, although I don't speak Chinese, it sounded like they were swearing at me; the prospects of getting a good meal without fat didn't look good. So throughout the day of the dinner, I made a point of munching on more fruit, rice cakes, and veggies than I normally would. I even had a late snack about 4:30. My plan was to avoid going to the restaurant feeling starved so that I wouldn't be tempted by all the oily dishes. Once there,

I ordered fish dishes and asked them to eliminate the sauces, plus a lot of steamed rice to fill me up.

The food was prepared with oil, but I kept the damage to a minimum. The truth is, if I were really crazy about Chinese food, I might have let it go and ordered the sweet-and-sour peanut sauce goo or the fattening dishes everyone else had ordered. But because I don't really care about that particular kind of cuisine, it wasn't worth becoming a victim of circumstance and just saying, "Oh, well, there's nothing I can do so I guess I'll just blow it tonight." Instead, I took care of myself.

Believe me, restaurant eating is one of the biggest problems my clientele (who dine out all the time) have. With Carrie Fisher, the problem was that she loved to munch on the bread or breadsticks as soon as she sat down, because it calmed her nerves. Fine, I said, just don't order pasta and more starches for dinner; keep it to grilled chicken, veggies, and salad. Kate Jackson wasn't as concerned with weight loss as she was with eating healthfully. So we eliminated oil from her foods at home, and she was fine. But she still doesn't order heavy cream sauces, pastas, or desserts when she dines out. Paul Stanley *lives* at restaurants so he made a point of learning how to order food completely oil-free and to enjoy his sweets when he craved them. Brian Wilson orders as religiously as I do. Madeleine Stowe, however, will order what she pleases at a good Italian restaurant. Not on a regular basis, though. Not every, or even every other, night, and that's key.

What follows is a cuisine-by-cuisine guide to good eating, designed to make menus, especially those at ethnic eateries, a little more user-friendly. The particular Chinese restaurant I went to was not as accommodating as one would hope. But many Chinese restaurants—*many restaurants*—are. Wherever you go, though, you just have to do the best that you can. If what you end up eating isn't as healthy and nonfattening as you hope, don't feel guilty about it, just enjoy it. Don't lay a guilt trip on yourself and ruin your (and probably your partner's) evening. Just try to make up for it the next day.

## To Have and Have Not . . .

Coffee shop to continental bistro, there are certain basics almost always on the menu. Here is what you should say "absolutely not" to (unless it's a special occasion) and what you should go for instead. Remember, though, anything that's on the recommended list can quickly become an "absolutely not" if it's doused with oil or cream sauces.

| Absolutely Not | Absolutely |
|---|---|

## APPETIZERS/STARTERS

| Absolutely Not | Absolutely |
|---|---|
| Fried hors d'oeuvres | Steamed veggies and artichokes (no oil or mayonnaise—dip in mustard) |
| Cream or onion (with cheese) soups | Broth soups and miso soups |
| Pâtés | Bread, breadsticks, and crackers (no butter) |
| Creamy dips | Shrimp and cocktail sauce |
| Caviar and egg yolks (high in cholesterol) | Fresh seafood—crab, lobster, oysters, clams, and mussels |
| Chips | Seviche |
| Antipastos (usually oil soaked) | Crudité and salsa |
| Anything fried, stir-fried, smoked, braised, sautéed, or marinated | |

## ENTRÉES

| Absolutely Not | Absolutely |
|---|---|
| Red meat | Fish |
| Organ meats (high in cholesterol) | Chicken or turkey |
| Anything sautéed, sauced, marinated, braised, simmered, or fried | Anything steamed, poached, baked, or broiled (without oil or butter) |
| Pastas with cream, butter, oil, or cheese sauces | Pasta with plain tomato sauce and herbs |

## SALAD ADD-ONS

| Absolutely Not | Absolutely |
|---|---|
| Grated cheese (a little Parmesan is okay) | All plain, fresh veggies |
| Veggies marinated in oil | Bamboo shoots |
| Seeds and nuts | Hearts of palm |
| Bacon | Water chestnuts |
| Regular salad dressings | Fresh seafood, canned tuna |
| Avocado | Light, diet, or fat-free dressings—or one you make yourself (see Box 2) |

## DESSERTS

| Absolutely Not | Absolutely |
|---|---|
| All pastries, cakes, pies, and ice creams | Fresh fruit |
| | Sorbets |
| | Nonfat frozen yogurt |

## Box 1.  Fish Facts

**S**ome fish are naturally fattier than others. Among them: salmon, mackerel, sea bass, trout, and black cod. To their disadvantage, they're more caloric so if you're trying to lose weight, order a low-fat fish like sole, halibut, flounder, or red snapper. To fattier fish's advantage is the fact that they contain more omega-3 fatty acids (thought to help guard against heart disease). Plus, because they have fat of their own, they tend to stay moist when cooked without the addition of any cooking oils. Be aware that within the fish category they're more fattening, but compared to most other kinds of entrées, they're still very low fat—and a very good choice.

### Nutritional Breakdown of Seafood

| 100g (3½ oz.) raw, edible portion | Calories | Fat gms | Chol. mgs | Omega 3 fatty acids gms |
|---|---|---|---|---|
| Albacore tuna | 102 | 3.0 | 25 | 1.3 |
| Catfish | 103 | 3.1 | 55 | 3 |
| Clams | 80 | 1.5 | 40 | trace |
| Cod | 70 | .7 | 40 | .2 |
| Crab, dungeness | 81 | 1.3 | 90 | .3 |
| Crab, imitation | 90 | .1 | 50 | — |
| Flounder | 90 | 1.4 | 50 | .2 |
| Haddock | 80 | .5 | 60 | — |
| Halibut | 105 | 1.2 | 50 | .4 |
| Lobster | 90 | 1.9 | 85 | .2 |
| Monkfish | 70 | 1.0 | 35 | — |
| Mussels | 75 | 1.6 | 25 | .5 |
| Ocean perch | 95 | 1.5 | 60 | .2 |
| Orange roughy | 65 | .3 | — | — |
| Oysters | 70 | 1.2 | 50 | .6 |
| Rockfish (snapper) | 97 | 1.8 | 40 | .5 |
| Sablefish (black cod) | 130 | 5.7 | 65 | 1.5 |
| Salmon | 142 | 7.0 | 65 | 1.1 |
| Scallops | 82 | .2 | 50 | .2 |
| Shark, thrasher | 90 | 1.0 | — | — |
| Shrimp | 90 | .8 | 158 | .3 |
| Sole | 70 | .5 | 45 | — |
| Squid | 85 | .9 | — | .3 |
| Swordfish | 120 | 4.4 | 50 | .2 |
| Trout, rainbow | 195 | 11.4 | 50 | .5 |

---

## Box 2. *The Skinny on Salad Dressings*

A ll restaurant salad dressings are laden with either oil, cheese, and cream and sometimes even all three. So ask for your salad sans dressing with a side of vinegar and mustard instead. Simply combine the two in a dish, then drizzle the mixture over your salad, and grind a little pepper on top. Many restaurants now have balsamic vinegar that, because it's sweet, doesn't really need to be cut with oil and can even be sprinkled over greens alone. If your vinegar-mustard mixture is too tart, add a bit of Sweet 'N Low or Equal or a teaspoon of Parmesan cheese. Another option: ask for a side of salsa and a few lemon wedges. Spritz the salsa with the lemon, then toss with salad. Other good combos:

- Worcestershire sauce/Tabasco sauce/light soy sauce/lemon
- Rice vinegar/light soy sauce/lemon

I still advocate bringing your own in a little jar. Skinny Haven and Weight Watchers make little foil packets (diet junk food, but not fattening) of dressing that you can keep in your purse or wallet.

---

## Box 3. *Salsa: The All-Purpose Sauce*

O nce strictly the stuff of Mexican restaurants, salsa is now a staple in all different kinds of eateries. It's also become more than just a dip for chips: because it's fat free, salsa makes a perfect sauce for fish and chicken. It it's not available for you to order on the side, make your own version. Ask for a plate of sliced tomatoes and onions, chop them up with your knife and fork, then mix in a little vinegar, mustard, and pepper.

The newest thing around are fruit salsas (for example, papaya salsa), also a great option if they are on the menu.

---

## Smart Ordering at Specialty Spots

## *BURGER JOINTS/FAST FOOD RESTAURANTS*

Thankfully, as I was writing this book, many fast food restaurants began to see the light. McDonald's, for one, had not only begun to make over its menu, but was even test marketing a leaner version of their usual, greasy burger. Wendy's now sells baked potatoes and has a salad bar. Still, fast food is fast food and the majority of it remains a hazard to both your health and hips.

Your best bet is a hamburger on, if possible, a whole-wheat bun. Ask for it well-done (if you can eat it that way—the longer meat cooks, the more fat it loses in the process), topped with lettuce, tomato, and ketchup or mustard. Go for junior hamburgers (they have fewer calories and fat) if the burger joint you're at offers them. If you're really trying to lose weight, skip the bun. Order extra tomatoes and pickles on the side, then munch on them instead of fries. This will be a high-salt meal (the pickles and the burger), but not a terribly fattening one.

Most places offer grilled chicken sandwiches now, but make sure you get them "your way"—with lettuce, tomato, ketchup or mustard instead of a fatty sauce. Salads are also newly hot fast-food items, but really take a good look to see what's in them. If you order a salad at McDonald's, avoid the one with ham and cheese, or just take it out of the salad yourself. Ask for their diet dressing or make your own dressing with lemon and mustard. (They surely can give you both on the side.)

Some places make it especially difficult to eat reasonably well, but *don't* give up. Find yourself at Kentucky Fried Chicken or some other greasy chicken joint? Always choose a breast (it's leanest) and peel the skin off the chicken. Order the corn without butter and opt for one serving of mashed potatoes instead of French fries. Pizza parlors tend to offer different kinds of slices these days, so choose wisely. Pizza Hut's thin and crispy pizza is less fattening than its cheese pan pizza; just adding pepperoni to a slice of Domino's adds almost twice as much fat. In general, look for thin crust, and vegetable toppings—or none.

A few good (okay, better) picks when you're stuck and starving:

McDonald's plain burger—263 calories
McDonald's Oriental chicken salad—141 calories
McDonald's nonfat apple bran muffin—90 calories

McDonald's frozen yogurt cone—100 calories
McDonald's low-fat milkshake—320 calories
Arby's boneless chicken breast—254 calories
Wendy's chili—240 calories
Wendy's grilled chicken sandwich—350 calories
Burger King's plain hamburger—240 calories
Burger King's salad with reduced-calorie dressing—42 calories (have three)
Burger King's BK broiler chicken sandwich (without sauce)—379 calories
Jack-in-the-Box's Breakfast Jack—307 calories

While most of the above are neither fat-free nor even border-line healthy, they'll help you avoid feeling like an outcast every time you end up in a fast-food restaurant.

## The All-American Diner/Coffee Shop

All of these restaurants have broiled chicken or fish. If you're caught at one where the only poultry and seafood dishes are breaded or fried, you're better off having them broil you a small steak without any butter or oil. Order a baked potato on the side, then accent it with Tabasco or Worcestershire sauce.

There is often some kind of turkey and mashed potato combo on the menu and you can probably get them to bring you the turkey without any gravy and with a baked potato and sliced tomatoes or a salad on the side instead of the mashed potatoes.

Most coffee shops and diners offer a chef salad, which you can ask for without the ham and cheese, with extra turkey, egg, tomato, and veggies. Have some crackers on the side and use mustard rather than butter as a spread. They usually have great baskets of assorted crackers.

At the very least, you can count on all of these places to have iceberg lettuce and tomatoes, and some sort of fresh fruit, and they all have salamanders (broilers) and grills so they can prepare you some chicken or fish without oils or butter. Also, if they have tuna salad on the menu, ask for plain tuna with some red wine vinegar on the side, and sliced tomatoes. Usually these places serve meals all day long, so they have quite a stock of food in their walk-ins (large refrigerators), so don't be afraid to ask for what you need.

## *Jewish Delicatessens*

Ordering here is pretty easy. Jewish delis generally have a lot of vegetable side dishes and always have sliced turkey breast—although make sure it isn't smoked, because the smoking process adds oil and a lot of salt and potentially carcinogenic nitrates to food. Likewise, stay away from the various kinds of smoked fish such as lox, smoked whitefish, and smoked cod.

There are always pickles and pickled tomatoes to eat along with your food; ask for the cracker basket, a water bagel, or a few slices of rye bread too. There's usually a good selection of soups, but don't order chicken soup with matzo balls—they're made with chicken fat. The broth alone, though, is fine.

It's possible to make a meal of the various steamed vegetable side dishes they serve. Order lots of sliced tomatoes and onions, but avoid the coleslaw because of its creamy sauce. There is usually a good variety of salads, just bring your own dressing or make a fat-free version at the table. The same goes here as at the coffee shop as far as getting grilled chicken or fish. For dessert, opt for the Jell-O with fruit (sugary, but it won't kill you).

## *Chinese*

The Chinese love to cook with three things: sugar, oil, and MSG—in short, all of the things you want to avoid. You can ask them to leave out the MSG but, if you're very allergic, be aware that it is similar to salt in that when they say "no MSG" they mean that they are not actually pouring MSG on the food—but many of the cooking ingredients they use already contain MSG. Remember, MSG is a flavor enhancer; it brings out a good salty punch to the palate. But the next morning your face looks outrageous—so puffy you can't recognize it. Eat a lot of steamed rice and drink a lot of water to wash it through your system.

The good news is that the Chinese also love to steam food. You can order a whole fish steamed with ginger and scallions, steamed dumplings and steamed bean curd (i.e., tofu). It's also possible to order steamed vegetables. With lots of steamed rice on the side, these dishes can make for a satisfying meal. Stay away from the cold noodles in sesame sauce, but do ask if they can bring you cold noodles with scallions and sprouts mixed in. Or start with one of the clear soups with garden vegetables, which will help to deaden your appetite.

# French

Beware the butter (beurre) sauces. Even a perfectly designed nouvelle cuisine plate of snow peas, baby carrots, and haricots verts that seems low-calorie may in fact be coated with butter. Insist that they give you the same plate simply steamed, no oil.

For starters, French restaurants usually have oysters, shrimps, scallops, or seviche, all good choices. Salads are fine too. Just ask for some of their fine wine vinegar and Dijon mustard on the side instead of the house dressing. Of course, enjoy the wine and bread as well. For entrées, the words to look for are in consommé, rotisserie, poached, and la nage (reduced poaching liquid). Try to get them to grill your fish or chicken without oil, but if they say they can't (they'll claim the food will stick to the grill), ask them to put them in the salamander, which is similar to a broiler or sauté your food in wine, broth, and shallots.

For dessert, go ahead and have a fruit tart, although try to leave the buttery crust. Or, go for a sorbet or a slice of angel food cake. Skip the sherbet, which contains milk fat. Sorbets? Oui!

# Greek

This type of cuisine can be fat-soaked and usually requires a lot of vigourous Greek dancing to burn it off. However, eating a whole grilled lamb isn't your only choice. *Plaki* is the word for grilled fish (avoid the souvlakia and go for the plaki or grilled chicken) and tzatziki is a mixture of yogurt, cucumbers, and garlic that you can eat with pita bread. Greek salads are okay, too, but ask them to leave off the dressing. The crumbled feta cheese (one of the lower-fat cheeses) on top is probably enough to give the salad flavor. If not, squeeze some lemon over the greens. To note: olives are a surprising ten calories each and almost all fat.

# Indian

Many Indian eateries will poach and steam food, just as Chinese restaurants do, so go ahead and ask. *Tandoori* is the word to look for, because this means baked in a clay oven, just be sure and ask what the marinade is. The chicken or fish tandoori is your best bet. They also have steamed rice and paratha, an unleavened bread that is good to fill up on. Vegetarian curries are also good choices—they will most likely contain some fat, but less than many of the other dishes.

# *Italian*

Pasta in itself is not that fattening. But most of the sauces are. Italian restaurants, though, have plain canned tomatoes and tomato sauce in the back. The chef can take the tomatoes and cook them with garlic, oregano, and basil and without oil—you'll never miss it (nor will your behind). You might also consider ordering plain pasta, then tossing it with tomatoes you cut up yourself on the side. Add a teaspoon of Parmesan cheese for flavor if you like. If you're really stuck, order the linguine with clam sauce, which isn't too bad. Sometimes you can get the chef to prepare a pasta dish of shrimp, broth, and garlic. Nine out of ten Italian restaurants also have fish, which they can grill or broil—always a safe order.

As for appetizers, you can order panzanella, a small salad of cucumbers and tomatoes. Again, ask for it without oil and with balsamic vinegar instead. Seviche and mussels in broth are also always good starters, although make sure they haven't been soaked in olive oil. If you're ordering the antipasto, get them to leave off the salami and put extra raw and pickled vegetables on the platter instead; a little mozzarella (one of the skim-milk cheeses) is okay too.

When dining in an Italian restaurant, don't be shy. The staff will never understand "no olive oil"—olive oil supports their country!—so insist, don't ask. Use the allergic trick here and ask them to cook your food in wine (that also supports their country).

# *Japanese*

Because there are so many seafood dishes to choose among, Japanese food is relatively healthy. Order the cucumber salad with rice vinegar and sesame to start or a bowl of the clear or miso soup. Sashimi with steamed rice is your best choice for an entrée, but there are others, too: any sushi that doesn't contain fried bits of food or avocado; yosenabe, a seafood and vegetable stew; broiled or steamed fish; chicken yakatori. Tempura, naturally, is not your wisest entrée choice and the teriyaki dishes, while not as bad, are made with a lot of sugar. One good way to keep your soy sauce (and, therefore, sodium) intake down is to fill your dipping bowl only halfway, fill up the rest with rice vinegar. To make sure you don't leave the table hungry, sample the side vegetables. I am the only person I know who devours the restaurant's artistic garnishes of carrot and daikon radish, and why not—they taste as good as they look.

Japanese restaurants always have tons premade, so ask for more than just a measly garnish.

## *Mexican*

This is one type of cuisine people who are concerned about fat and calories often avoid. A Mexican restaurant just might be the place you should throw caution to the wind and make it one of those special nights out. But if you wind up eating Mexican food often, you'll need to learn how to enjoy it and order wisely at the same time.

Naturally, you'll want to stay away from any of the fried dishes (chimichangas, for instance) and those that are loaded down with cheese (*never* nachos!) and sauces (i.e., enchiladas and flautas). Most Mexican sauces are made with lard or lots of oil; so, unfortunately, are most of the beans.

A Mexican restaurant's best asset is the salsa—it adds so much flavor to everything and is not fattening in the least. Have them bring you carrot or celery sticks or jicama slices so you can dip away and not even touch the chips. Gazpacho and seviche are both good starters too. Entrée-wise, most places will now grill or broil fish or chicken; then you can order more salsa to put on top. You might also try a chicken tostada without any beans (unless they're plain black or pinto beans, not refried), cheese, or guacamole—essentially a chicken salad. Use salsa to dress that, too, rather than the oily dressing the restaurant is most likely to serve.

As a side, steamed corn tortillas (they don't contain fat, but the flour tortillas do) are a relatively good choice. If they do have plain beans, (again, mix in salsa to give them more flavor), order some along with a few tortillas and plain rice and you have a complete (and low-fat) meal. Remember, most Mexican cuisine is designed to fill you up inexpensively, not entertain you with creative gourmet treats, so try to order foods that your body can burn, not just store.

## The Morning Menu: Having Breakfast/Brunch Out

Breakfast, the last bastion of home dining has now turned into a "power" meal during the week and a social one on the weekends. Some ways to cope with restaurants' morning menus:

*Eggs* are out if you have a cholesterol problem. Period. If weight loss is your goal and your cholesterol level is fine, go ahead and have eggs . . . that is, eggs that are poached, hard boiled, or soft boiled, not fried or scrambled, which are always cooked in butter. The best way to have them is poached over a piece of whole wheat toast: the bread will soak up the yolk and you won't feel the need to spread it with butter.

*Bacon and ham* are out of your life forever. The bottom line is that they come from pigs and pigs are raised on garbage, not healthy food, and you will "look like one too," to quote the old birthday song variation. Pork products are loaded with everything you don't need, i.e., fat and nitrates. You're better off ordering a lean steak with your eggs, although only on days when you feel you really need a hearty breakfast for, say, hiking or skiing. Turkey sausage is an alternative that's being offered in a lot of places now but, while some brands are better, others are still packed with chemicals (ask if they use an organic brand). Be aware, too, that turkey sausage is still fairly fattening.

*Muffins* can be deceptive, particularly if they're bran or oat bran. Don't assume that they're healthy or nonfattening just because you see those "B" words. That's like assuming the word *salad* is synonymous with nonfattening because it's made with lettuce, then ordering a chef's salad with oily dressing. A lot of muffins are loaded with oil, nuts, and raisins, making them high in calories, fat, and sugar. Many places now serve sugar-free muffins, which are usually healthier. You're safest, however, ordering a dry English muffin, then spreading a little jam (roughly 18 nonfat calories to butter's 35 fat calories) on it.

*Cold cereal and oatmeal* can be good choices if you eat them with skim milk and bananas or other fresh fruit for sweetness. Needless to say, stay away from sugar-coated cereals, especially granola — granola is often prepared with coconut or other saturated oils and lots of sugar.

*Fresh fruit* is almost always available and a great breakfast on its own or with some toast. If you're having fruit with breakfast, don't have any juice. Juice is high in sugar and you're already getting enough in the fruit. When you do order juice, cut it in half with mineral water.

*Waffles and pancakes,* common brunch fare, aren't too bad if you leave off the butter and syrup or whipped cream. Use jam instead. If you can get whole wheat French toast dipped in nonfat milk and egg white, and not cooked in butter, you're really doing well.

*Coffee and tea* will be less fattening if you have them with low-fat or skim milk. Avoid those little dairy creamers and never, ever use the powdered milk *substitutes*—they are often bolstered with palm and coconut oils. *Real* powdered nonfat milk, however, is a good alternative to cream. At the very least, ask for whole milk instead of the substitutes or real cream. Even on airplanes I insist on real milk instead of the little cream containers. They definitely have it on board. Remember, you can always burn off what is real, better than what is processed with oils and junk.

## Cocktail Cautionary: How to Stay Happy at Happy Hour

The cocktail hour has always been a problem for people concerned about their health and weight. You usually reach the bar starving or stressed out from work. Or if it's a cocktail party (just being at a cocktail party makes some people nervous), whether a social or business occasion, you're likely to feel anxiety at having to be "on." But the real purpose of cocktail hour and cocktail parties is to let people relax, unwind, and munch a little before dinner. It's supposed to be a very pleasant social experience. I personally love cocktail hour. However, I don't love what the peanuts, mini wieners, Swedish meatballs, and fried chicken wings do to my body. I tend not to be relaxed if I know what I am eating is going to make me feel slothful the next day.

Most people's resistance to cocktail hour and party fare is weakened by the first drink. They give into a few peanuts, then a few more, then suddenly they decide they've blown it, go out to dinner and order the fettucine, Caesar salad, and cheesecake, all the time thinking, "I'll diet tomorrow." The next morning they hate themselves, search through their closets for their "fat" clothes, and try to starve off the previous night's excesses.

Well, this syndrome—I want to have fun, I want to relax, I want to indulge and enjoy, but I do not want to be fat and ugly!—can become excessively boring. Yet it is possible to go to a bar at happy hour time or a cocktail party and enjoy yourself without having to pay the piper so dearly. Every single bar has things for you to eat: celery sticks and other raw veggies, orange slices, sometimes other kinds of fruit, too, that they usually put in drinks. I have even asked bartenders to bring me an apple from the back. Breadsticks are also good to munch on as are crackers: You can surely get these at a cocktail party and even the worst gin joint usually has saltines, which aren't great (they usually contain hydrogenated oils), but are much less fattening than greasy tortilla chips. Many places serve popcorn now—fine if it's not buttered. While salty, pretzels are not a killer either. Consider:

| Food | Calories | Fat | Sodium |
| --- | --- | --- | --- |
| 10 potato chips | 105 | 7 grams | 95 milligrams |
| ¼ cup peanuts | 210 | 18 grams | 155 milligrams |
| ⅔ cup pretzels | 100 | trace | 480 milligrams |

Unfortunately, many fairly low-fat snacks are fairly high in sodium. So whether you choose them or not should depend on how sodium affects you. If you have high blood pressure or blow up like a balloon just looking at salt, forget it. When push comes to shove, you can always ask the bartender to bring you one of the bread baskets served at the tables (presuming you are in a restaurant) and chances are your cocktail party host has some French bread out on the buffet table. Added plus: the bread will soak up the alcohol you're drinking a little and quench your appetite slightly so that, once you go to dinner, you won't overeat.

As far as alcohol goes, you'll be best off with wine spritzers, light beer, or plain mineral water (or seltzer). Because alcohol is a carbohydrate, you can burn off the calories, assuming you've consumed them in moderation. The problem drinks are those creamy and heavily sweetened liqueurs, hard liquor drinks made with fattening mixers (like Coke), and regular kinds of beer (beer is fattening because of the varied ingredients—yeast, malt, starch—used to make it). But even a few ounces, remember I said a few, of those varieties of alcohol aren't going to make you fat. People often blame their weight problems on alcohol, but unless you really sock it back, it's probably not a big factor. It might, though, make you eat more if you're prone to losing your willpower when you drink. In that case, you have to concentrate on the food around you in a drinking situation. Here's a good guide to go by.

Most important, remember to enjoy yourself. This is not a suffering or deprivation hour; it's a relaxation hour. Once you know the set of rules that work for you personally, cocktail hour will become a pleasure and not set you on the road to self-destruction.

The following menus will help you understand how to order at various restaurants. Once you have established "your rules" you will be able to eat anywhere in the world and really enjoy it.

## BAR TIME BASICS

| Go For | Avoid |
|---|---|
| Raw veggies (dip them in mustard if you like) | All nuts |
| | All dips |
| Shrimp or other fresh seafood (without cocktail sauce) | Chips |
| | Fried hors d'oeuvres |
| Fruit | Cheese |
| Crackers | Cheesy hors d'oeuvres |
| Bread or breadsticks | Meatballs |
| Popcorn | Mini franks |
| Pretzels | Olives |
| Chewing gum or Lifesavers | |

# SUNG TIENG CHINESE RESTAURANT

**343 Bleecker Street**
(Bet. 10th St. & Christopher St.)

## WE SERVE BROWN RICE

★ ★ ★
### WE USE NO M.S.G.

## HUNAN/SZECHUAN CUISINE

SMALL & LARGE PARTY ORDERS WELCOME

## APPETIZERS

Chicken or Shrimp

春 | 卷
鍋 | 餃
葱 | 水
排 | 餅
牛 | 骨
茄 | 串
 | 夾
 | 肉
 | 、
 | 油
 | 貼
 | 鍋

热 | 拼
棒 | 鶏
凉 | 麵
菠 | 棒
菜 | 凉
 | 麵

| | |
|---|---|
| 1. Egg Roll | 1.20 |
| 2. Dumplings (Fried or Boiled 6) | |
| 3. Crispy Scallion Pancake | 3.75 |
| 4. Barbecued Spare Ribs | 3.75 |
| 5. Barbecued Beef Skewer | 5.45 |
| 6. Eggplant Puffs Stuffed with Chicken and Shrimp Pate (4) | 3.95 |
| 7. Bo-Bo Platter (For 2) | 3.75 |
| 8.★ Hacked Chicken with Sesame Hot Sauce | 6.95 |
| 9.★ Cold Noodles with Sesame Hot Sauce | 3.75 |
| 10.★ Cold Spinach Noodles with Sesame Hot Sauce | 3.75 |
| | 3.75 |

## SOUPS

蛋 | 花 | 湯
雲 | 吞 | 湯
酸 | 辣 | 湯
青 | 菜 | 豆腐湯
賢 | 肉 | 玉米湯

| | |
|---|---|
| 11. Egg Drop Soup(1) | |
| 12. Wonton Soup | 1.20 |
| 13.★ Hot and Sour Soup | 1.35 |
| 14. Bean Curd & Chinese Veg. Soup (For 2) | 1.35 |
| 15. Creamy Corn & Crab Meat Soup (For 2) | 3.55 |
| | 5.55 |

## POULTRY

大 | 千 | 鶏
芝 | 麻 | 鶏
宮 | 保 | 鶏

| | |
|---|---|
| 16.★ Ta-Chien Chicken | |
| 18.★ Spicy Sesame Chicken | 7.25 |
| 19.★ Diced Chicken Szechuan Style | 7.25 |
| | 6.95 |

## CHEF'S SPECIALTIES

脆 皮 雙 鮮 **36.★ SHELLFISH SUPREME** ............... **9.95**
Crispy fried prawns & scallops, topped with toasted
sesame seeds, served with Hunan dipping sauce.

脆 皮 魚 **37.★ CRISPY WHOLE SEA BASS WITH** ......... **11.95**
**SPICY HUNAN SAUCE**

會 海 鮮 **38. FISHERMEN'S NEST** ............... **9.95**
Fresh scallops, prawns, and crab meat
with assorted Chinese vegetables.

炒 三 鮮 **39.★ TRIPLE DELIGHT** ............... **8.95**
Prawns, chicken and pork stir-fried with assorted
fresh vegetables.

干 貝 牛 4...BLE DELICACY ............... 
...with broccoli & pea pods.

龍 鳳 配 ............... **9.95**

*steamed in broth— no sauce*

*Avoid the word "sauce"*

## SEAFOOD

| | | | |
|---|---|---|---|
| 48. | Prawns with Snow Peas | | 8.75 |
| 49.★ | Scallops in Hot Garlic Sauce | *steamed* | 8.75 |
| 50. | Scallops with Broccoli | | 8.75 |
| 51.★ | Prawns Hunan Style | *steamed* | 8.75 |
| 52.★ | Jade Tree Prawns | | 8.75 |
| 53. | Prawns with Broccoli | *steamed* | 8.75 |
| 54.★ | Sauteed Shrimp & Chicken Combo | | 7.75 |
| 55.★ | Shrimp in Hot Garlic Sauce | | 7.75 |
| 56.★ | Shrimp Szechuan Style | | 7.75 |
| 57. | Shrimp in Balck Bean Sauce | | 7.75 |

## VEGETABLE

| | | | |
|---|---|---|---|
| 58. | Fried Bean Curd with Green Broccoli | | 6.25 |
| 59. | Vegetarian's Delight | | 6.25 |
| 60.★ | Broccoli, Zucchini and Eggplant | | 6.25 |
| 61. | Stir-Fried Zucchini | | 5.95 |
| 62. | Stir-Fried Broccoli | | 5.95 |
| 63. | Stir-Frlied Bean Sprouts | | 5.95 |
| 64. | Snow Peas and Bean Sprouts | | 5.95 |
| 65.★ | Eggplant in Hot Garlic Sauce | | 5.95 |
| 66.★ | Bean Curd Szechuan Style | | 5.95 |
| 67. | Bean Curd in Oyster Sauce | | 5.95 |
| 68. | Bean Curd Chinese Home Style | | 5.95 |
| 69. | Dry Fried String Beans | | 5.95 |

*whatever you can get steamed*

## DESSERTS & SODA

| | | | |
|---|---|---|---|
| 76. | Chilled Lichees | | 1.65 |
| 77. | Chilled Pineapple | | 1.65 |
| 78. | Almond Cookies | *Ask for* | 1.25 |
| 79. | Soda | *fortune* | 1.10 |
| 80. | Spring Water (11 oz) | *cookies* | 1.45 |

Whenever possible, we will prepare your order with sauces
or combinations of ingredients other than those listed.
Let us know your preference.

*They want to please you, so ask!*

# Mistral

| | |
|---|---|
| Onion Soup | 4.50 |
| Soup du Jour | 3.75 |
| Fried Calamari, Tomato Sauce | 5.50 |
| Goat Cheese Salad | 5.50 |
| Salad of Mixed Greens, Walnuts & Roquefort | 6.50 |
| Salad of Mixed Baby Greens | 4.00 |
| Caesar Salad | 5.00 |
| Salad of Tomato, Onions & Sweet Basil | 6.00 |

*with balsamic vinegar* (handwritten, left margin)

| | |
|---|---|
| Fresh Tuna Nicoise Salad | 11.00 |
| Grilled Chicken Salad with Artichoke Hearts, Avocado & Tomato | 9.50 |
| Angel Hair, Tomato, Basil, Garlic & Olive Oil *no oil* | 9.50 |
| Linguine, Primavera | 9.50 |
| Fettuccine, Three Cheeses & Pinenuts | 11.00 |
| Pizza Margherita: Tomato, Basil & Cheese | 7.00 |
| Pissaladiere: Onion Pizza with Anchovies & Black Olives | 7.50 |
| Vegetarian Pizza | 8.50 |

*no avocado* / *no anchovies no heavy dressing* (handwritten margins)

| | |
|---|---|
| Ahi Tuna, Grilled, Cracked Black Pepper | 15.50 |
| Whitefish, Mustard Sauce *no mustard sauce* | 13.00 |
| Norwegian Salmon, Grilled, Fresh Herbs & Lemon | 13.50 |
| Breast of Chicken, Cajun Style *no oil* | 12.00 |
| Breast of Chicken, Grilled, Steamed Vegetables & Lemon | 13.00 |
| Half A Chicken, Boneless, Rosemary & Garlic Cloves | 13.00 |
| Minute Steak, Grilled, French Fries & Salad | 13.50 |
| Steak Au Poivre, French Fries & Salad | 14.50 |
| Steak Tartare, French Fries & Salad | 14.50 |
| Lamb Chop, Grilled, Provencale Herbs, Au Jus | 16.00 |
| Omelettes | 8.50 |

*great grill with no oil* / *great* / *most likely has skin on* (handwritten margins)

| | |
|---|---|
| Tartes & Pastries | 4.25 |
| Tarte Tatin | 4.50 |
| Créme Brulée | 4.50 |
| Créme Caramel | 4.00 |

*Ask for fresh berries? sorbet?* (handwritten)

*Ask if marinade has oil — otherwise these are good choices*

Escargots In Mushroom Caps   6.50
Onion Soup   4.50
Soup Du Jour   4.00

Warm Marinated Salmon, Fresh Dill   8.50
Shrimps, Garlic, Parsley And Sherry Vinegar   8.50

*make or bring your own dressing*

Special House Salad   6.50
Caesar Salad   5.00
Salad Of Mixed Greens   4.50
Salad Of Tomato, Onions And Basil   6.50
Goat Cheese Salad   6.50
Salad Of Mixed Greens, Roquefort And Walnuts   7.00

Pissaladiere: Onions, Anchovies And Black Provencale Olives   7.50
Margherita: Tomatoes, Sweet Basil And Mozzarella Cheese   7.00
Vegetarian: Assortment Of Fresh Vegetables With Mozzarella Cheese   8.50

*no mozzarella*

*Same without the olive oil*

Angel Hair, Diced Tomatoes, Garlic, Sweet Basil And Olive Oil   10.50
Linguine, Multi-colored Bell Peppers, Onions And Cajun Shrimp   15.00
Linguine, Artichoke Hearts, Sun-dried Tomatoes, Basil And Olive Oil   12.50
Fettuccine, Dry Salami, Mushrooms And Parmesan Sauce   12.50

Norwegian Salmon, Grilled, Fresh Herbs And Lemon   16.00
Whitefish, Sauteed, Mustard Sauce   15.00
Sea Scallops, Sauteed, Provencale   17.50

*grill with no oil*

Breast Of Chicken, Grilled, Steamed Vegetables And Lemon   14.50
Chicken Mistral, Half A Chicken, Garlic Cloves And Rosemary   14.50
Lamb Chops, Sisteron Style, Provencale Herbs And Garlic   18.00

*can make with no oil please*

Steak Tartare   18.00       Steak, Echalottes   18.00
Steak, Au Poivre Vert   18.00       Steak, Beurre Maitre D'hotel   18.00
(All Steaks Are Served With A Small Green Salad And French Fries)

Crème Caramel   4.00
Crème Brulée   4.50
Coupe Mistral   7.50
Fresh Fruit Tartes And Cakes   4.50

*Ask for fresh fruit*

(split plate charge: $1 for appetizers, $2 for entrees)
not responsible for lost or stolen items.
we reserve the right to refuse service to anyone

# Maria's
## ITALIAN KITCHEN

### Appetizers

Zucchini Fritti *(Breaded Zucchini Wedges)* .......... 3.50
Capri Salad *(Fresh Buffala Mozzarella, Fresh Tomato, Fresh Basil, Topped with Balsamic Vinegar and Olive Oil)* .......... 4.95
Frittata *(Fresh Vegetable Omelet, Served with Marinara Topped with Mozzarella)* .......... 3.95
Stuffed Artichoke *(Seasoned Bread Crumbs, Fresh Garlic and Artichoke Bottoms)* .......... Seasonal
Minestrone Soup .......... 2.95
Soup of the Day .......... 2.95
Gourmet Pizza of the Day .......... 7.95
Caponata *(Cooked Eggplant, Olive, Tomato and Vegetables)* .......... 6.95
Garlic Bread *(Fresh Butter, Fresh Garlic, Parmesan Cheese)* .......... 1.50

### Salads

*Dressed with Maria's Famous House Italian Dressing*

Italian Green Salad *(Lettuce, Tomato, Garbanzos, Cucumber, Carrots, Pepperocini and Mozzarella)* .......... 3.95
*no mozzarella no dressing*
Chopped Italian Green Salad .......... 4.95
Caesar Salad *(Romaine, Homemade Croutons, Homemade Caesar Dressing and Parmesan Cheese)* .......... 5.95
Antipasto Salad *(Lettuce, Tomato, Garbanzos, Broccoli, Assorted Italian Cold Cuts, Cheeses and Caponata)* .......... 6.95
Chopped Antipasto Salad .......... 7.95
Broccoli Limone *(Dressed with Lemon and Garlic)* .......... 2.95
Green Bean Limone *(Dressed with Lemon and Garlic)* .......... 2.95
*great! order for an appetizer*
Calamari Salad *(Calamari and Celery Dressed with a Light Lemon Dressing)* .......... 6.95
Summer Salad *(Fresh Tomatoes, Cucumbers and Red Onions Dressed in a Light Vinaigrette)* .......... 3.95
Cleopatra Salad *(Feta Cheese, Red Onions, Olives and Romaine Lettuce Dressed with Olive Oil and Balsamic Vinegar)* .......... 4.95
*Ask for no olive oil*
**Add Gorgonzola Cheese Dressing** .......... 1.50
**Add Extra Virgin Olive Oil and Balsamic Vinegar Dressing** .......... 1.50
**Add Sesame Chicken Breast** *(Boneless Breast Lightly Breaded and Fried in Peanut Oil)* .......... 2.95
**Add Grilled Marinated Chicken Breast** .......... 4.95
*grill with no oil*

### Cold Hero Sandwiches

*(Served on French Roll with Lettuce, Tomato, Italian Dressing)*

Submarine *(Mixed Italian Cold Cuts)* .......... 4.25
Italian Ham & Cheese *(Proscuitto-Provolone)* .......... 4.95
Chicken Sesame *(Boneless Chicken Filet)* .......... 4.95
Genoa Salami with Provolone .......... 4.25
Turkey Breast .......... 4.95
*no dressing*
Add Extra Cheese .......... .50

### Hot Hero Sandwiches

*(Served on French Roll)*

Grilled Chicken Breast *(with Lettuce & Tomato)* .......... 5.95
*no mayo or olive oil*
Chicken Parmigiana *(Topped with Mozzarella)* .......... 4.95
Veal Parmigiana *(Breaded Veal Patty Topped with Mozzarella)* .......... 4.95

*Served with Pasta Marinara and Vegetables

## Seafood

Shrimp Parmigiana *(Breaded Shrimp, Fried in Peanut Oil)* .................. 10.95
Shrimp Maria *(Scampi Style Shrimp Prepared with Fresh Garlic, Butter, Lemon and
   White Wine. Tossed with Pasta.)* ..................................... 12.95
Shrimp Fra Diavolo *(Spicy Marinara Sauce, Tossed with Pasta.)* ........... 12.95
Clams with Linguine *(Red or White Sauce)*................................ 9.95
Green Lip Mussels with Linguine *(Red Sauce)* When Available............... 9.95
Pescatore with Linguine *(Shrimp, Clams, Mussels, Calamari, Fish,
   in a Red Fish Broth)* ................................................ 15.95
Calamari Fra Diavolo *(Spicy Marinara Sauce tossed with Linguine)* ......... 9.95

*ask for it plain without oil*

## Sauces To Go

Marinara ........................................... 4.00/pt.     8.00/qt.
Meat Sauce ......................................... 5.00/pt.    10.00/qt.

Each *Regular* Item Add ........................................... 1.25
Each *Special* Item Add ........................................... 2.00    2.00

*Regular Items*
*Eggplant • *Mushroom • *Onion • *Olive • *Bell Pepper • Fresh Tomatoes
*Zucchini • Fresh Garlic • Fresh Basil • Pepperoni • Extra Cheese

*Special Items*
Meatball • Sausage • Italian Ham • Artichoke Hearts • Sundried Tomatoes
Ricotta Cheese • Feta Cheese • Capicolla *(Spicy Italian Ham)* • Anchovy

Barbecue Chicken Pizza (with Red Onions, 10" Gourmet Size Only) ........... 7.95
Calzone *(Stuffed with Ricotta and Mozzarella Cheese)*
   Cheese Only ...................................................... 5.95
   Prosciutto or Spinach ............................................ 6.95
Any *Regular* Pizza Topping Add ........................................ 1.00
Any *Special* Pizza Topping Add ........................................ 2.00

## On The Lighter Side    *wonderful*

Angel Hair Pomidoro *(Fresh Tomato, Fresh Basil, Fresh Garlic. Lightly Sauteed
   with Oil)* No salt or oil upon request.
Pasta Primavera *(Fresh Vegetables Tossed with Pasta, Served Hot or Cold)* ... 8.95
Pasta Michelangelo *(Fresh Mushrooms, Fresh Spinach Lightly Sauteed with
   Olive Oil and Fresh Garlic Tossed with Pasta)* ........................ 8.95
*Grilled Lime Chicken Breast *(Boneless Breast, Wing Drummettes Attached
   Marinated with Fresh Lime. Grilled and Served with Fresh Vegetables and Pasta.
   Skinless on Request)* ................................................ 8.95
Chicken Primavera *(Boneless, Skinless Pieces of Chicken Breast, Wok Sauteed
   with Fresh Vegetables)* .............................................. 9.95
*Fresh Fish *(Broiled with Lemon or Topped a la Checca with Fresh Tomato,
   Fresh Basil and Fresh Garlic.)* .................................... Market
*Served with Pasta Marinara and Vegetables

*all great choices*

## Pasta
*(Spaghetti, Angel Hair, Rigatoni, Fusilli, Linguine, Penne or Fettucini)*

Marinara Sauce *(Naples Style, Light and Delicious)*
Meat Sauce ........................................................
Aglio Olio *(Oil and Garlic)* ...................................... 6.95
Bolognese Sauce *(Meat Sauce with Mushrooms)* ...................... 7.50
Alfredo *(Cream and Cheese Sauce)* ................................. 6.95
Fresh Broccoli Al Pesto *(Fussili with or without Cream Sauce)* ....... 7.95
Gnocchi a la Marinara *(Homemade Ricotta Dumplings a la Marinara)* .... 8.95
Ravioli a la Marinara *(Delicate Pillows of Ricotta Stuffed Pasta. Light and
   delicious)* ...................................................... 9.95
   Meat Sauce Add ................................................. 7.50
   Meatball or Sausage Add ........................................ 7.95
                                                                   1.75
                                                                   1.75

Special orders including sauces and pastas will be charged accordingly.

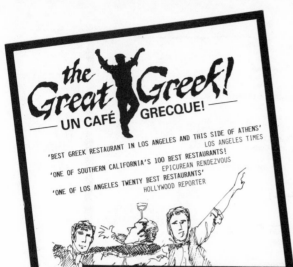

# Greek-Style Appetizers

## COLD SELECTIONS

**Yogurt Tzatziki**
*fresh yogurt, cucumbers thin-sliced, fresh garlic, herbs,* 4.65

**Eggplant Meltzanosalata,** 4.65

**Greek Caviar Tarama,** 4.65

**Feta Cheese, Black Olives,** 4.85

**Tabouli**
*cracked wheat, lemon juice, parsley, green onion, spices, tomato,* 4.65

**Greek Fassolia Beans** (Salata)
*with olive oil, fresh lemon,* 3.50

**Hummus** (Tahini)
*whipped chick peas, garlic, fresh lemon juice, sesame oil,* 4.65

**Fresh Baby Octopus Salad,** 6.75 —no dressing–just vinegar

## HOT SELECTIONS

**Stuffed Grape Leaves,** 5.65

**Batter-Fried Calamaria,** 5.65

**Greek Meatballs Keftethes,** 4

**Spinach Cheese Filo Pie,** 5.6

**Baked Pastichio**
**Deep-Dish Pasta,** 5.65

**Moussaka Izmir,** 6.95

**Fresh Horta (hot or cold)** no
*fresh boiled greens with olive oil,* ol
*fresh lemon,* 3.85

**Saganaki Pan-Fried Cheese,** 5

**Char-Grilled Fresh Octopus an**
grilled green scallions, 8.25

# —Salads-Classical and Nouveau Grecque —

**Greek Village Salad**
*tomato, cucumber, greens, feta, black olives, Greek dressing,* 5.85 — no dressing–no cheese

**Greek Taverna Salad**
*same ingredients as above, but without greens,* 5.85

**The Hollywood Savoy**
*as served in our American showplace restaurant in Paris, France—fresh endive, walnuts, avocado, vinaigrette,* 7.25

**Tabouli**
*cracked wheat, fresh lemon juice, pa green onion, spices, tomato,* 4.65

**Fresh Horta (cold or hot)** n
*fresh boiled greens with olive oil,* ol
*lemon juice,* 3.85

ask for
plain pita

*Order Our Famous*
**GRILLED PITA BREAD.**
*We ship it from Chicago…*
*It's the Best in America!*
1.95 *Per Order (serves two)*

# Pastas

**Macedonian Pasta (Shrimp)**
*thin pasta sauteed in a sauce of fresh tomatoes, shrimp, shallots, garlic, basil and feta cheese,* 13.95

**Pasta Tony Corfu**
*thin pasta laced with fresh veges— snowpeas, florets or broccoli, tomato, zucchini, carrot, garlic and feta cheese,* 11.95

**Pastichio Deep-Dish Pasta**
*the classical, meat and pasta-layered dish of Greece with bechamel sauce, served with fresh vegetable of the day,* 11.95

Served with Oven-Roasted Potatoes and Greek-Style Pilaf and Fresh Vegetable.

# Plate Specialties

## HELLENIC SEAFOODS

**Greek-Style Fresh Fish of the Day**
*Ask your waiter to describe our chefs' special fresh fish creation for today.*

grill with lemon only

**Sauteed Shrimp Agean**
*with feta cheese, shallots, herbs, tomatoes, white wine,* 15.65

**Grilled Swordfish Oreganato,** 15.35

no oil

**Batter-Fried Calamaria,** 11.25

**Lemon-Butter Char-Grilled Jumbo Shrimp,** 15.65

**Grilled Fresh Baby Salmon,**
*with a spray of lemon, oregano,* 15.95

## FRESH GREEK-STYLE LAMB

**Oven-Roasted Baby Lamb,** 15.95
**Broiled Loin Lamb Chops,** 16.35
**Broiled Lamb Souvlaki,** 14.95
**Rack of Baby Lamb,** market
**Sliced Tenderloin of Lamb,** 16.85

---

**Greek-Style Vegetarian Feast**
*Yogurt Tzatziki, Hummus, Eggplant Melitzanosalata, Greek Fassolia Beans, Tabouli, Spinach Cheese Filo Pie, Greek Salad, Fresh Vegetable of the Day, Rice Pilaf, Oven-Roasted Potato, Flaming Saganaki Pan-Fried Cheese, Pasta Corfu,* 17.95
(Per person, two or more persons)

**Special Vegetarian Platter,** 12.50

## CHICKEN AND BEEF

**Roasted Chicken Plaka**
*splashed with fresh lemon, oregano,* 13.25

**Broiled Chicken Breast Souvlaki**
*Chunks of marinated chicken breast sprinkled with fresh lemon and ground oregano,* 13.95

this means oil-ask for plain chicken breast to be grilled

**Broiled Beef Souvlaki,** 14.95

**Mixed Kebab Souvlaki**
*spit-grilled chicken breast and beef,* 14.95

**Chopped Peasant-Style Beefsteak**
*mixed with fresh chopped parsley, fresh onion, a hint of oregano, a touch of fresh garlic,* 11.95

## GREEK HOMELAND DELICACIES

**Baked Pastichio Deep-Dish Pasta**
*layers of pasta, meat, spices, tomato, eggs, bechamel sauce,* 11.95

**Moussaka Izmir -- A Specialty!**
*the national dish of Greece -baked eggplant, meat, spices,* 12.75

**Stuffed Grape Leaves,** 12.95

**Spinach Cheese Filo Pie Spanakopita,** 11.95

**Combination Greek Platter**
*Baked Pastichio Deep-Dish Pasta, Moussaka Izmir, Stuffed Grape Leaves, Spinach Cheese Filo Pie Spanakopita, Lamb of the Day, Oven-Roasted Potato, Rice Pilaf and Fresh Vegetable,* 15.25

---

**THE DELUXE DINNER** – Sit back and relax as 15 different, typically authentic Greek regional cuisine specialties created by our chefs are served to you in three, multdish presentations!
Greek tarama caviar . . tzatziki . . eggplant meltzanosalata . . hummus . . fassolia beans . . Greek village salata . . manestra pasta . batter-fried calamaria . . stuffed grape leaves . . spiced meatballs . . spinach pie spanakopita . . lamb specialty of the day . . pastachio pasta . . broiled souvlaki . . tabouli.
Served to Two or More Persons at $18.75 per person.
**ALSO ASK ABOUT OUR GREAT GREEK DINNER!**

## Specialties

All Dinners Served with Choice of Tomato Juice or Soup or Mixed Green Salad, Choice of Vegetable, Choice of Potato or Rice, Roll (Baked Potato 5 PM til 10 PM)

**BROILED PORK CHOPS**
*Two Pork Chops Broiled to Perfection, Served with Tangy Applesauce*

**HAMBURGER STEAK**
*Large Ground Beef Patty Topped with Onion Rings*

**ROAST BRISKET OF BEEF**
*Tender English Cut Brisket, Served with Mushroom Sauce*

**GRILLED BEEF LIVER**
*Try This House Specialty, Tender and Juicy, Beef Liver Smothered with Sauteed Onions or Two Strips of Bacon*

**BAKED MEAT LOAF** (Mushroom Sauce)

**CHICKEN FRIED STEAK**
*Tender Cubed and Breaded Steak, Served with Turkey Gravy*

**ROAST TURKEY DINNER** (All White Meat)
*Savory Dressing and Cranberry Sauce*

**SPAGHETTI AND MARINARA SAUCE**
*Parmesan Cheese and Garlic Toast (No Potato or Vegetable)*

**VEAL PARMIGIANA**
*Served with Spaghetti and Marinara Sauce,
Topped with Melted Cheese (No Potato or Vegetable)*

*[handwritten: no gravy — use mustard — plain bak... pot...]*

## Steaks

All Steaks USDA Eastern Choice, Topped with Onion Rings

| | | |
|---|---|---|
| TOP SIRLOIN STEAK . . 9.95 | TOP SIRLOIN STEAK & SHRIMP | |
| NEW YORK STEAK . . 10.95 | TOP SIRLOIN TERIYAKI STEAK | |

## Chicken

All Chicken Breasts Are Boneless and Skinless

**FRIED CHICKEN**
*One-Half Chicken, Fried to a Golden Brown and Finger Licking Good*

**CAJUN CHICKEN**
*Chicken Breast Marinated in Cajun Spices and Broiled to Perfection*

**TERIYAKI CHICKEN**
*Skewered Pieces of Chicken Breast with Tomato, Onion, Green Pepper, Pineapple Ring,
Served Over Bed of Rice, Broiled to Perfection (No Potato)*

**BREAST OF CHICKEN TERIYAKI**
*On Bed of Rice with Pineapple Ring (No Potato)*

**ATHENIAN CHICKEN**
*One-Half Chicken Broiled with Lemon Juice, Garlic, Oregano and Virgin Olive Oil,
If You Have the Time . . . It's Worth the Wait! You'll Love It.*

**BROILED BREAST OF CHICKEN**
*Served on Bed of Rice (No Potato)* *[handwritten: no oil]*

**CHICKEN PARMIGIANA**
*Breast of Chicken Topped with Mozzarella Cheese, Spaghetti with Marinara Sauce,
Parmesan Cheese, Garlic Bread (No Potato or Vegetable)*

## Seafood

**GRILLED or BROILED HALIBUT STEAK** *[handwritten: no oil]*

**STUFFED SHRIMP** *Stuffed with Crabmeat, Deep Fried to Perfection*

**SHRIMP PLATE** *Deep Fried Shrimp, Served with Cocktail Sauce, Cole Slaw*

**FISHERMAN'S PLATE** *Deep Fried Filet of Fish, Scallops and Shrimp*

**FISH AND CHIPS** *Tender and Mild, Deep Fried to a Golden Brown*

**BROILED FILET OF SALMON**

**GRILLED FILET OF SOLE**

**BROILED SWORDFISH**

*[handwritten: no oil / vegies / salad]*

**✳ MENU SELECTIONS ARE PREPARED WITH NO CHOLESTEROL, LESS FAT AND LOW CALORIE COOKING OIL FOR OUR PATRONS WHO ARE HEART & HEALTH CONSC...**

# • Breakfast
# • Luncheon
# • Dinner
# • Daily Specials
# • Beer & Wine

## Lancers
### Restaurant

*Ground Turkey Patty ... ...ut, French Fries*

## Sandwiches

**HOT MEAT LOAF SANDWICH** . . . . .5.75
*Served Open Face with Brown Beef Gravy
and Whipped Potatoes*

**HOT ROAST BEEF SANDWICH** . . .6.25
*Served Open Face with Brown Beef Gravy
and Whipped Potatoes*

**HOT ROAST TURKEY SANDWICH** 5.95
*All White Meat Served Open Faced with Gravy,
Whipped Potatoes and Cranberry Sauce*

**LANCER'S CHICKEN SANDWICH** . . 6.50
*Broiled Boneless and Skinless Breast of Chicken,
Lettuce and Tomato, Served on Grilled Bun*

**BARBECUE CHICKEN SANDWICH** . .6.95
*Broiled Boneless, Skinless Breast of Chicken, Topped
with Barbecue Sauce and Melted Mozzarella Cheese*

**THE CAJUN** . . . . . . . . . . . . .6.75
*Breast of Chicken marinated with Cajun Spices
on a Bun with Lettuce and Tomato, French Fries*

**THE CALIFORNIAN** . . . . . . . . .7.95
*Our Chicken Breast Sandwich Topped with
Avocado, Bacon and Swiss Cheese on a Bun,
with French Fries*

**THE WINDSOR** . . . . . . . . . . .5.95
*Sliced Turkey, Ham and Swiss Cheese with
Lettuce, Tomato and 1000 Dressing on
Rye Bread with Lancer's Cole Slaw*

**LANCER'S TALLY-HO** . . . . . . . .6.15
*White Meat Tuna on a Toasted English Muffin
Topped with Tomato, Melted Cheddar Cheese*

**MONTE CRISTO** . . . . . . . . . . .6.25
*Melted Swiss Cheese, Ham and Turkey
Between (2) Slices of French Toast*

**HAM AND CHEESE SANDWICH** . . . .5.95
*Choice of American or Swiss Cheese, Served
on Rye, Grilled If You Wish*

**TUNA MELT SANDWICH** . . . . . . .5.95
*Tuna & American Cheese, Grilled on Rye*

**REUBEN SANDWICH** . . . . . . . . .6.25
*Corned Beef, Swiss Cheese and Sauerkraut
Served on Grilled Rye*

| | Half | Full |
|---|---|---|
| **TUNA OR TURKEY SALAD SANDWICH** | 4.45/ | 5.75 |
| **TURKEY** ~~OR COLD ROAST BEEF~~ | 4.75/ | 5.95 |
| **COLD HAM** . . . . . . . . . . | 4.25/ | 5.45 |

*Above Served with Choice of: Potato Salad or
Cole Slaw or French Fries or Assorted Fruit
Served with Dinner Salad $1.00 Additional
Sandwiches Not Toasted, Unless Otherwise Requested*

*For an Additional 75¢ The Following Sandwiches
May Be Served with Choice of: Potato Salad or
Cole Slaw or French Fries or Assorted Fruit*

**BACON, LETTUCE AND TOMATO** . . .4.25
**GRILLED CHEESE SANDWICH** American Cheese 3.45
**AVOCADO, BACON, LETTUCE & TOMATO** 5.75
**HAM AND EGG SANDWICH** . . . . . .4.95
**BACON AND EGG SANDWICH** . . . . .4.75
**DEVILED EGG SANDWICH** . . . . . .3.25
**FRIED EGG SANDWICH** . . . . . . .2.50

*[handwritten: no mayo]*

**B...
IN B...**
*Thin Slice...
Savory Har...
Our Own D...
with Gree...*

**A RE...**
*Hot Tende...
Dipped in a...
Fren...*

*[handwritten: no may...]*

**CO...**
*Hot T...
Corne...
Serv...*

*(with Su...)*

**THREE...
RO...**
*Our Combi...
Tomato a...
Toas...*

**HAM AND CHEESE
CLUB SANDWICH**
*Generous Portions of
Cold Sliced Ham and
American Cheese on Toast
Served with French Fries*
5.95

**THE CALIFORNIA
TRIPLE-DECKER
AVOCADO CLUB**
*Turkey, Bacon, Lettuce, Tomato
and Avocado, Served on Toasted
White Bread with French Fries*
6.50

*[handwritten: no mayo / whole wheat bread]*

## Side Orders

**FRENCH FRIES** . . . . . . .1.75
**HASHED BROWNS** . . . . . .1.75
**COTTAGE CHEESE** . . . . .1.75
**VEGETABLE** . . . . . . . .1.75 *[handwritten: steamed]*
**COLE SLAW** . . . . . . . .1.75
**SLICED TOMATOES** . . . .1.85
**SIDE OF MIXED FRUIT** . . .1.95

## Eggs 'n' Such

*All Egg Dishes Served with (3) Large Eggs*

| | |
|---|---|
| BURGER PATTY AND EGGS | 4.95 |
| TURKEY PATTY AND EGGS | 5.25 |
| LINK SAUSAGE AND EGGS | 4.95 |
| BACON AND EGGS | 4.95 |
| HAM AND EGGS | 5.45 |
| CANADIAN STYLE BACON AND EGGS | 5.45 |
| CORNED BEEF HASH AND EGGS | 5.25 |
| THREE EGGS 3.25 TWO EGGS 2.95 | |
| TWO PORK CHOPS AND EGGS | 7.85 |
| ONE PORK CHOP AND EGGS | 5.85 |
| LOX, BAGEL AND SCRAMBLED EGGS | 7.95 |
| NEW YORK STEAK AND EGGS | 8.95 |
| TOP SIRLOIN STEAK AND EGGS | 7.95 |
| RANCH STYLE BREAKFAST | 4.75 |

*Three Eggs with Two Sausage Patties*

*[handwritten] poached / no hash browns*

**NO. 1**
**BREAKFAST SPECIAL**
Three Golden Brown Pancakes
with Two Eggs and Syrup
83.95

**NO. 2**
**LANCER'S BREAKFAST**
TWO Strips of Bacon, TWO Eggs,
Hashed Brown Potatoes,
Toast and Jelly
84.25

**NO. 3**
**LANCER'S EXTRAORDINARY
FRENCH TOAST**
Cinnamon Swirled Honey-Nut Bread.
84.50
**REGULAR FRENCH TOAST**
83.40

**NO. 4**
**CHOPPED HAM AND
SCRAMBLED EGGS**
Served with Hashed
Brown Potatoes, Toast and Jelly
85.25

**PIGS IN A BLANKET**
(3) Link Sausages,
Wrapped in Pancakes,
Served with Syrup
84.25

**EGGS BENEDICT**
Two Poached Eggs and
Canadian Bacon on an
English Muffin. Topped with
Hollandaise Sauce.
Served with Fresh Fruit (No Potato)
85.95
Served 6 am til 11 am Monday thru Friday.
Weekends Until 3:30 pm

**HUEVOS RANCHEROS
LANCER'S STYLE**
Three Eggs Scrambled,
Topped with Salsa,
and Refried Beans
Three Corn Tortillas
83.95

---

## Appetizers

| | | | |
|---|---|---|---|
| BAKED POTATO | 1.75 | GARLIC BREAD | 1.45 |
| DEEP FRIED ZUCCHINI | 2.95 | DELICIOUS ONION RINGS | 2.75 |
| *Topped with Parmesan Cheese* | | *Deep Fried to Perfection* | |
| SPICY CHICKEN WINGS | 4.50 | DEEP FRIED CALAMARI RINGS | 4.95 |

**POTATO SKINS** .... 3.95
*Stuffed with Cauliflower and Broccoli,
Topped with Cheddar Cheese and Served with Sour Cream*

## South of the Border

**STEAK OR CHICKEN PICADO** .... 7.95
*Chunks of Steak Sauteed with Bell Pepper, Fresh Tomatoes, Fresh Mushrooms and Onions,
Served with Guacamole, Refried Beans, Rice, Tortillas and Salsa. Choice of Soup or Salad*

**GUACAMOLE CHICKEN BREAST** .... 7.95
*Breast of Chicken with Guacamole and Salsa, Refried Beans, Rice and Tortillas.
Choice of Soup or Salad*

**TOSTADA SALAD** .... 7.45
*Chunks of Chicken Breast, Shredded Lettuce, Tomato, Guacamole, Jack and Cheddar Cheeses,
Refried Beans, Sour Cream and Salsa. Served in Large Tortilla Shell*

**TACO SALAD** .... 6.45
*Seasoned Ground Beef, Shredded Lettuce, Tomato, Refried Beans, Jack and Cheddar Cheeses,
Guacamole and Sour Cream, Served in Large Tortilla Shell*

## Salads

*Served with Crackers or Roll and Butter. Choice of Dressing*

| | HALF | FULL |
|---|---|---|
| CHEF'S SALAD | 5.45 | 6.45 |
| *Mixed Lettuce, Topped with Julienne of Ham, Turkey and American Cheese, Egg, Tomato* | | |
| SPINACH SALAD | | 5.45 |
| *with Hard Boiled Egg, Bacon Bits, Sliced Tomato Wedge, Mushrooms, Avocado* | | |
| FESTIVAL PLATTER | | 6.65 |
| *Delicious Combination of Cold Roast Beef, Sliced Ham and Turkey.
Served with Potato Salad, Hard Boiled Egg and Tomato Wedges* | | |
| CHINESE CHICKEN OR SHRIMP SALAD | 6.25 | 7.25 |
| *On Bed of Shredded Lettuce with Chicken or Shrimp, Chopped Scallions, Mandarin Oranges,
Crispy Noodles, Topped with a Honey Sesame Dressing* | | |
| CAJUN CHICKEN OR SHRIMP SALAD | 6.25 | 7.25 |
| *Shredded Lettuce with Chunks of Breast of Chicken
or Shrimp, Scallions and Spicy Cajun Dressing* | | |
| COMBINATION SALAD | | 7.25 |
| *Mounds of Tuna Salad, Turkey Salad, Hard Boiled Egg, Sliced Tomato Wedge,
on a Bed of Crisp Mixed Green Salad* | | |
| COBB SALAD | 5.25 | 6.25 |
| *Served with Crisp Bacon, Turkey, Crumbled Bleu Cheese, Hard Boiled Egg,
Avocado and Tomatoes on a Bed of Mixed Greens* | | |
| CAESAR SALAD | | 5.95 |
| *Romaine Lettuce with Caesar Dressing, Topped with Croutons and Parmesan Cheese* | | |
| DELUXE FRUIT SALAD | | 6.50 |
| *Assortment of the Season's Fruits, Choice of Cottage Cheese or Sherbet* | | |
| COTTAGE CHEESE WITH PEACHES OR PINEAPPLE | | 4.45 |
| SHRIMP AND AVOCADO SALAD | | 7.25 |
| TURKEY OR TUNA SALAD | | 6.10 |
| STUFFED AVOCADO with Turkey or Tuna Salad | | 6.95 |
| MIXED GREEN SALAD (with Crackers only) | | 3.75 |
| *Hard Boiled Egg and Tomato Wedges* | | |
| SMALL MIXED GREEN SALAD (with Crackers only) | | 1.95 |
| SPECIAL TURKEY SALAD | | 6.45 |
| *Served with Jell-O Squares and Assorted Fruit* | | |
| GREEK SALAD | | 6.45 |
| *Mixed Greens with Feta Cheese, Greek Olives, Cucumber, Onions, and Tomato* | | |
| LOX & BAGEL PLATE  Sliced Onion, Tomato, Olives, Cream Cheese | | 7.95 |

*[handwritten] no dressing*

## Diet Plates

*Served with Scoop of Cottage Cheese, Assorted Fruit,
Quartered Tomatoes and Melba Toast or Ry-Krisp*

| | | | |
|---|---|---|---|
| CHAR-BROILED GROUND BEEF (Small) | 4.95 | (Large) | 5.95 |
| BROILED BREAST OF CHICKEN (Skinless and Boneless) | | | 7.75 |
| BROILED HALIBUT STEAK | | | 8.95 |
| SLICED ROAST TURKEY | | | 6.45 |
| CHAR BROILED TURKEY BURGER | | | 5.45 |

## Chili

| | |
|---|---|
| CHILI AND BEANS, with Saltine Crackers | 3.45 |
| CHILI SIZE DELUXE | 5.25 |
| *Ground Beef Patty Smothered with Chili and Beans, Topped with
Melted American Cheese, and Onions. Served on a Toasted Bun* | |

MENU SELECTIONS ARE PREPARED WITH NO CHOLESTEROL, LESS FAT AND
LOW CALORIE COOKING OIL FOR OUR PATRONS WHO ARE HEART & HEALTH CONSCIOUS

---

*(partially obscured center column)*

.... 5.45

*ders Served with Golden Hashed
...eese or Tomatoes and Toast
...utter & Jelly or (2) Hot Cakes
...ns Add 50¢ Each)*

...(3) Large Eggs

...OMELETTE .... 5.95
*...Light Blend of Eggs, Fresh
...ion, Flavored with Feta Cheese*
5.55;  with Cheese 5.85
...E .... 4.95
...ELETTE .... 5.25
.... 3.95
...ELETTE .... 5.25
...TTE .... 5.25
...E with Swiss Cheese 5.25
.... 5.75
*...ef, Guacamole and Sour Cream*
...OMELETTE .... 6.45
...ELETTE .... 5.25
...TTE .... 5.25
...TTE .... 5.95
*...ato and Cheese*
...E .... 5.35
.... 5.95
.... 5.95
*...Sausage, Mushroom, Tomato*

...es, Waffles
...Blintzes

...CAKES:
...75  (12) .... 3.95
...tack 3) .... 2.95
...ueberry Topping  Add 1.25
...CH .... 4.85
...Eggs, Sliced Ham, Syrup
.... 4.75
...ge & 2 Eggs
.... 4.85
...ips of Bacon or 2 Link Sausages
.... 3.45
...ueberry Topping Add 1.25
.... 4.45
.... 5.45
*...Served with Sour Cream, or
...Preserves.*

## Side Orders

| | |
|---|---|
| BACON OR SAUSAGE | 2.10 |
| FRIED HAM | 2.55 |
| CANADIAN STYLE BACON | 2.65 |
| BURGER PATTY | 2.10 |
| ONE EGG | 1.15 |
| THREE EGGS | 1.95 |
| HASHED BROWNS | 1.75 |
| BAGEL (Plain) | 1.25 |
| BAGEL & CREAM CHEESE | 1.75 |
| CINNAMON TOAST | 1.15 |
| ENGLISH MUFFIN | 1.15 |
| *Toasted with Jelly* | |
| BREAKFAST ROLL | 1.25 |
| TOAST & JELLY | 1.00 |
| RAISIN TOAST | 1.35 |
| DOUGHNUTS | .75 |

*[handwritten] no butter— / poached / eggs*

# APPETIZERS

**Boap Todd (Zucchini Fritter)** .............................................. 3.25
*Crisp zucchini fritter served with plum sauce.*

**Poa-Pia (Thai Spring Roll)** .................................................... 3.95
*Ground pork, bean thread, and bamboo shoot wrapped in a spring roll and deep fried served with plum sauce.*

**Rung Nok (Vegetable Slivers)** ............................................ 3.95
*Taro, fried crispy. Served with a special Thai sauce.*

★ **Tod Mun Pla** ..................................................................... 4.25
*Kingfish and fresh herbs ground together with red curry, deep fried and served with cucumber sauce.*

**Shrimp Fritter** ...................................................................... 4.95
*Ground pork and shrimp mixed with Thai herbs, wrapped in a bean curd skin and deep fried to a golden fritter crispness served with plum sauce.*

**Koong Ka Bog** ...................................................................... 4.95
*Marinated whole shrimp wrapped in a special pastry shell and deep fried. Served with plum sauce.*

**Or Try Our Famous Satees**

**Nuur Satee (Beef)**

**Kai Satee (Chicken)** ............................................................. 5.50
*Sliced chicken or steak, marinated in coconut milk and Thai herbs then charcoaled on a skewer and served with our famous peanut sauce.*

*saving grace—they can skew chicken + veg\[ as well*

# SOUPS

**Chicken Rice Soup** .............................................................. 2.75
*Rice and chicken in a special broth garnished with scallions.*

**Rice Noodle Soup** ................................................................ 2.75
*Rice noodles and chicken in a special broth garnished with scallions.*

**Kang Jude Pu (Crab Meat Stick Soup)** ............................ 2.95
*Crab meat stick with mushrooms and scallions in a clear broth.*

★ **Tom Yum Koong (Spicy Shrimp Soup)** .......................... 2.95
*Shrimp and mushrooms simmered in a corriander, lime leaf, and lemon grass hot and sour broth.*

★ **Tom Kha Kai (Chicken Coconut Soup)** ......................... 3.50
*Sliced chicken in a coconut milk, mushroom and herb creme broth.*

*great for curbing the appetite!*

# SALAD

**Sala Thai (Our House Specialty)** ...................................... 3.50
*Dried bean curds, lettuce, bean sprouts, egg, tomato, onion and cucumber topped with our famous* ~~Toons peanuts dressing.~~

*great salad— ask for rice vinegar*

# YUM

*Sliced steak, ground pork, shrimp, squid, or Thai sausage soaked in lime juice then mixed with chili pepper, onions, tomato, cucumber corriander and lettuce. Served room temperature. Delicious!*

★ **Thai Sausage** .................................................................... 8.95

★ **Ground Pork** ..................................................................... 8.95

★ **Sliced Steak** ...................................................................... 9.50

★ **Squid** ............................................................................... 10.95

★ **Shrimp** ............................................................................ 10.95

*★Indicates the hotness or spicy of each dish. Please consult your waiter or waitress to request an increase or decrease in flavorings.*

# PLA (WHOLE FISH)

★ **Pla Lad Prig** ............................................................ 14.95
*Whole fish fried crisp and covered with our Chef's spicy hot chili and garlic sauce, served on a sizzling platter.*

★ **Pla Chu Chee** ........................................................... 14.95
*Whole fish fried crisp, topped with curry paste and coconut milk.*

**Pla Gien** ..................................................................... 14.95
*Whole fish fried crisp, topped with mushrooms, ginger and scallions served on a sizzling platter.*

**Pla Peow Whan** ......................................................... 14.95
*Whole fish fried crisp and topped with sauteed vegetables and pineapple in a Thai sweet and sour sauce.*

**Pla Bae Sa (Steamed Whole Fish)** ........................... 14.95
*Whole fish steamed to perfection and topped with vegetables, ginger and preserved plums.*

# SHRIMP AND SQUID

★ **Pla Muk Pad Tua (Squid with String Beans)** ......... 10.95
*Deep fried squid sauteed with string beans and chili paste.*

★ **Pla Muk (Squid with Chili Sauce)** .......................... 10.95
*Sauteed squid with chili pepper, onion and other Thai Herbs.*

★ **Koong Kra Prow (Shrimp Basil)** ............................. 10.95
*Shrimp sauteed with onion basil leaves and chili pepper.*

★ **Kang Koong (Shrimp Curry)** .................................. 10.95
*Shrimp with red curry, coconut milk and bamboo shoots.*

**Koong Kra-Tiem (Shrimp Scampi)** ........................... 10.95
*Sauteed shrimp with green peas in a corriander and garlic sauce.*

**Koong Kao Pod (Shrimp with Baby Corn)** ............... 10.95
*Shrimp sauteed with baby corns, mushrooms, and scallions.*

**Koong Ob-Mo Din (Shrimp** 
*Broiled shrimp with baby corn, mush
thread.*

*Ask them to steam some whole fish or shrimp*

*can they steam??*

# PLUK (VEGETABLES)

★ **Ma Kuur Pad (Eggplant)** ........................................ 6.95
*Eggplant sauteed in soy bean, garlic, chili pepper and basil leaves.*

★ **Pad Tua (String Beans)** .......................................... 6.95
*String beans sauteed in a chili paste, garlic and Thai herb sauce.*

★ **Kang Pluk (Vegetable Curry)** ................................. 7.95
*Mixed vegetable cooked with red curry and coconut milk.*

**Mixed Sauteed Vegetables** ...................................... 7.50
*A colorful assembly of vegetables, cooked to perfection.*

**Ka Na (Broccoli)** ...................................................... 6.95
*Sauteed broccoli with oyster sauce.*

# THAI STYLED FRIED RICE

Mixed Vegetable Fried Rice ........................................ 7.50

Chicken, Beef, Pork or Sausage ................................. 7.50

Shrimp or Crabmeat Stick .......................................... 7.95

Combination Fried Rice (all the above) ...................... 8.95

Extra Rice ................................................................... .50

*plain*

Curried Rice ................................................................ 1.00

Toons Famous Peanuts Sauce (side) .......................... 1.00

To Take Home (8 oz) .................................................. 2.50

# 10

## Give Your Kids a Break: How to Keep Your Children Lean and Healthy

**T**HE EFFECT YOU have on your children's health and weight begins at the moment of conception and lasts until they grow up and move out of the house—if not longer: the eating habits you help your kids to form in childhood will likely be the eating habits they maintain in adulthood. In the beginning, when you are pregnant, what you eat affects the growth of the embryo into a full-fledged child. Once the child is born, whether you breast feed or not, you are in control of what the baby needs to sustain life. Beyond that even, you are in control of determining what kind of body this child will eventually have.

There are many theories as to why some children are overweight. One is that fatness is due to genetics. I think this may be true, but only in some cases. More often, it's a cop-out and denies the truth that what children are fed from day one is the deciding factor. If you are eating poorly when you are pregnant, you are already setting your child up for fatness and creating fat cells. If you continue to overfeed growing children more food than their bodies can use efficiently, you will have fat children. It's mostly up to you. A child will have little or no say in what he's to be fed over the next few years. The food choices you make for your child are really an extension of the umbilical cord.

As big a responsibility as feeding a child is, it also creates a wonderful connection between the parent and child. Providing food is a way of providing comfort; it's a way of sharing with our loved ones. Every parent has the desire to see his or her child eat well. We all want our childen to be strong and healthy, but whether or not most parents are doing what they should to ensure it is another story. Unfortunately, the scales in this country are tipped more toward overweight children with high cholesterol than thin, healthy children.

What to feed our children has become one of the biggest dilemmas in American life. I get calls all the time from women who have their own diets under control, who know how to lose weight or eat healthfully themselves, but are crying for help for their children. This upsets me, and I'll be blunt about my feelings about this matter: If your child is overweight it's *your fault*. And you should feel guilty. Even if the problem is hormonal and not what you're feeding your kid, it's still your obligation to get that kid to a doctor and find out what's going on. But it's especially your duty to intervene if your children are putting on weight precisely because of what they are putting in their mouths.

I had a client who called me in to clean out her refrigerator and educate her and her family on how to eat more healthfully. Sharon was in her early forties and worked out regularly, but knew that in order for her workouts to be more effective, she would have to get her diet straightened out as well. She had two preteen twins, a boy who was athletic and wanted to eat healthfully, and a girl who, reaching the age at which many girls start to gain weight, was paranoid about getting fat. I came over and threw an amazing amount of junk out of her kitchen and gave her cooking lessons.

That was four years ago and to this day Sharon has never looked better. She goes through periods when her weight slides a little, but she basically eats pretty well. I still see Sharon because we became friends during her consultation. The other day I was at her house and, when I opened the refrigerator, I couldn't believe my eyes—everything from Wonder Bread Light to fattening salad dressings to oily leftover Chinese food stood on the shelves. I asked her what happened and she quickly said that she didn't eat any of that stuff, her kids did. "Sharon," I said, "this is the same food that gave you a weight problem and your husband a cholesterol problem. How can you give it to your kids?" Sharon's next defense was that the housekeeper did the shopping; it was her fault. My next admonition was, "How can you let your housekeeper spend your money buying crap for your family? You wouldn't let her buy your children cigarettes or all the chocolate and candy they wanted, would you?"

"Of course not, but that's the food they want to eat," she replied.

"Of course, they want to eat junk," I said. "The junk tastes good because it's loaded with sugar and salt and, besides, they are children and children quite naturally think they're indestructible. You can't give your kids that much power, because in the long run, it's not fair to them." We cleaned out her refrigerator one more time.

Sharon's answer to me—"Well, that's what they like"—is one I hear from mothers again and again. All children would probably love to have cookies for breakfast, ice cream for lunch, and Ding Dongs for dinner. But you don't feed them that because you know it's not healthy. Instead, though, you go and feed them unhealthy, fattening foods disguised as real meals, like SpaghettiO's. Read the labels on the foods going into your children's bodies and have mercy on them. My daughter may rebel against me as she grows older and join a junk food cult, but at least I will know that I didn't give her fat thighs, high cholesterol, gray skin, and rotten teeth. Really, give your kid a break.

Another client had a problem very similar to Sharon's. A woman hired me to come to her house in Beverly Hills and clean out her refrigerator and cupboards. She had just lost 30 pounds by taking some doctor's pills (and as of the writing of this book, had gained back more than the 30 pounds she'd lost) and wanted to know how to eat so she could stay thin. She also wanted to have me help her thirteen-year-old daughter who was starting to gain weight. "I don't know what to do," she said. "She comes home from school and roasts marshmallows over the stove!"

I looked at the woman and said, "Who's buying her the marshmallows? May I suggest that you do not buy this junk, since you are very wealthy and can afford better food than Hamburger Helper and marshmallows?"

This wealthy, educated woman could afford to buy better food but, in truth, even though I pointed that fact out to her, affordability has little to do with the problem. One of the real reasons is just plain laziness: being too lazy to read the labels, to search out a better market, to go to a different store to get meats without chemicals and hormones. Yet no one is lazy when it comes to running to the doctor. But you can keep paying his bills or you could use that money for healthier foods that would probably keep the kids out of his office in the first place! I'll brag about my nine-year-old daughter here: she hasn't been sick enough to warrant a visit to a doctor in six years!

I am not trying to play holistic doctor nor am I saying that food is the all-time panacea—believe me, I believe in medicine. My mother tried to cure my hay fever with vitamin C and pantothenic acid for one whole summer, and I finally went sneezing to the doctor for real medication! But I do know that food is the ultimate source of vitamins, minerals, and everything else you need to have a healthy body. I agree that a lot of our produce could be healthier were it not for pesticides. But the fresh foods available today give us everything we need nutritionally. It's just that most people don't consume enough of the produce, grains, and lean proteins they need. One salad doesn't cut it. Just like one day of exercise doesn't get you the results you want and need. Eating well has to be a LIFESTYLE! And adopting this lifestyle is not that difficult—for adults or children. As we grow older we realize that to eat more healthfully we have to make changes in our own lifestyles. Why not form your children's lifestyles in such a way that they won't have to struggle to make changes later in their lives. Smoking is "not cool" these days for kids; eating junk food is going out of fashion, too.

Just as you create rules for yourself, it's essential to create rules that apply to your individual children. I have to watch my weight, but that doesn't mean I put my daughter on a diet. She has a growing body and needs more and different kinds of fuel than I do. Still, I try to keep her diet as healthy as possible, although it's virtually impossible to control every morsel a child puts in his or her mouth. I have always packed a healthy lunch for my daughter to take to school and there was a time when the lunch box would come back with Twinkie wrappers and Frito bags! She had traded off her healthy items for junk food all through the first and second grades. In third grade (she's now in fourth) her lunches were the envy of her class. The health food industry has put out such a variety of goodies, treats, and fun things to pack that her friends began to ask me to pack them lunch as well! Also, they are at the age where they know who is overweight and who isn't, and they also know whose mom is or isn't, too. Kids get the idea very young.

When Nolina did trade her lunches, though, I never got angry or upset; it was kind of funny. I never made it an issue or a battleground because—this is one point I want to make clear—children change their eating habits as fast as they grow out of their shoes. Today she loves her lunch, and tells me all her friends envy her and wish their mothers would buy healthier foods. Believe me, it's becoming hip.

Children are attracted to junk food just as they are to junk television. And just as you can't entirely censor out what your children see on television or anywhere else, you can't censor out the entire world of food. Face it. This world is 80 percent junk food. How can they escape it? But don't just give up—you can exert some control. You wouldn't let your child sit in front of a TV all day watching soaps—and you shouldn't let your child consume food that is equally junky all day long either. Most people wouldn't give their children alcohol or drugs, and yet they consistently give them the worst food imaginable. Why? Mostly, because it was the food that they were raised on themselves. It's the food they associate with their own childhood. However, it's this same overprocessed junk food that gives them problems today with their own weight and health.

## Setting Standards for Kids

Recently I worked with a very wealthy family with three children. Two were overweight, and the third had high cholesterol. Their mother had fought weight problems all of her life, as had her mother. She had gone through every quick gimmick diet in the book and basically was living on lunches out, popcorn, and yogurt-covered raisins. Putting her diet aside for the time being, I went through the pantry for the children. Absolute, complete, junk food. We gave away enough to feed the homeless for two months. I restocked the house with healthy foods, worked with the chef on fat-free menus, and began to educate the whole family on eating for the future. The children began to lose weight. When the family was off to a two-week trip to Hawaii, I advised them how to order and have a good vacation without suffering. For example, I told their mother, the kids should have only one creamy fruit drink a day, not three to four. She looked at me and said, "But what do I do when my son starts to pig out and just keeps eating?" "Simple," I said, "Stop him!" In this case it was a matter of tough love. If your child is overweight, you have to lay down the law. They may look at you like they hate you now (and most of them will even say they do), but they will thank you when they grow up into a society that ostracizes the overweight.

This does not mean that feeding your children properly requires becoming a food freak with almost religious fervor or standing on a soapbox, berating the poor kids about what they should and shouldn't eat. Children have a right to enjoy food as much as any adult. You can't—nor should you—eliminate candy and other goodies from a child's world, but you can moderate them. Whatever happened to the word *treat?* These things were supposed to be special. These days children have access to sweets and junk all day long. No wonder they're fat. There has been a great loss of respect for mealtime and structured eating hours. The prevailing attitude these days seem to be "just stuff your mouth with any quick convenience food, when or wherever you want."

My position on what Nolina eats is this: in my house the food is healthy. It is not "vegetarian," or "Pritikin," nor is it dictated by any other strict rules. It is good, healthy, enjoyable food. This is the house I live in, and the money I work for pays for the food I buy and eat. I do not allow Coca-Cola in my house or other junk foods. But I keep Nolina's favorite frozen yogurt around (and some sugar-free pies from the health food bakery) for treat times at home. And, when she's out and about, I allow her to indulge in the world around her. I do not go running across the room at a birthday party and snatch the hot dog and soda out of my daughter's hand in a health-fanatic fit. When we eat out I let her order what she wants, within reason, which is always the great standards — spaghetti, pizza, or an occasional hamburger. She can go with everyone to McDonald's after her dad's baseball game and enjoy herself. If she is at the park, she can have the ice cream or popcorn or whatever the other kids are having. At the movies she can have her beloved red licorice or KitKat bar. In addition to letting her have treats, though, I try to teach her about my food decisions and why I am making them. I tell her what is good and bad, and why. After all, she sees me go for candy once in a while. I like to enjoy myself as well. But just as I wouldn't let her write on the walls, wear dirty clothes to school, or dye her hair, I won't allow junk food in my house. It is my standard for myself and my family. Just as many homes have religious standards or educational standards, I have standards for a fit and healthy lifestyle in my home.

I'm not saying you should make sugary, salty junk food the enemy or hold that eating it is a sin. Just make your kids aware of their choices and let them know where you stand on those choices, exactly as you would want them to understand your principles on everything else. And keep in mind that it's easy to be hypocritical where food is concerned. You don't want your children to swear, but you yourself do once in a while. Likewise, you probably have some other habits that you wouldn't want your child to repeat. For example, I use one Equal in my coffee in the morning, but I don't want my child to have foods made with chemicals. But kids must be made aware that they can't do everything their parents do and that there are rules they must abide by. Yet it's a thin line to walk: children so often model themselves after their parents.

When I was growing up, food was the main attraction in our home. We were served everything from the average spaghetti dinner, to cow's tongue or fish with béarnaise sauce, every gourmet creation my mother could think of. I distinctly remember hating many meals and for a long period of time wanting to eat nothing but peanut butter sandwiches and Oreo cookies. I literally did not want to eat anything else. My mother let me do it for about a week, then started to demand I eat other foods. Of course, years later, what stuck with me was how wonderful it was to have all that variety of great foods. I have changed my style of eating, but not the great pleasure that food brought to my life. Rebel as I did against many Sunday dinners, I still ended up loving to cook and eat. In that way I still modeled myself after my mother. I happen to have adjusted my food to make it less fattening and more healthy, but I still take my cues from what my mother taught me. Likewise, your children will model themselves after you. They may rebel against this sandwich, or that cereal, or whatever, but you are setting the pattern for their long-term relationship with food.

Also keep in mind that, as has been noted before, we're the children of the Weight Watchers generation. People in their twenties, thirties, and forties are part of the body obsession culture—and we're the generation with severe eating disorders, too. While it's been said that French women love their bodies, most American women dislike their physiques and pick apart their bodies. It's a neurosis that I for one would like to see my daughter grow up without. We need to teach our children that as long as they are eating healthfully and getting enough exercise, they are fine. Being bigger, doesn't mean being fatter, and we should respect the individual structure we are given.

If your child is overweight, then help the child learn lean eating habits from the start. If your child has to wear glasses or braces, you teach him or her how to deal with those physical problems. It should be the same with weight. Most parents either make their child so upset about it or try to overcontrol it or ignore it. Fatness is not a disease, it is a physical problem that can be corrected. More parents are willing to spend a ton of money on a nose job before they will take the responsibility of a child's weight problem. It's as if it just happened without them. You don't have to make them neurotic about their weight, it's just another side of child rearing you have to cope with. No matter what your kids do on their own, they will always come back to the truths that you teach them. With what you know now, though, you can give your children all the benefits of food. It doesn't have to be one or the other. Let your children know that food can be wonderful, pleasurable, sensual, fulfilling, *plus* healthy and nonfattening.

# What to Do When Your Child Is Overweight

You really have to understand one thing very clearly. When there is excess fat on a body, that means the body is screaming to you "I DO NOT NEED MORE FOOD! I am not using it up. I am storing it as excess, because I don't need it to fuel the energy I'm expending right now." A growing child needs plenty of fuel to build on, so if your child is carrying excess weight, then you are grossly overfeeding him or her.

Thinking seriously about what and how much a child needs to eat should begin right from the start. Although it's not possible for many women, I highly advocate nursing your child for as long as you can. What I don't advocate, however, is giving babies cereals and baby pastas that contain fillers. These are foods often used to fill kids up when they're still hungry after they've had their milk source. Don't get me wrong—I don't believe in "diets" for babies. I believe in cute, plump babies, not skinny babies, but not overstuffed fat babies either. Instead of feeding them fillers to satiate their appetite, start by putting whole, real foods into your baby's body. Mash some boiled brown rice, banana, or acorn squash; peas, apples, or bananas—foods that will help your child grow healthy and strong, instead of helping her or him develop a lot of unwanted fat cells. Every mother knows the need to fill a baby, to give it what it needs to be quiet or calm. A baby that is unhappy and crying grates on a mother's nerves more than anyone can imagine. Sometimes the answer is to feed babies, but this doesn't mean you have to fill them with stuffing, or ply them with bottles of milk. Give your babies real food.

Once your children are older they'll have a hand in helping you figure out what it is they need. While it might seem that your children should be consuming every source of vitamins and minerals every day, they don't really need to and, in fact, left to their own devices, children balance their diets very well. They crave what their bodies need at any given time, then fulfill those needs by eating just enough. What trips them up is being allowed to fulfill those needs with sugary, high-fat foods. As every adult knows, the more junk you eat, the more you want. Kids, of course, have a natural penchant for sweets—breast milk is sweet so they're already used to it. Unfortunately, most sweet foods are also loaded with fat, so kids—like adults—develop a taste for it, too. The end result is that, while some children may not be eating an overabundance of food, the food they're eating is excessively fattening. And, they may get so filled up on junk that they won't be hungry for the nutritionally sound food they really need. If you're wondering why your children aren't eating the right foods, consider the fact that they're probably already full.

The reason most children are overweight is because they have access to all kinds of goodies all day long. Sweets used to be saved for a special occasion, now I see mothers with jars of cookies and candy in their houses, which the kids help themselves to on a regular basis. Mothers think they have to pack a "treat" or dessert at lunch and then give their kids a junky snack after school, then again after dinner. No wonder these kids are fat! You are not being good to your kids by giving them these treats all the time, you are spoiling them in a destructive way. No child needs dessert every night. Heavy desserts and treats should be reserved for special occasions. Let them snack on fruit. Believe me, if they are hungry enough and there are no doughnuts or cookies, they will eat fruit and enjoy it.

Children should understand that a snack is a special in-between-meals treat to keep them from getting too hungry before the next meal. A snack is not whatever they want to be eaten whenever they please; when they can have it and what it will be is determined by *you*. I do not allow my daughter to go into the refrigerator any time she wants because I believe in mealtime. Admittedly, it's just not possible to patrol a kid constantly so I just make sure that if my daughter does go into the cupboards or refrigerator looking for a snack, whatever she finds will be something healthy that her body can use. For example: popcorn, fresh nuts, fruit (grapes, berries, bananas, orange sections, sliced apples), flavored rice snacks, low-fat string cheese, yogurt, applesauce, and graham crackers as opposed to Mallomars (nice for an occasional treat, but not everyday).

Snack time is an important time for a child, even an overweight child. By the time we are adults we have pretty much gotten away from the word *snack*. We call it a "coffee break" or "grazing." Well, snack time is officially the time when you want to eat something in between a full meal, and children hardly ever eat a full meal. One of the biggest arguments between children and parents is whether or not the children will "finish what's on their plates." Well, that's not the way children consume food. They like to eat as much as they please during a meal and have a snack later. They are the original grazers. This is fine. No one is asking you to stand guard in the kitchen all day to make sure that they choose a proper snack—just have *nothing but* proper snacks around. My point is that as long as your house is free of junk products your children will be fine.

They will get all the junk they want outside of your house. Sure, you can even keep a few fun treats around, like yogurt popsicles or carob-covered raisins. Just make sure the bulk of your children's diet is good food. They will survive the rest.

I find that many parents feel like they're depriving their kids if they don't keep all kinds of junk around. After all, they have fond memories of indulging when they were kids; why should their own children go without? It always shocked me that they weren't as concerned with the fact that they were setting their children up for weight problems later in life, a future battle to fight, if not a present one—being fat as a child is humiliating. But instead of feeling guilty about that, parents will feel guilty for disciplining their children. Or perhaps it just that they're simply to weak to impose rules.

One mother paid for a long-distance telephone call consultation just to tell me she didn't feel it was fair to deprive her child of Coke and ice cream after school (not to mention various other junk foods) because the child's friends were able to eat whatever they pleased. Yes, it's true that some children eat nothing but junk food and look as skinny as rails, but that doesn't mean that they are healthy. Or that the eating won't catch up with them later as the pounds pour on. Frankly, life just isn't fair. Some kids are born to have acne, some are uncoordinated, some are plain ugly! What is really not fair is that she is allowing her child to take control of her own diet and as a result the child is fat. Her daughter doesn't know enough about what she should and shouldn't eat to be able to make the decisions for herself. It's the parent's responsibility to guide the child and, if the child is overweight, to begin dealing with it right away so it doesn't become a lifelong problem.

What *do* you say to your children when they ask why their friends are allowed to have treats, but they aren't? Tell them that just because so and so can eat all the junk food right now doesn't mean that it isn't going to catch up with her later on in life. Also there is the old cliché we've all used on our kids: "I don't care what they do at Johnny's house, in this house we do it my way!" But, really, it's not about what the other children can or can't eat, the point is, you are the one to make the rules. "But my daughter Sally hates fruit," you say. You have allowed Sally to hate fruit. The world of fruit is too wide for anyone to hate it all. And if Sally gets hungry enough, and the options she has are fruit, Sally will learn to love fruit.

Remember, the reason that you give your children the same products you had when you were growing up is that they represented the security of your home. Your childhood. At my house, we don't pull out chips, greasy popcorn, and sweets. We have bowls of fruit, butter-free popcorn, or one of the new rice puffs to munch on while we watch a movie or television program. I started this because fruit is what I like to eat, but I didn't think that Nolina would want it so I gave her popcorn instead. But then she ended up eating all my fruit and skipping the popcorn! Go figure. Now she looks forward to the fruit because this what represents comfort and family time to her. There is nothing she likes better than when we curl up to watch TV with a big bowl of grapes or sliced apples. These foods will become her "comfort" foods as she grows older. This sounds dull in comparison to the other junk, but if you try it for a few nights, you will realize that your body and your children's will stop craving the junk and start craving the fruit. All of you will feel more energetic and less sluggish, too.

You owe this to your children. They will adjust to the healthy food served in their household and, in fact, they might as well adjust to it now—healthy and nonfattening is the way much of the food will be in the twenty-first century. These days, children are bombarded with "Don't Smoke," "Just Say No to Drugs," "Don't Drink and Drive," but they are also hearing about the dangers of high cholesterol as early as *the third grade.* They want to eat well and be healthy. My daughter is very proud that I am slim and in good shape. She knows it's due to the way I eat and she wants to be like me. No child wants to be fat. They may say they want junk, but they also want to pierce their ears, drive a car, and go on dates when they're not ready. Put the foods that will help them have a better body and a longer, stronger life in front of them and they'll rebel— but only for about one second. Then they will eat and later they will thank you for not having to battle with their weight and health.

One client, a famous and wealthy psychiatrist, called me because both she and her daughter needed to lose weight. Her daughter was eleven and went to one of the most expensive private schools in the country. What I learned from this woman is that people will admit that they themselves have lousy eating habits and eventually take responsibility for their problems, but when it comes to their children's problems, they are incredibly defensive and unaware of what is going on. While the psychiatrist was perfectly ready to discuss her own food troubles, every time we got to her daughter's problems she skirted the issue as if to say that someone or something else was responsible. Certainly not she. The school brought in all kinds of junk food, she told me. They had McDonald's delivered sometimes and the rest of the time served fatty, unhealthy lunches. The snacks and the peer pressure her daughter felt to indulge in them was yet another problem . . . and on and on.

All the time she was telling me this, I couldn't help but think, if I was paying as much for my daughter's education as this woman was, I certainly wouldn't let my money be used to make my child fat, not to mention unhealthy. Sure, a child might be subject to peer pressure for refusing to snack or eat the fatty foods from the cafeteria along with her friends. But she will also be subject to peer pressure and rejection if she's fat, so teach your child how to eat correctly in the cafeteria. Just as you teach your children not to take drugs or smoke under peer pressure, educate them in what it takes to stay healthy. Pack your children's lunches or talk to the school and have them set up a menu for the child who is overweight so that she can eat at the same time and not feel left out. If your children go to public school—trying to get a public school to change their menu is like beating your head against a wall—then make sure your kids bring their lunches the majority of the time.

Many parents have just avoided discussing healthy eating with their children because they don't know the answers or feel that what the kids eat is out of their control. But you *are* in control and it is your responsibility to make sure your child is getting the proper foods—or to educate him or her on how to get them. Not only should you not let yourself be a victim, you shouldn't let your child be one either. Fat is a family matter, and for a child, being overweight has profound social and medical effects. A fat child is made fun of and discriminated against, and, more urgently, is subject to high blood pressure, high cholesterol, and prediabetic states. The more junk you let your children pour into their bodies, the more you poison them. Just as you are educating yourself on pros and cons of different foods today, you need to educate your children. This doesn't mean putting your children on adult "diets"—their bodies have different requirements than adults; plus dieting is harder for them to cope with emotionally. As you learn to listen to your own needs and wants from foods, tune in to your child's needs and wants, too. Create the same standards with food as you do in other areas of their lives.

I would like to say one last thing about why children have weight problems. They simply are not active enough. While their parents are out there jogging, going to gyms, hiring private trainers, buying expensive equipment, and generally trying to do anything to bring physical activity back into their sedentary lives, their children are taking buses or getting rides (it is too dangerous in most places to let your children walk alone) to school and sitting around watching television. No longer do children play kick-the-can or other street games or ride bikes after school. They play computer games—great for the mind perhaps, but not for the body. Kids just aren't expending enough energy.

Remember, the formula for being overweight is simple: calories *in* must equal calories *out* or the body will gain weight. Just living, keeping the body functioning and going through your daily routine expends about 75 percent of a person's energy. The other 25 percent needs to be burned up by activity. Children's bodies typically burn more than adults' because their daily activity includes growing—their little bodies are very busy building more cells and so on, which is a lot of work. So if your children are overweight you are feeding their bodies more (probably fat) calories that they can use. It's simple mathematics.

The answer, then, is to get your kid into activities, even if it's just walking the dog every evening. All schools offer after-school programs of some kind and there's always one, if not more, physical activity that suits a child. I hated gym and barely passed it. But when one gym program offered folk dancing I couldn't get enough! The activity doesn't have to be something you were involved with as a child or even a sport as long as it gets your child to move. I have taken my daughter hiking since she was three and walked her up and down some pretty lengthy trails, always encouraging her to use her legs and go for it. Many times cars will pass us as people decide to drive to the end of the hike. Nolina just sighs and says, "Why can't people just learn how to use their legs and walk?"

Bottom line: if your children are overweight, simply cut out all the fats and oils at home, get them to increase their physical activity and don't make a big deal of those special times when they eat junky, fattening foods. Give their bodies food that they can burn, real burnable food. If you are consistent, the weight will come off. But if every time your children go to a baseball game and have hot dogs, peanuts, and ice cream, you figure "Oh what the hell, they liked it so much" and continue with the same routine, you'll have a fat child, who will be a fat adult—due to you. Respect yourself and respect your children and give them a better, healthier life.

## Fighting Finickiness

You would be amazed what your children would eat if you just kept making it available to them. Not forcing it on them, just exposing them to it. This is especially true because children change their minds every day. One day they just love oatmeal, and the next day they tell you they hate it, how could you even think of serving it? Kids will tell you that they hate something, then when they find out their best friend loves it, change their minds. There is no rhyme or reason to a child's food likes and dislikes. The minute you think you have them figured out, they change. Perhaps it's one of the two powers they have in their world. You can put me to bed, but you can't make me sleep. You can prepare the food and put the plate in front of me, but you can't make me eat. No matter what kind of food you present to your children, they will always find those words "I hate this, why did you make it for me?" and look at you like you are both stone-stupid and mean.

Every parent has experienced the dinner table tug-of-war with their children. The sad thing is when it becomes a battle. You have to learn and believe in one thing: your children will eat, and they will eat until they are full. They know how to moderate their intake better than you do. And if they do not like what is being served, they can eat it or just go hungry. There were weeks when I thought my daughter would eat nothing but string cheese. Then there were weeks when 70 percent of her intake was bread. I tried to fight it and get her to eat other things (especially vegetables) but it usually became a bribe or a threat. But the truth is, she usually got over her one-food-of-the-week periods pretty quickly, and, besides, it takes a lot to starve a child or have them reach a state of malnutrition. Offer children a wide variety of foods and they will choose among them and usually choose fairly well. You can encourage certain foods or employ little tricks (like slipping grated veggies into their burgers), but forcing your child to eat, eat, eat only creates an eating problem and, often, a fat child.

Here's a perfect example of what I mean by exposing your kids to lean, healthy foods. I always cut up some raw vegetables to munch on while I prepare dinner, which is also the time when my daughter Nolina sits and talks to me about her day. Sometimes she does her homework or watches a program on TV. Nine times out of ten she ends up nibbling on whatever I have chopped up. She is hungry, the veggies are right there, and she is emulating me. It's natural. I don't have to scream eat your vegetables at dinner, because she has already eaten fresh veggies beforehand and that makes life a lot nicer. One night my husband got upset that Nolina would not eat her vegetables at dinner. I told him quietly that she had eaten a whole red bell pepper, jicama, and carrots while we were munching and making dinner. As far as I was concerned, that was plenty. She didn't have to eat her steamed vegetables, because she had already consumed a nice amount of raw ones. Now nibbling vegetables is turning into a habit—Nolina is so crazy about red bell peppers in mustard that she insists I put them in her lunch.

I'm not saying that your children are always going to eat what you put in front of them without protest. I just believe that you have a greater chance of getting them to eat nutritious foods if you keep them around the house. If your kids say they only like Capt'n Crunch's cereal so you only buy Capt'n Crunch's cereal, well then, of course, they're never going to try healthier, juice-sweetened whole wheat flakes. Yet, by the same token, I don't think you need go to the other extreme and insist that your kids eat perfect four-food group meals at every sitting. It would be nice if they did, but it's highly unlikely that they will, and it may not even really be necessary.

When my daughter started third grade, she announced in a very determined manner that she wanted nothing but fruit and cheese and corn chips in her lunch. Anything else she would throw out. Well, I felt like the father on *Family Ties*. In one episode, Michael J. Fox tried to tell him not to pack the apples in their lunches because they just throw them out. "I know," said his TV dad, "but I have to pack them anyway." Likewise, it seemed like I was a terrible mother if I didn't pack all the so-called proper lunch goods in Nolina's box. I had visions of getting notes from the principal accusing me of sending my child to school with an inadequate lunch. But knowing that my daughter, who now professed to hate sandwiches, wouldn't eat one even if I sent it along, I reconsidered the matter. The truth is, fruit and string cheese, plus healthy no-salt corn chips is not a bad lunch. And with the pickles and natural fruit leather I got her to let me include, it actually turned out to be a great lunch, just not a traditional one. If that's all she wants to eat for lunch for a while—fine. Once again, though, this only lasted for about two weeks until she decided she liked other foods in her lunch.

I have other ways of getting her to eat what she should. For instance, during a period where she refused anything green I put on her plate, I decided that she had to consume one, just one green vegetable a day. I took her to the store with me, showed her the whole produce section and said, pick one. She enjoys the novelty of choosing it herself. For a while it was cabbage. Then okra. Then spinach. Now it's snowpeas. It changes regularly and she stays with one vegetable for about two weeks. That's okay. In fact, it's great. Another great way to get a child interested in vegetables is to use the old Popeye routine. In other words, pick an idol for the child. Some person or figure that they admire and teach them how healthy that person eats. I used the opposite method on a little girl who wanted to be an actress when she grew up. I taught her to watch how Roseanne Barr eats, as opposed to Julia Roberts. Or pick someone in your world. Nolina will also eat anything her dad eats. I mean anything. She is completely infatuated with her father, and that means if he eats it, it must be good. Fortunately, my husband likes the healthy food I make.

Even if you have nothing to offer a child but junky, child-delight dinners (hot dogs, pizza, Chef BoyarDee ravioli in a can) you're going to hear "I hate this" at some point in time. "Ewww, why did you make this?" they'll say with such a horrible expression on their faces one would think you just committed child abuse. So don't be paranoid about pleasing your children's palates. They will learn what you teach them. Granted, rebelling along the way, but learning.

## A Meal-by-Meal Guide to Good Children's Food

The following is a list of foods for kids. All of them serve a child well, not only because they're healthy, but because they're flavorful and even fun, the way kids like. The idea here is that you can do things very simply and have the peace of mind that you are not destroying your children's bodies with rotten food. They're going to rebel against whatever you serve at some point—even if it's Kentucky Fried Chicken and Hostess Cupcakes they will eventually say "I hate this!"—but the bottom line is that they live in your house and will eventually become accustomed to the type of food you serve, no matter what. Children all over the world are raised on millions of different kinds of cuisines, eating things that we perceive as bizarre or even grotesque. They eat what is available to them, what their parents, siblings, and extended family eat. Just as other tribal or cultural habits are formed, so are food habits. Eating is a form of language passed down in every culture.

And it's a language that is changing in America today. The desire for health and life extension exist in everyone of us, but not until recently did people begin to understand that food is an integral part of achieving those goals. The trend hasn't passed children by either. Children are aware that food is changing—with every television commerical for food shouting the words "healthy and natural," how could they not? With healthy food available that won't assault their senses, kids today have a better chance at eating correctly from the start. Thankfully, chemical-free food that's low in fat and sugar is in both our and our children's future. Just as brown bread now owns more than half as much shelf space as white bread, so will the other products I am introducing you to be predominant on grocery store shelves one day. Most of these healthy foods will also be—and already are—convenient.

The majority of the foods on these lists can be cross-referenced to the shopping guide (Chapter 5), and those with asterisks indicate that the recipe is included in Chapter 8. The majority of the foods are for children who do *not* have a weight problem and are active and healthy; variations for heavy kids, when necessary, are included in parentheses.

However, one rule of thumb: even if a child does not have a weight problem, it's a good idea to trim the fat from his or her diet. I don't mean completely eliminating it, just keeping it low so that the child doesn't develop a taste for—and bad habit of seeking out—fatty foods. Something also important to remember is that, as I mentioned in Chapter 4, U.S. RDA means recommended *dietary* allowance, not recommended *daily* amount. The point is, it's virtually impossible to have every vitamin and mineral every day and even those who set the standards acknowledge it. So lighten up at each meal and try to keep an overall view. Make sure your children get all the necessary nutrients over a period of five days and they'll be in good shape.

## *Breakfast*

Once again I urge you to drop the old standards you were raised with and tune in to what is happening at your house in the morning—what your children are actually consuming. Boys will usually eat a bigger breakfast than girls and if your child isn't eating in the morning it's a good idea to try and wake him or her up about ten minutes earlier than usual. Children don't stuff themselves at night and it is natural for them to be hungry about a half an hour after they've awakened.

**Eggs.** Serve them poached over whole grain toast or scrambled with Pam or in safflower margarine. If you're scrambling the eggs, leave margarine off the toast. If the kids really miss ham with their eggs, try the Shelton Farms salami or bologna. They're also great chopped into a mostly egg white omelette.

**Toast.** Spread sugar-free jam on top or, if your child isn't having eggs with it, add a touch of soy-based or safflower margarine.

**Fruits and fruit juices.** Always keep fresh fruit on the table. (If your child is heavy, cut the juice with mineral water and stick to citrus juices.)

**Natural and whole grain cereals with low-fat (or nonfat) milk.**
Granola is fine (except for overweight kids), but check the label—many
are loaded with too much sugar, nuts, coconut, carob chips, and oil for
any kid. I do not allow the commercial cereals in my house. No matter
what is written on the label, to me they are still junk food. There is an
endless list of natural cereals that taste and look like corn flakes, Cheerios, nuggets, Shredded Wheat, and all kinds of puffs that are completely
healthy, burnable, and packaged to appeal to your child's imagination
(see the shopping guide). Add fruit, and if your children insist on something sweet on top, a little honey is not that fattening and certainly not
bad for their health.

**Hot cereals.** These are great provided they are not the instant versions, which contain chemicals. Top them with some sugar-free jam, cinnamon, fresh fruit, or raisins. A little honey is all right, but don't add
butter or margarine to the cereal—this food is hearty enough without
the added fat.

**Nonfat yogurt or cottage cheese.** Children do need calcium for strong
bone growth, so if your child does not have a weight problem, then just
keep dairy products to low fat or nonfat. (If your child is overweight and
you're serving dairy at breakfast, you can skip it at lunch. Limit to nonfat
and add calcium sources like spinach and broccoli to his/her diet.)

**Low-fat Cinnamon-Vanilla French Toast\* or oat bran pancakes.**
Serve this without butter and accompanied by sugar-free jam or one of
the new all-fruit syrups (the French toast recipe calls for whole wheat or
oat bran bread). If your child has no weight problem a little maple syrup
is fine, just don't smother it. Make a large batch and freeze it. Then you
have your own version of the junk-food toaster-oven kind. There are
many brands of oat bran and whole wheat pancake mixes available. Ar-
rowhead Mills is one I've seen at most markets cross-country. They are
also freezable. Top with sugar-free jams or syrups.

**Turkey sausage.** Although some brands are healthy, they still have a lot
of fat so I broil the sausage, then drain it before serving. (For weight
control, skip these.)

**Bagels or English muffins.** Look for whole-grain or fat-free versions.
Spread them with healthy cream cheese or light cream cheese once in a
while. (If your child has a weight problem, spread it with no-sugar jam.)

**Whole wheat cinnamon rolls with raisins, a variety of bran muffins, and even whole wheat croissants.** These are good substitutes for sugary pastries, but make sure the muffins aren't loaded with nuts and sugar. (Lay off the croissants completely for children trying to lose weight.)

**Applesauce or berry applesauce over sliced bananas.** Any fresh fruit variation is fine.

## *Lunch*

I am a firm believer in packing your children's lunch. Even in the best private schools, the food is lacking miserably in nutritional value and is very high in fat, chemicals, salt, and sugar. However, my daughter thinks buying a "hot lunch" at school is a novelty. So every once in a while I let her. But one of the changes I would like to see in this country is a reevaluation of our schools' foods.

The following is a list of the different foods you can pack in your children's' lunch boxes in whatever combinations you see fit. Keep in mind, though, that kids are always changing their minds. Try to listen to them so they don't go to school and throw out the food you gave them or trade it all away. But also try to erase the old standard menu—sandwich, celery sticks, chips, apple, cookies and so on—from your mind and start with a fresh attitude.

Again, children do not have to have all four food groups at each meal. If you stop being concerned with what you think they should have, and start becoming aware of what they are actually going to eat, you can save your time and money and move onto other battles (like getting them to clean their rooms).

**Fruit.** As many pieces as they like: grapes, an orange, a banana, berries, plums, and so on.

**Individual cartons of natural applesauces.** (Make sure they don't have added sugar or corn syrup. They now also have cherry, strawberry, and apricot flavors in mini sizes.)

**Small yogurts.** For overweight children, make sure the yogurts are nonfat, and don't let your child eat more than two to three nonfat dairy foods per day.

**String cheese, slices of another low-fat cheese, or small containers of low-fat cottage cheese.** Look for the Soyco cheese slices, individually wrapped like Kraft slices. Great for kids with high cholesterol. (Again, for overweight children, look for nonfat cheese and cottage cheese.)

**Dried fruits.** Make sure to buy the kind without sulfites. (Overweight kids should stick with the tiny boxes of raisins and avoid the other dried fruits, which are high in calories.)

**All varieties of rice crackers and low-fat grain crackers.** As with the cereals, there are aisles full of healthy cracker alternatives for children. I put them in Baggies with natural cheese slices and some pickle slices, or for variation, you can spread them thinly with peanut butter about two to three times a week. You can also spread peanut butter between two slices of apple or, the old favorite, on celery. (Overweight kids should skip peanut butter altogether. Don't feel that you're depriving your child. It's better that they don't develop a taste for it, and they will thank you for growing up thin. Use a sugar-free jam or an apple butter instead.)

**Turkey sandwiches, tuna or Garlic Herb Chicken Salad\* sandwiches.** If your child has no weight problem, then look for mayonnaise based on soy (Nayonnaise) or a safflower-based mayo (Hollywood). The best is to get off mayonnaise altogether and use the recipe on page 198 for a spread based on tofu, nonfat yogurt, herbs, and spices. If you can't make this, then use an oil-free salad dressing. Also, look for natural tofu-based egg salad and bean spreads for sandwiches in the deli section of your local health food store.

**Chicken/turkey salami or bologna.** Find these in the frozen food section of your health food store. If you can't find the natural kind, the commercial fat-free versions are the next best thing. You can make sandwiches with them; my daughter likes the slices just plain in a Baggie.

**Leftover anything they liked from the dinner before.** Like a slice of healthy Crustless Pizza\* or quiche, cold chicken or turkey. (Do not serve quiche—it is a healthy dish, but fattening. Stick to the lean leftovers and lean pizza for heavier kids.)

**Pickles.** Look for salt-free, bottled without preservatives.

**Raw vegetable slices.** Let your kids choose. Last week, Nolina's favorite was raw fennel. Expose your kids to different foods and they will come up with their own ideas. Trust me, they may wrinkle their noses, but if you offer them a variety they will find one they like. Try the cute, mini bunny carrots that come in bags in the produce section. Most kids also love cucumbers; try cucumber sandwiches.

**Healthy, sugar-free granola bars and sugar-free all-fruit strips.** There are just as many natural, sugar-free granola bars as there are ones laden with sugar, chocolate, and chemicals. Most commercial granola bars are as nutritional as a candy bar. The same goes for fruit leather. It should be fruit, not sugar. Health Valley now has fat-free granola bars out as well. Hain makes truly fat-free granola bars, and Barbara's makes granola bar "lights." (Make sure overweight children only get the granola bars that don't have nuts or carob chips. Just give them the plain or apple cinnamon ones. Alternate the fruit strips with the raisins.)

**Natural corn chips and baked cheese puffs.** The variety is amazing. Hain has Mini Rice Cakes in Ranch, Barbecue, Teriyaki, Honey Nut, Apple Cinnamon, and more. There are endless brands of what I call rice puffs, which also come in great flavors. There are oat bran puffs, and Barbara's light cheese puffs. There're Poprice and Turbo Twists, and Skinny Haven has a variety of Skinny Munchies that come in lunch-size bags. (Just the light cheese puffs for heavy kids.)

**Air-popped popcorn.** Many stores carry prepopped popcorn, just read the labels for additives. Don't let your child just fill up on popcorn and never serve it buttered. Spray the popcorn with butter-flavored Pam and sprinkle it with a salt-free seasoning.

**Fantastic Foods instant soup in a cup.** Not loaded with chemicals and as appealing as the junkier ones in the same kind of convenient packaging. (Whenever trying to keep a child's diet very lean, stick to soups like chicken vegetable, vegetable, tomato, miso broth, or turkey rice, not cream soups.)

**Fortune cookies.** They are low in calories and sugar—and fun (plus, great for the overweight children).

**Any health store brand of oat bran or healthy cookies.** Health Valley makes a great fat-free cookie now.

**More healthy edibles to toss into your kids' lunch sacks:**
Hard-boiled eggs (not for the child with high cholesterol).
Kashi brittles.
Natural fruit drops in assorted flavors.
Panda black licorice or All Natural Raspberry Flavored Chew.

For more lunch suggestions see Chapter 7.

## *Dinner*

With both parents working, dinner has become a problem for many families in America today. I get calls all the time: "Help, how do I get a decent meal on the table for my family when I work full-time?"—especially these days when "full-time" almost always means working ten-hour-days. This is a valid question, and unless you can afford to hire help, you are stuck in the quickly eroding superparent role. When both parents are working someone must be, or take on the chores of, "the wife." And no one is naive to the fact that "housewiving" is a full-time job in itself, particularly because it includes preparing the meals—and that means everything from doing the shopping and planning to doing the cooking.

All this is twice as difficult if you are a single parent. At times you wonder how either you or your children will ever get fed. You find yourself weakening and giving into whatever is most convenient. Shopping for food becomes another tedious chore that you drag yourself through as quickly as possible in the hopes of trying to get that one hour of "quality time to yourself" before Monday hits again. The result is that you may get a decent bowl of cereal into your kids in the morning, and you may even pack their lunches, but by the time you get home from work you are too tired to be Julia Child let alone just prepare a decent dinner; preparing a healthy one would seem to be an even harder task to master.

But it *can* be done—and more easily than you may believe. There are so many new healthy and lean foods in your supermarkets that it is now just as easy to make a quick, healthy meal as it is to make a quick, junky meal—and I don't mean coming home and making brown rice and tofu patties either. I'm talking about great food that will benefit you and your family. What follows is eight days' worth of family dinner menus that prove the point. As before, an asterisk means that the recipe can be found in Chapter 8 and advice for the overweight child will be in parentheses.

NOTE: I don't eat red meat because I find it too hard to digest, and, besides, I just don't have a taste for it anymore. I never wanted to feed my daughter red meat either because of all the chemicals and hormones contained in most of the cuts available. But when I found organic pork chops and other red meats at Mrs. Gooches, a local supermarket, I bought them. Now Nolina has meat—not on a regular basis—but on occasion. If she chooses to eliminate red meat from her diet ultimately, that is her choice. In the meantime I have allowed her to experience it in a healthy way.

**Day 1: Spaghetti.** This sounds so obvious, but there are many variations, it is quick, kids love it, and, if you use the right sauces, it's very healthy. Switch the shape of the noodles on the kids: there are sea shells (this was great when my daughter thought she was a mermaid), rotelle, penne, rotini, vermicelli, wagon wheels, and more. Make sure the sauce is a natural one with no chemicals or preservatives, and hunt down one of the ever-growing number of sauces made without oil. To make it a complete meal, toss in some thawed frozen veggies and some ground turkey or ground chicken. (Definitely serve the oil-free sauce for the overweight child, and don't serve bread and butter as an accompaniment. Instead, serve a salad.)

**Day 2: BBQ Chicken.** You don't even have to have an outdoor grill. Take the chicken and cover it with barbecue sauce that is not loaded with sugar, salt, and chemicals (see the shopping lists or see page 221 for a recipe). Place the chicken in the broiler, while you boil water for some frozen peas or other frozen vegetable of your child's choice. Served with a whole grain roll, this is an easy, well-rounded, and satisfying meal.

**Day 3: Tacos.*** Opt for corn/lime/water tortillas (and there are many out there now) instead of those with an ingredient list that starts with lard and includes a long lineup of chemicals. Again, use ground turkey or leftover chicken pieces instead of ground beef. Assemble the tacos with some shredded lettuce and chopped tomatoes. Salsa for a topping can be bought fresh at any market or try Pritikin Mexican Sauce, which is great heated and drizzled on top of the tacos. Grate some low-fat cheese to sprinkle on top of the tacos and add a little sour cream. (No sour cream for overweight kids and only a little cheese.) Instead of serving those killer refried beans as an accompaniment, just heat a can of plain kidney beans and mash them with some chicken broth (you can do the same thing to make mashed potatoes).

**Day 4: Halibits.*** Like Chicken McNuggets, but no, not the McDonald's prefab deep-fried junk—the healthier version on page 210. It is always a good idea to try and understand children's attraction to junk/fast food. Usually it is not the actual food as it is the design, texture, packaging, and marketing of the product. Granted, you can't normally duplicate all of this in one meal, but you can try to imitate what your kids find most attractive about certain fast foods. With McNuggets it's the bite-size pieces with a crunchy coating and dipping sauce that appeals. So I cut up chunks of halibut (you can use chicken, too) and coat them with beaten egg and wheat germ, then sauté them in a healthy oil and let my daughter dip them in ketchup. This takes five to ten minutes. (For overweight children, eliminate the oil and sauté the nuggets in a little chicken broth and Pam.)

**Day 5: Pizza.*** If you can make one of these yourself, great (see recipe, page 211). But if you don't have time and, of course, don't want to pick one up from a take-out place because you know it's fattening and unhealthy, why not try one of the new, healthy pizzas now in the frozen food, or deli, section of the supermarket? I always have a few in my freezer for those nights when I am working late. This is a healthy all-in-one-meal, to which you can add some soup or salad if you like. (If your child is overweight, just take off most, but not all of the cheese, and look for Pizza Lite, a healthy and lean alternative.)

**Day 6: Soup and Sandwich.** This is an old standby meal, but can be made in a healthy and lean manner. Don't trust soup can labels—just because they say the product is low-sodium or light does not mean that they are healthy. Look for the natural manufacturers cited in the shopping list and try different varieties. (Westbrae's individual packages of miso soups with noodles, for instance, are wonderful.) Or make a big pot of soup from scratch on Sunday to serve to the kids during the week. A good hearty soup is a complete meal and is easy to prepare. As for the sandwiches, trying making a grilled cheese on whole grain bread with low-fat cheese, but use Pam, not butter, to do the grilling. I have served my daughter tomato and cucumber sandwiches with mustard many times and she loves them. See recipes for a chicken salad, tuna salad, and potato salad mix in Chapter 8.

**Day 7: Burgers.** Once again, forget the traditional beef burger and switch to turkey burgers. Ground turkey is available everywhere now and tastes great. Sometimes I mix the ground meat with mustard, ketchup, or barbecue sauce to give it a kick. Make sure you make the patties flat and skinny like McDonald's does and serve them with lettuce, tomato, pickles, whole grain buns, and steamed red potatoes (instead of fries). You can slice some low-fat cheese and avocado (except for over-weight children) or add various other garnishes.

**Day 8: Stuffed Potatoes.** Take a large russet potato and pop it into your microwave or oven. While it is baking sauté some ground turkey or chicken quickly in a pan sprayed with Pam or defatted chicken broth. Add some Parsley Patch Garlicsaltless seasoning (or plain garlic powder). Grate some low-fat cheese and chop a few scallions and tomatoes. Remove the potato, slice it down the middle and scoop out the stuffing. Mix the stuffing with the other ingredients and pour a little of your favorite fat-free salad dressing over the top. Reheat for about two minutes until the cheese melts and serve. Obviously, you can add your own variations, use nonfat plain yogurt if you please, different seasonings, and even some healthy pasta sauce. It's a quick and easy meal and kids love anything that comes compact and in one serving.

**Another dinner solution.** Look for the frozen meals in your health food store. They offer many great choices that you can microwave and serve with a clear conscience. My daughter especially loves Shelton Farms turkey pot pies or frozen quiche.

## Out of Sight, but Not Out of Mind

Okay, you say, I have my children on a healthy eating course at home and I pack them a fun, nutritious lunch for school. Now what about the times when I can't control what they eat? It's true, there are times when you do not have control over the food your children are eating; that is when you have to let go. Just as you learn to adjust your own diet to your social life and situations around you, you have to let your children adjust to their world. Unfortunately, if you look at the food most often offered to children when a parent is not around, it's 90 percent junk. But as long as you know the home base is clean and healthy (not boring and safe—there's a difference) you can have a clear conscience about letting your kids enjoy themselves when they're out and about.

A perfect example of when to let go: at birthday parties. The mother of one of Nolina's best friends cannot seem to let go at any time. The woman's little girl was invited to every birthday party of my daughter's and each time the woman would follow her child around with a piece of apple or vegetable, insisting that she eat it before lunch—even though my lunches were always healthy pizza or turkey dogs! The mother would also stop her daughter in the middle of a meal if she felt she had had enough. The woman was completely obsessed with what her daughter was consuming at every second. It was annoying to be around, not to mention painful for the child.

Obviously, this is an extreme case. But it's important for every parent to realize that at birthday parties and similar events, children are involved in their own little rituals. Sameness is very important. Anyone who has kids is aware that you never give two children the same age an unequal amount of anything unless you like minor warfare. I have another friend who, along with her husband, is a vegetarian. They are very strict with their diet and are raising their children that way at home. Fine. But if they were to take their children to a birthday party and watch over everything they ate outside the home (which, thankfully, they don't), their children would eventually rebel. Let kids be a part of the party, a part of their crowd. Food is not a religion, it's part of our lifestyles and you cannot impose your lifestyle completely to the last degree on your child. Do the best you can, give them something worthwhile to emulate, but ease up when the time is appropriate.

# 11

# *The Joy of Eating*

L IFE CAN BE very long—or short, depending on your perspective that day. But either way you look at it, no one wants to go through life without enjoying favorite foods. No one wants to go through it being fat and unhealthy either. And, even on the worst days when things are pretty black, we still all want to extend our lives. Food is not just involved in the matter of survival, it is part of our background, culture, religion, relationships, and an intricate part of our fabric. Most joyful, sorrowful, and deeply emotional moments are based around food. Things that pull at the heartstrings seems to pull at the stomach as well.

I have a friend, thirty-two and single, who finally met a guy she thought might be Mr. Right. They had been dating for about two weeks when she noticed that besides the fact that he was very slender, few of their dates revolved around food or restaurants. And it wasn't that he was being cheap, because he spent money on their dates. She finally realized that he didn't like food! She asked him one day and he told her that food didn't really interest him very much and that he rarely had a desire to eat. When he did eat, he told her, it didn't matter much what it was. Now my friend is a slender, well-balanced eater, who has a healthy passion for food—and who quickly lost her passion for him. How could he not love food? Could she spend her life with a man who never savored the glory of couples sharing food? The answer was no. It was as if there were a great hole in his soul. A passion for eating, I think, is symbolic of a passion for life.

I can't count the endless stories I've heard about men who cannot stand it if their wives/lovers/girlfriends pick at a salad or barely order when they are taken to a fine restaurant. Just as women want to see men eat, men want to see women eat (but they do not want to see them the least bit fat—the Catch-22 I addressed in Chapter 3). No one wants to see anyone sit at every meal, hands tied in knots, struggling not to enjoy himself or herself. I'm not saying we all want to see each other act like gluttons, but the act of eating definitely bonds us together. How nice it is to meet someone and find that you like the same foods or restaurants. I dated a guy once who loved to eat in Denny's and coffee shops. Needless to say we didn't last. I didn't like to be so limited by his choice of restaurants. Considering that we spend so much time at meals, food is an intricate part of a relationship. It is part of all forms of loving relationships—parent to child, friend to friend, lover to lover, and on and on. We feel loved and taken care of when someone cooks for us. It is a great turn on when a girl makes dinner for a guy. And an even greater turn on when a guy makes dinner for a girl.

To sum it up, we love each other, we feed each other, we share one of the finest things, and most necessary things put on this earth—FOOD, GLORIOUS FOOD. Which of course brings to mind the old cliché, "The way to a man's heart is through his stomach." To this day, I believe I truly hooked my husband by giving him a warm, home-cooked meal every night—and the rest of the evening wasn't so bad either.

I wish that everyone would take time out—it doesn't matter when or where—and enjoy at least one relaxed meal a day. I know it sounds very European and that most of us don't have the luxury to stop for a leisurely breakfast or lunch or even to carve some time out in the evening for a decent dinner. But nonetheless, try and give yourself some love and self-respect in the form of food each day. Allow yourself something to look forward to and a quiet time to sit and eat. Even one of the most famous American businessmen, Lee Iacocca, has said that he doesn't do business over meals and that meals are a relaxing and important part of his day.

Right now you're probably thinking, "Yeah, sure. Lee might have the time and luxury to do that, but my life isn't like that." Well, think again. If you've already read this far in this book, you obviously want to be healthier than you are right now; you want to get a handle on your eating habits. Well, what that takes is an appreciation of food—discovering all that food can be at its best, not just diving into fast food or easy take-out dinners. That, flat out, is not a healthy or caring way to treat yourself. You need to eat. Why not make it the right food and savor the experience?

I hope this book will give you the impetus to make sure that healthy food is at your disposal all the time. No more complaining about it being too difficult to eat healthfully. You now know that there are many nutritious and delicious alternatives to the garbage most people resign themselves to eating; and you know now, too, that there is room for indulgences in your life. There's no reason to be living your life in either a state of deprivation or one of debauchery and its partner, guilt. There is an excellent middle ground where you can be happy: happy with the foods you eat and happy with the way you look and feel. Both are important to your sense of well-being. I have an extensive list of clients who are so happy with what I have taught them, the way they look and feel, that it fills me with great satisfaction.

Don't forget that the key to getting your food intake in balance is accepting the body you've been given, not some model's or movie star's. There is nothing more attractive than a person who feels good about himself or herself. We all know people who are really not that good looking, but attract the opposite sex like crazy because of what they exude. This is not an excuse to stay heavy, and unhealthy—there's nothing to flaunt about fat. But know your body's limits and do the best you can.

I had a client, married with two children, who came to me for both exercise and diet consultation. She was about sixty pounds overweight and had an exquisite face. Really beautiful. I was a little surprised when she showed up for her first exercise session in neon-bright, leotards and tights, making no attempt to hide her rather large behind. After the session I measured her and we discussed her goals, where she would like to see the inches come off first, and so on. She slowly got up from her mat, sighed, then looked straight in the mirror, tossed her gorgeous chestnut hair and said with absolute confidence, in a slow drawl, "But I still look good." I laughed because it was so refreshing to hear someone, who despite carrying sixty extra pounds, had high self-esteem. I was so used to clients with five to ten pounds to lose constantly degrading themselves, that I appreciated her attitude. And it was true that she was beautiful, but those added pounds were unhealthy. She lost about fifty-five of them and, believe me, she looked a lot more than good.

If Americans would stop being so obsessed with their bodies, their diets, and the perfect image, they would have a lot more time to focus on the positive changes going on in the world of food and nutrition. Yes, if we could all just, "Shut Up and Eat!"

My family and I have a wonderful "eating life." We have a quiet dinner every night and lazy weekend breakfasts on a regular basis. We have our holidays and weekends at the cabin of what seems to be nonstop eating. We have our movies, baseball games, picnics, restaurants, and the treats that go with them. We even have some gooey, junky, fattening foods sprinkled here and there (I love a good croissant, well actually two, on Sundays) and we are still thin and healthy. Does it sound like I'm bragging? I'm really not. We have accomplished no more than it's possible for you to accomplish. This is what I want to teach the world. We can all live life and enjoy food with our loved ones . . . and feel great about our bodies too.

# Bibliography

"Salt, Sodium and Blood Pressure." American Heart Association pamphlet, 1979.

"Thin Fat," *American Medical News,* September 8, 1989.

Baker, Russell. "The Cholesterol Thing," *New York Times,* November 29, 1989.

Blumenthal, Dale. "A New Look At Food Labeling," *FDA Consumer,* November 1989.

Brody, Jane. "Huge Study of Diet Indicts Fat and Meat," *New York Times,* May 8, 1990.

Brody, Jane. "Personal Health," *New York Times,* December 7, 1989.

Burros, Marian. "Eating Well: Decoding a Nutrition Label," *New York Times,* July 12, 1989.

Burros, Marian. "Are the parts of the turkey better than the whole?" *New York Times,* November 15, 1989.

Carper, Jean. *Jean Carper's Total Nutrition Guide.* New York: Bantam Books, 1987.

*Encyclopedia of Food Additives.* Boca Raton: Globe Communications Corp., 1987.

Flipse, Robyn. "Beyond Oat Bran: Other Foods That Lower Cholesterol," *Environmental Nutrition,* July 1989; Vol. 12 No. 7.

Greene, Gael. "How to Eat Healthy at New York's Great Restaurants," *New York Magazine,* August 15, 1988.

Hecht, Ken. "Oh, Come On Fatties," *Newsweek,* September 3, 1990.

Hughes Market. *Nutritional Breakdown of Seafood.*

International Food Information Council. "Sorting Out the Facts About Fat," *Food Insight Reports,* 1989.

"Nearly half of all adults eat food prepared away from hone on a typical day, survey finds," *Journal of the American Dietetic Association,* October 1988; Vol. 88, No. 10.

Lecos, Chris W. "Food Labels: Test Your Food Label Knowledge," *FDA Consumer,* March 1988.

"Cutting Cholesterol," *Nutritional Action Healthletter,* September 1989.

Kantor, Mark A. "Nutrition, Cholesterol and Heart Disease Part IV: The Role of Dietary Fiber," *Nutrition Forum,* July/August 1989.

Saltman, Paul; Gurin, Joel; Mothner, Ira. *The California Nutrition Book.* Boston: Little, Brown and Co., 1987.

Stern, Bert. *The Food Book.* New York: Bookmark Books, 1987.

Stern, Judith S. "Decoding Food Labels," *Vogue,* October 1988.

The Sugar Association. "Carbohydrates: A User's Guide," *On Your Mark,* August 1989.

"What is a gram of fat . . . and how many should you eat? *Tufts University Diet & Nutrition Letter,* October 1989; Vol. 7, No. 8.

"Ask the Experts," *Tufts University Diet & Nutrition Letter,* January 1990; Vol. 7, No. 11.

# Index

INDEX

Vitamins
  body's need for, 66–68
  fat-soluble, 68

Waffles, 248
Walking, 11–12
Wants
  anticipating, 36
  making trade-offs for, 36–37
  sacrificing needs for, 35–36
Weight loss, 79–80
Wheat flour, 107
Wheat Thins, fat content of, 111
Whole grains, 82
Whole wheat flour, 107
Williams, Robin, xiv

Wilson, Brian, xiv, 72, 160
Winfrey, Oprah, 6, 27
Women, need for calcium, 67–78
Work, impact of, on eating habits, 45–48
Workout time, putting in extra, for holidays, 172
Workout, calorie burning cardio-vascular, 74

Xanthum gum, 97

Yogurts, 281
  best and worst choices in, 106–7
Yolanda's BBQ Sauce, 221
Yo-yo dieting, 79